Diana and Beyond

Diana and Beyond

*White Femininity, National Identity,
and Contemporary Media Culture*

RAKA SHOME

University of Illinois Press

URBANA, CHICAGO, AND SPRINGFIELD

© 2014 by the Board of Trustees
of the University of Illinois
All rights reserved
Manufactured in the United States of America
1 2 3 4 5 C P 5 4 3 2 1
♾ This book is printed on acid-free paper.

Library of Congress Cataloging-in-Publication Data
Shome, Raka, 1966–
Diana and beyond: white femininity, national identity,
and contemporary media culture / Raka Shome.
pages cm
Includes bibliographical references and index.
ISBN 978-0-252-03873-0 (cloth: acid-free paper)
ISBN 978-0-252-08030-2 (pbk.: acid-free paper)
ISBN 978-0-252-09668-6 (ebook)
1. Diana, Princess of Wales, 1961–1997—Influence. 2.
Diana, Princess of Wales, 1961–1997—In mass media.
3. Women, White—Great Britain—Social conditions.
4. National characteristics, British—History—20th
century. 5. Popular culture—Great Britain—History.
I. Title.
DA591.A45D536276   2014
941.085092—dc23   2014018805

To all women of color, and underprivileged women in and from the Global South . . .
    For the indignities and injustices

. . . the white woman is what the white man "produces." . . . If her body is in filmic language the place of "suture," what she sews together—what it "coheres"—are the white man's production . . .

—Rey Chow (1990, p. 84)

Contents

Acknowledgments

Any such project is always the outcome of numerous moments of friendship, conversation, support, love, intellectual guidance, and encouragement that its author receives over the years. While they may not always be directly evident, they nurture the author to arrive at a stage where she is able to bring years of thinking into some kind of fruition. Thus, numerous people need to be thanked for all that they have given me over the years. While I know that I do not have space to mention every kind individual whose professional path has crossed mine, I hope they know that I am a better intellectual and human being for having known them.

I must first however thank a few organizations whose financial support enabled me to complete the project. The Karl Wallace Research Award from National Communication Association several years ago enabled me to purchase many media materials that were crucial in this project; a generous grant from the Waterhouse Family Institute at Villanova University in the Department of Communication, as well as funding from the Organization for Research on Women (ORWAC), were crucial in assisting me to purchase copyright licenses for the numerous images presented in the book. I thank these organizations for their support of this research.

Raymie McKerrow is a model senior colleague and mentor. On so many occasions, Ray has guided, advised, and supported me—from the time I submitted my first whiteness essay in a journal he was editing, to now, when I am still engaging new forms of whiteness. He deserves special thanks for his kindness and for being a wonderful human being. Soyini Madison is an ideal intellectual conversationalist. With Soyini, I love discussing ideas and challenges of bringing issues of the Global South into the Western academy. And

Soyini always "gets it." She too has supported me on so many instances and I have also learned much from her. I especially cherish the soul-stimulating (at least for me) intellectual conversations we frequently have. Larry Grossberg supported my initiatives in postcolonial studies in the field of communication from the beginning of my career as junior faculty. Over the years, Larry has also offered helpful advice on how to navigate the discipline of communication and the academy when doing cultural studies work. I thank him for all the times he has generously made himself available for advice and professional support. Many other colleagues and friends have been supportive in numerous ways along the way and they deserve my deep thanks: Chris Berry, Carol Blair, Tom Frentz, Angela Ginorio, Marsha Houston, Youna Kim, Wenshu Lee, Swapna Mukhopadhaya, Tom Nakayama, Kent Ono, Radhika Parameswaran, Anita Ramasastry, Terhi Rantanen, Shakuntala Rao, Vince Waldron, and Phil Wander. Ramona Liera-Schwichtenberg also deserves thanks for having introduced me to cultural studies and for her intellectual support in graduate school. To the numerous students who have been in my classes over the years, although many of you have gone on to establish your own successful careers, I thank you for all insights you have shared in my classrooms.

It is highly unusual, I know, to thank someone you do not know. Yet, this someone has been more of a teacher to me than anyone else I have encountered in my professional life. I have learned so much from this individual's work; her ideas have influenced me heavily over the years. Her thoughts have continually impressed upon me the importance of recognizing the ethical demands on an intellectual's imagination. When I get stuck, it is to her work that I turn. And inevitably I find the answer to some question that may have stopped me in my writing or thinking track. A big "thank you" to Professor Gayatri Chakravarty Spivak for the courageous ways in which she has made visible the links between geopolitics and knowledge and for forever changing the way in which we understand knowledge production. She remains one of the greatest intellectuals of the 20th and 21st centuries.

At the University of Illinois Press, my editor Larin McLaughlin deserves great thanks for her patience and for supporting the project. Thanks also to Dawn Durante for her technical guidance and support. This project benefited from the reflections of two wonderful reviewers. I thank them for the questions and suggestions that have enriched this book. Sections of this work have been presented at University of Wisconsin—Madison, Södertörn University, Northern Arizona University, and the International Communication Association conference. Sections of Chapter 6 were presented as a keynote in 2012 at the Stockholm Multicultural Center, Botkyrka, Sweden. I thank the organizers of these events that enabled me to test out some of the ideas of this book. Parts of Chapter 4 were published in *Critical Studies in Media Communication* (December 2011). An essay I published on white femininity and national identity in *Feminist Media Studies* (December 2001) bore earlier imprints of my some my ideas here.

Numerous nonacademic friends have sustained me over the years. Indeed, I am grateful for the friends I have outside the academy, who keep me grounded. While space does not permit me to mention all of them (you know who you are), I must acknowledge my dear friend Seema Saxena Buckshee for her humor, eccentricity, eternal optimism, and love—and for her ability to see otherness even without academic training. A shout out as well to Susmita (Lily) Ghosh for her spiritual wisdom and finer observations on life and its struggles. And to Jaba for her friendship.

To my sister, Rhea for all her love and support over the years, and for her incredible culinary skills; to my mother, for her kindness, love, and humor, and for the patience and faith with which she keeps moving through life. To my maternal grandmother, my *Dida*, who is now no more. You would have been so proud.

1. White Femininity in the Nation, the Nation in White Femininity

All around the world a strange thing happened. It got bigger everyday. It stretched beyond the wildest imaginings of even the most devoted followers of celebrities. Diana who was flesh and blood, the English woman who died in the tunnel in Paris had already become a myth and more than that, a symbol of things that are good.
—Keith Morrison, *Dateline NBC*, September 14, 1997

[A] decade after her death, Diana remains an inescapable presence in British life: mostly but not always benign: a restless and seductive ghost. It's time to peer into the many corners she still haunts.
—*Time Magazine*, "How Diana Transformed Britain"
  (August 16, 2007)

In 1997 when Princess Diana died I, like the rest of the world, was fascinated by what was happening. I was struck, in particular, by the emotions and sense of familiarity being expressed by the people—British and non-British—toward a white upper-class heterosexual British woman they did not know. I was intrigued by how a media narrative of a white heterosexual upper-class British woman was able to secure so many affective attachments of love and desire from people—white and not white, Western and not Western. I thought to myself then, here was a thoroughly British (and particularly English) woman who, through multiple mediations, was being hypernationalized and transnationalized, and with no seeming contradictions rupturing this double movement. What script of white femininity was being so successfully spun and mediated such that this highly British woman became a simultaneous signifier of a national popular and a global popular? What ideologies of white femininity did this script tap into and stabilize such that this woman soon became an idealized signifier of a modern woman of the millennium? Why would a similar idealization not have

RQ5

occurred of a nonwhite woman, an immigrant woman, or a non-Western woman? Even though 15 years and more have passed since the death of Diana, that moment of her death, which unleashed a media phenomenon unprecedented in history, was an important cultural and political moment. It was a moment in which we saw the hypermediated construction of a national myth organized around the body of a white upper-class heterosexual woman whose every aspect was being linked to "the people," both in the United Kingdom and beyond, and who came to signify a new (white) postcolonial British identity—at once cosmopolitan and national. Thus, when Diana died and a frenzied mediation followed, I excitedly waited for some for some academic book to emerge that would zero in on this aspect: the mediated relationship between white femininity and nation that the Diana phenomenon made visible. As academics started producing essays and edited collections about the Diana phenomenon, what struck me is that the whiteness of the phenomenon and, specifically, the white femininity angle was hardly being theorized or analyzed. Yet, it was so visible, so in our face (at least if you were nonwhite).

Available research on Diana has focused attention on her death as a performance of various aspects of the public sphere (Ang et al, 1997; Kear & Steinberg, 1999; Merck, 1998; McGuigan, 2001; Richards, Wilson, & Woodhead, 1999; Taylor, 2000; T. Walter, 1999).[1] Scholars have addressed the Diana phenomenon from various perspectives—as a ritual of mourning, as a sign of an emerging feminine public sphere, as a site for the production of an emotional national sphere, as an example of a global "structure of feeling," as a location through which race was negotiated, and as a narrative of humanitarianism through which a neoliberal regime of governmentality was staged (Rajagopal, 1999). All of these are indeed important lenses through which to comprehend the Diana phenomenon. While these works have provided significant insights into this cultural phenomenon—and some have specifically also focused on its gender politics (for example, Campbell, 1999; Braidiotti, 1997)—there is very little work to date that has discussed explicitly how this entire national spectacle, which continues to be revisited even today, was enabled by a _spectacularization of white femininity_. Although Richard Dyer (1997), prior to Diana's death, had discussed her image—in a section of his influential book _White_—as an example of idealized whiteness, his work—given its emphasis—was not focused on issues of nation and national identity. Overall, work linking white femininity to national identity in a comprehensive manner is still limited.[2] This book hopes to offer a contextually situated analysis of the numerous facets of white femininity that the Diana phenomenon mobilized and stabilized in the production of a (new) national narrative of Britishness in the 1990s and beyond. Additionally, this book links the representations of Diana's white femininity to images of several other privileged white women in popular culture at the turn of the millennium in order to call attention to a larger neoliberal formation of citizenship in North Atlantic nations (especially the United Kingdom and the United States) that was being expressed through particular images of privileged white women. Thus, while Diana's image remains my point of entry into, and exit out of, such discussions, throughout this book, I touch on a constellation of images of privileged white women in order to illustrate a larger formation of white femininity through which many neoliberal logics of national identity and citizenly belonging were being rewritten in the late 20th and early 21st centuries. My hope is that this project will offer useful insights for comprehending larger neoliberal logics of "selfhood" in the late 20th and early 21st centuries that were not only gendered, but also enacted through bodies of numerous privileged (and primarily heterosexually identified, upper-/middle-class, and able bodied) white women in North Atlantic nations.

Although there are works on the Diana phenomenon that have focused on the issue of race, these works have not moved this focus to the level of theorizing what the phenomenon revealed about the intersections between white femininity and the nation. For instance, Paul Gilroy (1997), Mica Nava (1999), Yasmin Brown (2001), and Emily Lomax (1999) offer useful and interesting discussions of the problematics of race that surfaced in the Diana event in 1997. Gilroy harshly, and in my view correctly, remained skeptical of linking the Diana phenomenon to the promise of a more ethnic Britain. Nava and Brown, on the other hand, saw the multicultural face of Britain represented through Diana's death as a positive sign of a changing England. Lomax remained more critical and saw the representation of multiculturalism occurring through the Diana phenomenon as a ploy of what she called "ethnic marketing" (1999, p. 74). And Nava, more recently, in her book *Visceral Cosmopolitanism* (2007), has addressed the representational politics of the Diana and Dodi romance in order to argue that it indicated a healthy cosmopolitanism that offered possibilities for reimagining Britain through multicultural logics. I respectfully disagree with this argument (but address this disagreement in a later chapter). Overall, in focusing solely on how national and global ethnicity were represented through the Diana media phenomenon, these works do not *explicitly* analyze or theorize the complex functioning of white femininity in this *national* performance.

With the Diana phenomenon, the relative absence of a focus on white femininity is especially to be commented upon. The sheer range and volume of images available about this white woman (including the many tropes of white femininity through which she has been represented) supersedes media representations of most other white women in history. While the full complexity of this unprecedented event cannot be captured in one book, it is the case that there are numerous complexities regarding the operations of white femininity expressed in this phenomenon that are of value to cultural theorists interested in understanding how the white female body remains a site for the performance of a national (re)vision. Given all this, I felt that the Diana phenomenon needed to be revisited as a case study in order to better understand the relationship between nation and white femininity. Such an examination, while certainly contextual—given that whiteness functions in different ways in different times—nonetheless would provide larger glimpses into the circuits of power through which white femininity and national identity articulate each other in contemporary culture (something that has not been theorized as much even today and especially when contrasted with the numerous studies done on white masculinity and the nation).

Indeed, the Diana case offers an example *par excellence* through which to comprehend how representations of iconic white women signify shifts in a national common sense. Few white women in history have had such an archive of images organized around them through which shifts in a nation's modernity has been imagined. And very few white women in history have risen to a level where they symbolized not just a national popular but also a global popular. And furthermore, very few white women in our mediated times have simultaneously signified so many universalized narratives of white femininity: angel, good mother, global savior, icon of beauty, and a goddess, Diana Taylor (2003) notes that Diana's physical existence was "redundant"; she existed always as an image, a representation that was more real than her corporeality and "that continues to defy the limits of space and time" (p. 154). Indeed, Diana's image simply refuses to disappear. In the first few months of 2011, we saw it vehemently assert itself with the Royal Wedding of Prince William and Catherine Middleton. Following that, we have seen almost every act and every fashion style of Kate Middleton being compared to those of Diana. And, more recently, the birth of Kate and William's baby, William and Kate's "hands on" no-fuss parenting style, the new 2013 biopic of Diana where she is played by Naomi Watts, and the 2013 resurrection of the investigation of Diana's death following new claims of conspiracy continue to prove to us that Diana does not perish.

Diana's fashion designer Victor Edelstein once commented on the universal quality that the image of Diana has acquired.

There are certain women in the world who have that [universal appeal]. . . . it's hard to put your finger on it . . . its beauty, its kindness, its vulnerability . . . I think in a way there's a very human need to have one's goddesses since the beginning of time, people have needed that. . . . Humanity needs it somehow. Doesn't happen with men. They are not gods in the same way. It's always women.[3]

Edelstein's explanation is inadequate. When he states that "certain" women have "that," what is unremarked is that in world history, it is only white women who have risen to the level of a mythology, and it is only white women around whom narratives of universal love and desire tend to be scripted. The question is: Why? What enables that? What genealogies, stories, myths, and desires have already been solidified and given meaning in Western (and due to imperialism even in non-Western) cultures through the body of the white woman that they enable white womanhood to acquire a status of universal goodness, beauty, caring, and desire? As a national signifier of white femininity, Diana is also one of the few white women in contemporary times whose body has simultaneously traveled from the national to the global (and not always in this order or through a neat linearity)—although now the likes of Angelina Jolie are also signifying such movements (which I discuss in later chapters) Although I am using the terms *national* and *global* separately here, I do not suggest that they exist in a binary relation to each other. Rather, they constitute a network of interconnections in that the relations of the global are always shored up by, and situated in, competing national logics just as national logics are simultaneously informed by larger global relations. The global and the national are thus not neat separate objects or domains. They constantly inform each other through shifting transnational circuits of power that may inform what a national landscape might look like at a particular moment just as shifting transnational relations of power that may inform the nation (or national identity) at a particular time also impact the kinds of global logics that may confront us in that time (and beyond).

The signification of Diana in the 1990s was one in which we saw the British nation simultaneously assert itself as highly national yet also global. One of the foci of this project is to invite a rethinking of contemporary white national femininity through a lens of the geopolitical and global. How do representations, articulations, and actions of privileged white women of the Global North impact, inform, and intersect with larger geopolitics? How does the body of the privileged white woman—symbolically and materially—circulate through transnational relations of power and in the process maintain and reify (and sometimes unsettle) the hegemonic logics of those relations? One of the claims of this project is that white (national) femininity is always imbricated in larger global relations and logics. And some of the different ways in which white femininity remains situated in, and is productive (as well as also being an outcome) of, larger geopolitical and global currents is one important emphasis of this book. A gap in existing research on Diana (as well as on contemporary white women in general) is precisely a focus on the global relations of white (national) femininity. In this book, the global articulations of white national femininity and the ways in which transnational linkages constitute national identity formations through the body and image of the white woman (in Anglo-dominant contexts) will be dealt with extensively.

And Beyond

"And beyond" in the book's title is important. *Beyond,* along with *Diana,* frames this investigation of the relation between white femininity and national identity. Although Diana (the representation) is my central focus, I address numerous other white female icons of the late 20th and early 21st centuries—many of whom have not only articulated themselves through references to Diana (for example, Angelina Jolie, the Spice Girls) but who, along with the Diana, signal a larger millennial (and even postmillennial) neoliberal formation of white femininity in North Atlantic nations that need to be analyzed. For instance, in almost every chapter, while localizing the Diana phenomenon in the Blairite times of New Britain, I have broadened my discussion to address other white female celebrities who have been visible during these millennial times. Indeed, while the Diana phenomenon is contextually based, many of its logics about (white) national femininity provide a lens through which to read many other white women at the turn of the century. Thus, on the one hand, the book is about the Diana phenomenon. On the other, it calls attention to a broader reinvention of white womanhood in North Atlantic nations such as the United Kingdom and United States in the late 20th and early 21st centuries through which we have been witnessing a complex neoliberal management of the (gendered) self and a containment of any Other that might threaten that self. Cherie Blair, Angelina Jolie, Madonna, Christy Turlington, Sandra Bullock, Mia Farrow, Jemima Khan, Goldie Hawn, Donna Karan, Camilla Parker Bowles, the Spice Girls, Sarah Ferguson, Naomi Campbell, Oprah, Julia Roberts, Cindy McCain, and many others have small roles in this book. The black female icons in this list are included because, as will be discussed later, neoliberal logics of race today often articulate privileged black women through scripts of privileged white femininity.

This approach of constantly linking the Diana phenomenon to related representations of white femininity in the late 20th and early 21st centuries is a productive framework for studying popular icons in contemporary culture. While research on celebrities and popular figures sometimes tends

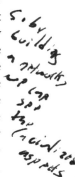

to focus singularly on one icon—for example, a Madonna, or an Elvis, or a Marilyn Monroe—and this can be a useful approach—it is easy to forget that representational and racial logics through which a particular celebrity or icon is given meaning, as well as producing meaning, intersect with the positioning of other celebrities around the same time. This is especially true perhaps of female icons given that racialized female bodies in popular culture are regulated through similar gendered logics at a given moment that are often responses to larger political and social anxieties of the nation (and the world at large). Saying this is not to encourage generalizations. It is rather to recognize, methodologically and politically, that the logics that underlie media representations of particular constructs such as white femininity, in a given moment or context, become particularly visible when we address a range of related formations of white female icons in a time period and across similar contexts (in this case neoliberal national contexts). Thus, my hope is that this project will be particularly useful to those interested in the broader significance of the Diana phenomenon for understanding millennial formations of (white) femininity.

Finally, "beyond" in the title hints at the constant beyond that lies beyond a particular formation of white femininity—the beyond that is always there to reinvent new futures for the nation through new formations of white femininity. To that extent, "beyond" makes an implicit statement that white femininity is not a frozen homogenous timeless structure. It slips and slides through the beyonds of time. And it is a geo-contextual formation.

The Diana Renaissance

Even though more than 15 years have passed since the death of Diana and although the explosive intensity of images from 1997 has lessened, the circulation of images and stories about Diana is unrelenting as I indicated earlier. The recent Royal Wedding was just one example where Diana's image reemerged quite forcefully and voluminously. But beyond this special occasion, at an everyday level, her image continues to be everywhere: from coffee mugs to comic books, brooches to calendar art, wall posters to Diana dolls. In fact, there is now an entire online industry dedicated to collecting and selling Diana artifacts. One simply has to go to Ebay to witness the selling and buying of Diana artifacts—newspapers, books, magazines, postcards, calendars, comic books, DVDs, videos, television programs, dolls, pins, buttons, mugs, collector's spoons, and even brochures of events she attended. Such products are often sold at fairly high prices. And bidding tends to be quite fierce. In fact some of the media materials for this research that were sometimes hard to acquire or access directly from a producer, publisher, or a merchant after all these years were acquired from such eBay auctions on Diana. What especially interested me, as I often bid for some of the items, is how fast the bids moved and how far they climbed. An item starting with an initial bid of $5 could end up, after fierce and quick competition, with a price of $40 or $50 dollars (and sometimes even more). This illustrates the material investment people are still willing to make in the story of Diana.

The last few years in particular have witnessed a renaissance in images and narratives about Princess Diana. The year 2007 alone—the tenth anniversary year of Diana's death—witnessed a multitude of popular cultural articulations of Diana. In July 2007, the Concert for Princess Diana took place at the Wembley Stadium in London, organized by her sons, Princes William and Harry. Reportedly, 70,000 people attended the concert. Tickets sold out several months prior to the event. In 2006, the Oscar-winning film *The Queen* captured the imagination of the world. While purportedly focused on the life of Elizabeth II, *The Queen* was, in many ways, a response to Princess Diana's royal victim status by showcasing the Queen's side of things. Anyone who has seen the film would agree that it rescued the queen from the depths of unpopularity into which she had sunk after Diana's death. In February 2007, the British newspaper the *Daily Mail,* in a Sunday edition, attached a special DVD supplement on the life of Diana narrated by Richard Attenborough that contained some unseen footage of her life. In 2005, in Hyde Park, London, a water fountain was opened (it was first inaugurated in 2004 and then reopened in 2005 given the problems that arose after the 2004 inauguration) to signify the "natural" spirit of Diana. Further, the last few years in Britain have witnessed intense inquisition into Diana's death. And this has generated all kinds of stories about whether she was killed by the royals, whether she was pregnant, or whether other conspiracies were involved. In September 2007, there was a national televised coverage of the memorial marking the 10th anniversary of Diana's death that was organized by William and Harry. Just the very next day, the BBC reran the original televised coverage of Diana's funeral from 1997. In September 2007 (the September 4 issue), *Hello* magazine devoted itself to Diana's memory and assessed its relevance for the people on the 10th anniversary of her death. The *Hello* issue published several surveys. One of the surveys claimed that around 52% of British people thought that there should be a statue in the memory of Diana while another survey stated that 9 out of 10 women "say that Diana's place in history is assured." Between August 20 and 23, 2007, the Britannica blog conducted a forum on the celebrity culture of Diana in which academics, sport stars, and media commentators addressed the relevance of Diana 10 years after her corporeal death. At this same time, the television film *Who Killed Diana* (2006) that recreated the Paris tragedy also aired in Britain (it initially aired on British TV channel, Sky One) as well as in the United States. A special 50-pence stamp to commemorate the 10-year anniversary of Diana's and Mother Teresa's deaths was released by Ascension Island (a U.K. Overseas Territory). The visual on the Diana stamp depicted Diana and Mother Teresa together.

References to the story of Diana seem to be increasing in recent years. In 2009, Bluewater Productions published a comic book immortalizing Diana in their *Female Force* series (issue 1, July 2009). The publisher stated that while the series was not explicitly designed for kids, many mothers buy it for their kids. He specifically noted, "we want girls to learn what she has done."[4] In 2009, the *National Constitution Center* in Philadelphia displayed an exhibition of Diana titled *Diana: A Celebration*. It presented over 150 artifacts loaned from Diana's ancestral estate, Althorp House. The tickets were priced at $25 for adults. Celebrity figures such as Angelina Jolie and Paris Hilton have recently declared that they want to be seen as the Diana of the 21st century. In the recent 2011 Cannes Film Festival, a new controversial film *Unlawful Killing*, which has been banned in Britain and which raises new questions about Diana's death, was screened. Again in 2011, there was a planned auction of many of Diana's letters written to her ex-colleague at the kindergarten where she worked prior to her marriage. In 2013, the Diana biopic starring Naomi Watts, which is said to focus primarily on her complex relationship with Pakistani doctor Hasnat Khan, hit the screens in the United Kingdom in September. The film was released in the United States later—which was also around the time this book was going into production. So I did not have the opportunity to view it—and thus comment on it. In 2013, another significant occurrence took place: a photograph emerged of Diana. The photograph is of her as a teenager lying in bed with a "mystery man" seated behind her. This photo has created a sensation. It was later revealed that Adam Russell (grandson of Stanley Baldwin) was the young man in the photo. While the details of the photo are not that important perhaps, what is important is that any unseen or unknown image of Diana that surfaces rocks the world—even today.

Some of the most interesting recent references to Diana, however, are the following. In 2011, the Barbuda beach was to be named after Diana by the two-island nation-state of Barbuda and Antigua. The beach constitutes a pristine strip of land by the ocean. Diana allegedly visited this land often to escape the world. The decision to name the beach as such evokes naturalized associations between white femininity and pristine landscapes. Reports also note that several initiatives are being planned to brand the beach as a natural wonder. There are also (apparently) plans for erecting a monument to honor the legacy of Diana.

In June 2011, on Diana's 50th birthday, *Newsweek* ran a much publicized cover page that shows Kate Middleton walking with Diana as Diana might have looked at the age of 50 (figure 1.1). Diana's image is doctored with technology—slightly old, a little ghostly, but as glamorous as ever. What is interesting about this cover image is that there was no real need for Kate Middleton to be featured on the cover. After all, it was about "Diana at 50." The theme would have held even if the cover image simply focused on Diana. Kate's image next to a ghostly Diana thus becomes noteworthy. And Kate, unlike Diana, is not looking in front but sideways at Diana and wearing a big smile on her face. While such imagined visual moments are always complex to read, it can be argued that there is a visual assertion being made about the continuity of the symbolism of Diana in the future (which Kate Middleton now symbolizes). Indeed, this image seems to signify powerfully that the "ghost" of Diana (or her remains so to speak) is very much alive and continues to make its mark on British society (and the world at large). As I noted earlier, Diana does not seem to die. In fact, ever since Kate Middleton's appearance on our public screens, she has been frequently referenced (visually) through Diana. Frequently the shots through which Kate is framed remind us of Diana—such as the shot of her (dressed in blue) leaving her apartment in Chelsea, when she was dating William, while being hounded by the press. This is similar in its framing to the much-circulated 1980s image of Diana (dressed in blue) leaving her Sloane Square apartment while being chased by photographers. Further, Diana's engagement ring on Kate's finger, which the media loves so much, makes it difficult to view this new princess outside of the legacy of the actual "people's princess."

In 2011, Monica Ali, the acclaimed British author of *Brick Lane* (2004), published the highly publicized novel *Untold Story* (published first in paperback 2012), which imagines a fictional Diana had she continued to live. And in 2010, a Chinese clothing company *Jealousy International* used a Diana look-alike model wearing lingerie to promote the company's brand. The promotional ads urged customers to "feel the romance of British royalty." This lingerie promotion sparked controversy and outrage in Britain. The company had first unveiled the brand via huge billboards at Shenzen Airport. A section of the company's website presented the Diana lingerie range with the slogan "free your mind, free your style." This slogan clearly links Diana's fashion (and sexuality) to a neoliberal sense of freedom, an issue I take up in a later chapter. It also suggests how growing neoliberal logics in

Diana at 50 If She Were Here Now By Tina Brown

JULY 4 & 11, 2011 THEDAILYBEAST.COM

Newsweek

| AFGHANISTAN General Rod's War | COMING HOME Young Exiles Return to a New South Sudan | REPORT CARD 2011's Crazy First Six Months | PLUS Simon Schama Paul Theroux Laila Lalami Simon Winchester |

Figure 1.1. "Diana at 50" from the July 4/July 11, 2011 *Newsweek* cover. (The Newsweek/Daily Beast Company LLC. All rights reserved. Used by permission and protected by the copyright laws of the United States. The printing, copying, redistribution, or retransmission of this content without express permission is prohibited.)

non-Western nations are often glamorized through ideologies of whiteness and, in this case, white femininity.

These examples provide ample evidence that not only has the story of Diana not died, it has, in fact, become so commonplace and ubiquitous that we forget that it is always there—always circulating in mass culture and its various currents. The story of Diana seems to have become even more powerful today than in the earlier days of her entry into public screens. Consider this brief example. On May 24, 2010, *Larry King Live* conducted a panel discussing Sarah Ferguson's latest scandal where she allegedly offered *News of the World* access to Prince Andrew for a huge sum of money (she apparently did not know who they were as they were undercover). We learned later that this had been a scam to trap Sarah. During one of the commercial breaks in this program, there was a streaming of some images, and one such image was of Diana. The image of Diana had no relevance to the panel discussion; she was not even mentioned in the panel as the whole focus was on the ethicality of Sarah's conduct. Yet, Diana's image was just displayed as the panel took a break. It is precisely this kind of a commonplaceness that Diana's image has acquired—where, on the one hand, we never forget who she was and, on the other, we rarely bat an eye when we see her image in likely and unlikely places. It is this that makes the script that we call Diana so culturally significant. Diana is an assemblage—a media assemblage to be specific—constituting a constellation of meanings about white femininity through which the places of numerous other white women, and sometimes even nonwhite women, and their relation to the nation and the world are seen. For example, even though Eva Peron of Argentina became a world figure much before Diana, after Diana's death, in a peculiar temporal reversal (illustrating the complex power inequalities between the Global North and Global South) media reports sometimes discussed Peron *as* Argentina's Diana.

Sara Ahmed's (2007) work on whiteness has intimated that the power of whiteness is secured through its habitual performance—the repeats and repetitions of its practices—as there is no ontology to whiteness. Put differently, whiteness is not an original property of bodies. Rather, it secures its ideological power through a constant repetition of its logics—through stories, myths, images, and narratives that, in a given moment, secure a particular orientation of whiteness. This orientation locates itself in particular kinds of (white) bodies (as opposed to others). With the Diana phenomenon this argument becomes especially relevant in underscoring the importance of analyzing her representations for understanding contemporary white femininity. The vast gallery of images and narratives that exist about Diana spanning almost 30 years is extremely repetitive. It is often the same images and narratives that are repeated, replayed, and recirculated. If we close our eyes and think of Diana, images such as the following would appear on our mental screens: Diana hugging an African baby, Diana sliding down a water ride with William and Harry, Diana in her bridal dress walking into Saint Paul's, Diana in a glamorous slim-cut cocktail dress that highlights her gym-toned body, Diana in a landmine site in Bosnia, Diana touching an HIV patient or consoling a cancer patient in a hospital, Diana on a yacht with Dodi, Diana with Mother Teresa, or the damaged (and now visually fetishized) car from the Paris chase that killed both her and Dodi Fayed. While the plethora of images about Diana is overwhelming, the reality is that it is through a constant repetition of only a limited number of images or stories that the Diana phenomenon, for the most part, produces its meanings about white nationalized femininity. Through constant repetition, a multifaceted script of white femininity has been stabilized that today has acquired so much power that it has become a framework for depicting the "modern" woman of the late 20th and early 21st centuries and a cipher for postcolonial white British identity in the millennial years. Britain before Diana and Britain after Diana function as temporal markers through which old Britain is distinguished from the late 1990s' New Britain, which was apparently ushered in by Tony Blair's New Labor government.

When I first began thinking of writing a book on white femininity and national identity, I was not particularly focused on the Diana phenomenon. Rather, as a media and communications scholar, I wanted to understand the ways in which media representations of white women play a role in producing a national common sense about white femininity. I wanted to understand how media narratives about white femininity produce assemblages of meanings about white women and, more particularly, white women's relations with the nation and vice versa. And I wanted to explore this particularly by focusing on an iconic white woman in contemporary times, for iconic subjects—especially celebrity figures—are intimately linked to everyday aspects of people's lives. They offer us scripts for being human (Dyer, 2004). The Diana phenomenon provides a rich context for such explorations. For, as suggested earlier, very few white women have been visualized, mediated, and scripted as being of "the people" as has been Diana. While many other white women in earlier times might have served as national and even global icons, the media was not as pervasive, intrusive, interactive, and instantaneous in those times. The assemblage of images about white femininity produced through Diana's iconicity functions today as a huge ocean in which we see various waves of white womanhood—waves that often signify diverse articulations of "modern" Britishness and the "modern" woman.

Celebrity Culture and Gender

Because I have addressed Diana's iconicity, it is only appropriate that I say a few words about the significance of celebrities—themselves products, and productive, of contemporary media ecologies—in the late 20th century and early 21st century. Diana was (and still is) a celebrity *par excellance.* And the Diana phenomenon, in particular, expresses specific logics, to some of which this book calls attention, about the intersections of celebrity culture, cultural politics, national identity, and global struggles over (what constitutes) modern subjectivity. Richard Dyer's influential (1979, 1986) work analyzed stars as a semiotic system that articulates larger ideological and political relations in society. In particular, for Dyer, stars/celebrities express prevailing "ideas of personhood" (2004, p. 9) in society. Dyer's work paved the way for the study of celebrities. Specifically, there has been a significant focus on how celebrities, and often their private lives, function as screens upon which larger social anxieties are played out, and how celebritization (a term that is increasingly in use these days) produces forms of cultural authority and notions of cultural normalcy while also functioning as a space of cultural change and struggle. In their introduction to the inaugural issue of the journal *Celebrity Studies,* Su Holmes and Sean Redmond (2010) note that a celebrity "exists at the core of many of the spaces, experiences, and economies of modern life" (p. 7). They note elsewhere that celebrities have a profound effect "on their [i.e., the audience's] identity, self-image, and sense of belonging" (Redmond & Holmes, 2007, p. 4). Graeme Turner (2004, p. 92) discusses celebrities as situated in, and as well productive of, what he calls "para-social" relationships. Chris Rojek (2001) describes such para-social relations—where people share a connection with an icon that feels extremely intimate, and yet the icon may not know such people individually—as "second-order intimacy" (p. 52). Second-order intimacies are "relations of intimacy constructed through the mass-media rather than direct experience and face-to-face meetings" (p. 52).

The Princess Diana cultural phenomenon expressed many of these features of celebrity culture. It offered, as well as normalized, new modes of belonging (in Britain and the world). It illustrated unprecedented levels of intimacy with the people, and it functioned as a (shifting) screen upon which larger relations about modern national belonging (in Britain) were played out. Where the Diana phenomenon, as a celebrity phenomenon, becomes important is in its representation of how female (and especially white female) celebrities are often "celebritized" in ways that normalize—or if not that then at least make prominent—larger national desires that are usually informed by specific nationalized gender logics (and crosscut by race, sexuality, globality, and class). Many of the themes through which Diana felt "intimate" to us—motherhood, global humanitarianism, love for children, a "cool" fashion style, explorations of inner self—are ultimately national themes that encouraged particular ways of thinking about Britishness in the millennium. Even Diana's relationships to Muslim men—while not endorsed by the nation—revealed (as I point out in Chapter 5) a kind of mediated policing of Muslim men who dare to be close to white women. As I illustrate later in the book, such mediation itself was situated in, and expressive of, the anti-Muslim climate of Britain in the 1990s.

Thus, the Diana phenomenon offers an important space through which to comprehend what Holmes and Negra (2011) call the "gendered politics of fame" (p. 9). Pointing out how celebrity studies have been primarily dominated by men and that there have been very few feminist interventions, Holmes and Negra (2011) note that in contrast to a "star," a celebrity connotes a "representational structure" that is consumed by a person's "private life or lifestyle" (p. 13). And given that women are primarily associated with the private and the domestic, and that celebrity culture is primarily constituted by women, it therefore tends to be gendered in particular ways. That is, the politics that celebrity cultures produce, and within which they are often ensconced, express larger social issues around gender relations. To that extent, the Diana phenomenon (as a nationalized phenomenon) invites us to consider the ways in which the (white) female celebrity body is nationalized and renationalized in contemporary times through modes and logics that are different from those of (white) male celebrities. While the aim of this book is not to theorize celebrity politics, it is my hope that some of the insights of this book will make a modest contribution to the rich and emerging field of (feminist) celebrity studies.

Recent Research on White Femininity

This book situates itself within larger conversations in feminist scholarship that have explored white women's social locations as constituting sites through which racialized and colonial relations are produced (Blee, 2002; Cherniavsky, 1995, 2006; Davy, 1997; Deliovsky, 2010; Dyer, 1997; Frankenberg, 1993; Grewal, 1996; C. Hall, 2000; Hurtado, 1996; Ingraham, 1999; Kaplan, 1995, 2001; McClintock, 1995; Najmi & Srikanth, 2002; Rafael, 2000; Sharpe, 1993; Stokes, 2001; Stoler, 1995, 2002, 2006; Tapia, 2011; Thobani, 2010; Ware, 1992, 2001; Ware & Back, 2001; among others). This body of work, following the innovative works of scholars such as McIntosh (1988) and Dyer (1988) broke new grounds not only by turning the study of race back upon whiteness, but also by emphasizing how race in Anglo-dominant social contexts is centrally tied to ideologies of white femininity. This project remains heavily indebted to the lines of thought opened up by this important literature.

Despite important moves made in this literature, some of its trends need to be commented on. I briefly mentioned some earlier but elaborate them more fully here. First, for the most part, studies investigating white femininity or white womanhood have tended to reside largely at the level of examining the racialization of white women. There are very few works that extend such discussions explicitly to levels of nation and national identity (Grewal, 1996; McClintock, 1995; Stoler, 1995; Ware, 1992 are some exceptions)—and specifically, to the *complex* ways in which white femininity is made to perform the nation and the ways in which the nation performs itself on and through the body of the white woman. In saying this I do not mean to diminish the importance of works that have focused on white women in the empire (given that during high imperialism, the empire was also inextricably linked to the nation).[5] But even when such studies focused on white women in the empire, the issue of how the functioning of white women in the colonies was explicitly linked to (colonial) national identity formation, while often implied in such works, has not always been specifically articulated or theorized

(Grewal's 1996 work is an exception here). Indeed, apart from the few notable exceptions mentioned here, the whiteness turn in feminist studies has, for the most part, paid insufficient attention to the specific processes through which white femininity remains *nationalized*. For instance, now there are some influential anthologies on gender and nation that have done much to advance our understanding of the relationships among gender, sexuality, and nation (for example, Alarcon, Moallem, & Kaplan, 1999; McClintock, Mufti, & Shohat, 1997). These works, however, do not focus as much on the interrelationship between white femininity and national identity. This is not a criticism of these influential works. It is, rather, to make the overall argument that, for the most part, the explicit relationship between white femininity and the nation, especially as it plays out in *contemporary* times, has been undertheorized in feminist scholarship of the nation. A recent exception that should be acknowledged, however, is Tapia's (2011) book on the intersections of race, the maternal, and death, in which one chapter also focuses on Princess Diana's death. The chapter addresses how death and the maternal come together in visual culture to produce racialized citizenship that is grounded on "commemorating whiteness" (p. 43). This is certainly an interesting insight that illustrates how commemorative visual culture often links race and death through a logic of maternalism.

Second, of the studies that engage the nation by exploring white femininity more explicitly (for example, Grewal, 1996; Rafael, 2000; Stoler, 1995, 2002; Ware, 1992) the focus has been on the role of white women in historical colonial contexts—that is, during the age of high imperialism when the lines between "us" and "them," "the colonizer" and "the colonized," were more rigorously drawn, maintained, and visible. Both Grewal (1996) and Ware (1992), for instance, have engaged in incisive studies that address the role of British women in India during high British imperialism. Similarly, Stoler has brilliantly examined the Dutch imperial context and discussed the role of white women in those contexts. And Rafael, in his book on U.S.-Philippines historical relations, has devoted a few sections to how white women played a role in enacting a benevolent "white love" that was used to justify U.S. colonialism.

While this project is influenced by these important works, its exploration of white femininity and national identity is located in a *contemporary* Anglo-dominant national context. In most Anglo-national societies today, the challenges faced by the nation-state are quite different than what they were during pre—Second World War days of the empire. Today, due to globalization, the presence of postcolonial populations, and advances in gender and sexual politics, the very boundaries of several Western nations are being complicated. The lines between us and them are no longer drawn in overt black and white ways. Unlike periods of high imperialism, the challenge for the nation in the late 20th and early 21st centuries is to manage, contain, negotiate, and even utilize difference while at the same time striving to maintain a larger (white) national commonsense. The problem with such management and utilization of difference is that it often produces a logic where *cultural difference overrides racial tensions* and even becomes a lid to keep them from erupting. Indeed, as new identities and new imaginaries that produce new demographics begin to mess up the contemporary logics of the modern, Anglo-dominant nations desperately seek new grounds on which to anchor themselves through some sense of a unified identity, all the while seeking to manage and absorb the (often unpredictable) explosion and implosion of difference (even as they try to contain that very difference). In such conditions of differential messiness, in such moments of *differance,* what happens to the script of white femininity as it functions to anchor and write new national modernities? How is it deployed to mediate difference while keeping in place the structural borders of (national) whiteness? What old articulations are resecured and what new ones become visible in such mediations? And do such mediations signal a shift, or a recentering, of Anglo-centric logics of the (national) modern?

Third, in much of the current research, limited attention has been directed to the ways in which popular cultural representations of white femininity produce a nationalized public sphere (see Banet-Weiser, 1999; Dyer, 1997; Kaplan, 1995; Negra, 2001; Shome, 2001; Tapia, 2011 for exceptions). Although there exists scholarship on media images of white women, the scant attention to how media representations of white femininity are explicitly linked to national modernities is to be noted. In particular, there is very little work on the mediated relationship between *white femininity and national identity* in *contemporary times* that speaks to racial anxieties that inform neoliberal rationalities of the late 20th and early 21st centuries. This is especially to be observed, given that, on the parallel side, significant work exists on how representations of white masculinity function to produce the nation (including in contemporary times) (Carroll, 2011; DiPiero, 2002; Jeffords, 1988, 1994; Nelson, 1998; Pfeil, 1994; Robinson, 2000; Savran, 1998; Wiegman, 1995 among others). This project argues that media representations of white women are important to focus on in order to comprehend spectacles of national identity formation. Popular cultural representations of white femininity embody condensed desires and violences of the nation through which various exclusions, contradictions, ironies, and tensions of contemporary Anglo democracies manifest themselves.

In my own field of communication studies, as in other fields, there has been an explosion of work on whiteness (Cooks & Simpson, 2007; Crenshaw, 1997; Moon & Flores, 2000; Nakayama & Martin, 1999; Nakayama & Krizek, 1995; Dubrofsky, 2006; Projansky & Ono, 1999; Shome, 1996, 2000; Warren, 2003 to list a few). But there has been almost no work in communication studies that focuses on the relationship between *white* femininity and national identity in contemporary times. While some communication scholars have indeed addressed the communicative constructions of white femininity (such as Moon, 1999; Carrillo-Rowe, 2000; Shome, 2001; Zacharias, 2003), there is still a significant absence of work that unpacks the communicative and mediated articulations between white femininity and national ideologies. I should note that my argument is *not* that there is no work on gender and nation whether in communication studies or in the broader field of feminist studies. Indeed, as I discuss later, there exists a rich literature on gender and national identity. Rather, my argument is that there are hardly any works (other than a handful I noted earlier) that focus *comprehensively* on the mediated relationship between white femininity and national identity in contemporary times—especially at the turn of the century.

Fourth, while excellent work has been done on white femininity in critical whiteness studies, there is limited work that has addressed the transnationalization of white femininity, particularly in the context of nation and national identity. Some notable exceptions are Cherniavsky (2006) and Kaplan (2001, 1995). Vron Ware (2001) writes that "the politics of the geo-body are clearly crucial to this discussion [of whiteness], since ideologies of 'race', ethnicity, and belonging are fundamentally bound up with the histories of the nation and how it is defined by competing forces" (p. 185). Without a recognition of the "interconnected global system," Ware argues, "a discussion of national anything is meaningless" (p. 185).[6] I thus suggest that the white female national body needs to be understood as a "geo-body" by which I mean, following Ware, a geopolitical body. The Diana phenomenon manifested not just the nationalization of white femininity but also the ways in which the nation often stages its modernity through a transnationalization (and a geo-politicization) of itself through the body of the white woman.

White Femininity and the Nation

Eva Cherniavsky (2006) makes an interesting point about white women in contemporary mediated times. She suggests that in an age of mechanical reproduction, white womanhood is becoming less and less something that we can understand as located in the body of white women. Rather, white womanhood, and whiteness more generally, is depthless today. In an age of mechanical reproduction, it is the constant depthless consumerist reproduction of visual representations and images of white women that produce and stabilize hegemonic logics of white femininity. For media and communications scholars, this suggestion is relevant. While much work in critical whiteness studies has focused on how whites experience and articulate their privilege, Cherniavsky's point calls for a subtle shift in perspective that is significant for my argument. The implications of Cherniavsky's point invite us to recognize that in an age of mechanical reproduction, whiteness (and white femininity), as an assemblage of power, is constantly reproduced through media circuits and their technologies. This depthlessness is symptomatic of our heightened media and visual environment within which race is constantly reworked today. At the same time, this consumerist depthlessness also underscores how the image and the narrative of whiteness cannot be adequately understood by focusing only on individualized subjects of whiteness as though they have an internal coherence to themselves. Whiteness acquires meaning today through constant mediated reproductions and repetitions of diverse images and logics of whiteness. And these images and logics, that are subject to constant and relentless media techniques of cut-and-paste (which are central to how commercial media functions), ultimately produce a larger assemblage of meanings about particular modes of whiteness that are made desirable (or sometimes othered) in a given national moment and context.

Princess Diana's representations constitute an example of the highest order of such mediated cut-and-paste reproduction of white femininity. The "story" of Diana actually cannot be garnered and made sense of in an autobiographical or chronological manner. We learn less of Diana's significance when we read her biographies. We learn far more about her significance when we engage her story through the numerous cut-and-paste visual narratives and images that do not follow any neat or deep linear chronology. A significant part of this depthlessness of Diana has to do with the quality of "liveness" of her image. Although dead, she never seems dead. Susan Stewart of *TV Guide* (1997) noted after her death,

> I know for a fact that Diana existed apart from television: I once shook her hand. It was exciting . . . but almost meaningless. [. . .] There are at least a dozen film clips of Diana more vivid in my mind than our actual off screen meeting. (cited in Taylor, 1999, p. 205)

Indeed our exposure to Diana (not the person whom we never knew, but the script, the image, the story, the representation) rarely reflects a coherent, organized, and unified process. An image of her from the mid-1980s was

easily reproduced during her funeral in 1997; an image from 1997 could easily
be reproduced today to make some comment about contemporary Britain.
While surely complete media programs of Diana do exist—voluminously
in fact—our everyday exposure to Diana is often through the cut-and-paste
techniques with which iconic images of her are constantly given new life in
popular culture as they are inserted and reinserted into contexts and stories
that may have nothing to do with the context of the original image. This
project, then, is an exploration of the mediated relationship between white
femininity and national identity. Through various analyses of the Diana
phenomenon, as well as numerous other contemporary iconic and celebrity
white women, this book probes the ways in which a modern national body
is mapped onto, and articulated through, the figure of the white female
middle-/upper-class heterosexual body. An important argument of this book
is that white femininity constitutes a central ideological force in the performance of national identity. And this performance becomes especially visible
and visual (in our media-saturated times) during moments of national shifts
or crises. This book suggests that white femininity is a nationalized category
that is always already imbricated in the production of various borders and
boundaries—of gender, race, sexuality, class, globality—in the staging of a
nation's sense of the modern.

White Femininity and National Identity

Before proceeding further, I want to clarify my use of the terms *white femininity* and *national identity*. *White femininity*, as I use it, "is not meant to suggest
a physical body or property with some ontological origin" (Shome, 2001, p.
323). Rather, it emphasizes an ideological construction through which meanings about white women and their place in society are naturalized, stabilized,
and legitimized in national narratives (Shome, 2001). There is, thus, a con-
ceptual distinction between *white women* and *white femininity*. The former
relates to individual subjects, while the latter is much more structural, having
to do with ideological scripts through which the former is influenced, shaped,
constrained, and produced (Shome, 2001). Given this, white femininity is to
be understood not as a static unchanging script. As a script that is a product
of capitalist patriarchies in Western societies, it takes on different dimensions
and formations at a given moment in a nation's sense of itself. It is because
of this that the specificities of its workings warrant attention. Further, white
femininity is not a given category, just as race is not a given. The contours of
white femininity can never be known in advance. Because we study white
femininity not to understand white femininity *per se* but rather to understand

how it gets deployed in the performance of a nation's sense of self at a given moment, the politics of white femininity is a politics without guarantees (to use Stuart Hall's admittedly overused phrase). White femininity is always a *doing* and not a *being*. It is always pushed and pulled, routed and rerouted, to script national desires. And, it is in the pushing and pulling, routing and rerouting, that it functions as a site of cultural politics.

My understanding of national identity derives from the sophisticated work on nations and nationalism that exists in cultural and social theory.[7] Following the foundational work of Benedict Anderson (1983), I see nations as "imagined communities" that are constituted of stories, myths, images, and symbols through which notions of belonging are staged and ideas about who is an appropriate national subject secured. But while nations are imagined communities, to be sure, it is the issue of what Partha Chatterjee (1991) had queried "whose imagined community?" (p. 3) that is of most interest to many postcolonial scholars. Although Chatterjee had initially raised this question to respond to Anderson and suggest that Anderson's argument already assumed a Eurocentric model of the nation, his question invites us to recognize that it is the *kinds* of bodies and identities through which the imagination of the nation is produced at a given time that makes the imagined community of the nation a site of material and discursive *struggle*. That is, the nation is not simply an imagination. The imagination itself is enabled by, as well as productive of, gross material and cultural inequities.

The mutual articulatory relationship between white femininity and national identity is an important topic for study. Numerous feminist scholars of nation and nationalism have pointed out that women's bodies, identities, and representations are central in the staging of national narratives (Alexander, 1997; Eisenstein, 1996; Hill Collins, 1994; Kandiyoti, 1991; Mayer, 2000; McClintock, 1995; Puri, 2004; Spivak, 1993; Thobani, 2007; Walby, 2006; Werbner & Yuval-Davis, 1999; West, 2009; Yuval-Davis, 1997a, 1997b; Yuval-Davis & Anthias, 1989 among others). Kaplan, Alarcon, and Moallem (1999) emphasize the "continuous repetition of gender and sexuality and their symbolic power both in the historicity and temporality of the nation" (p. 9). Similarly, Radcliffe and Westwood (1996) argue, "nationalism is constituted from its origins as a highly gendered relationship dependent on the marking on women's and men's bodies of the ideologies of national difference" (p. 135). And Jyoti Kim-Puri (2005) states that the "flawed promises of nationalism as an all-inclusive, horizontal community are especially visible from the positions of women and marginalized groups" (p. 137). Indeed, the fact that women (and other minority groups) are "of" the nation but not "in" the nation (McClintock, 1995) is something that has been recognized for a while now by feminist scholars of nationalism who argue that nationalisms spring from "masculinized memory, masculinized humiliation, and masculinized hopes" (Enloe, 1990, p. 44). National narratives too often construct a normalized and idealized woman (white, heterosexual, middle- or upper-class, and citizen) who becomes the "iconic signifier for the material, the passive, and the corporeal to be worshipped, protected, and controlled by those in power to remember and forget, to guard, to define, and redefine" (Kaplan, Alarcon, & Moallem, 1999, p. 10). As a mechanism (biological and cultural) of national reproduction, the woman's body and what that body should and should not do, becomes a site of national control, for it is through women that the nation reproduces its morality, citizenry, familial relations, and domesticity, future and present.

Ranchod-Nilsson and Tetreault (2000), however, have cautioned that the "chameleon quality of nationalism" means that while nations are indeed gendered, "we must be alert to the specific gender meanings invoked at particular times and places, and the ways in which those meanings change over time" (p. 7). Walby (2006) pushes this point further as she argues against any easy generalizations of the relation between gender and nation. Different nationalisms, in specific times and contexts, and also in relation to other political projects of the nation, may prefer particular models of gender relations over others. There is no one "preferred vision of womanhood" (p. 119). These arguments are important to keep in mind especially as there sometimes tends to be an implicit assumption in the literature on gender and nation that gender differences (including the nature of the unequal relations between various groups) in the nation are stable. Yet, nothing can be farther from the truth. For example, while motherhood may be a trope often used in nationalist mediations, *the type* of motherhood required in a particular time might signal very different gender relations than at other times. I illustrate this explicitly in a discussion about the struggle over the signification of "motherhood" that was played out in competing narratives of postwar, outdated, imperial-oriented maternity of the queen (that was not desired by the nation), and the cool, active, and modern motherhood of Diana (that was very much desired as a model of the active and entrepreneurial citizen promoted by New Labor). Thus, to say that national discourses utilize the female body to enact patriarchal desires is not enough. It is important to also recognize the ongoing struggles over different visions, meanings, and images of womanhood, including white womanhood, in a particular national hegemony (Walby, 2006). Contradictory currents of white womanhood are present in a national formation, for hegemonies are never watertight and homogeneous formations. They have their internal ambiguities as well (Gitlin, 1979). Such ambiguities or contradictory currents will usually be negated or contained within the hegemonic formation for that is how a formation becomes hegemonic—through the containment of that which can unsettle it (Hall, 1997). While focusing primarily on the dominant logics of white femininity in Blairite Britain, this project also calls attention to some competing and contradictory narratives of white womanhood that underlie those logics.

White femininity centrally informs the nation, for in Anglo-national contexts, the nation is not interested in reproducing itself through Other women but through white women, and, in particular, the white heterosexual, upper-/middle-class woman whose body is deployed strategically to secure, as well as produce, dominant national desires. As a biological and social reproducer of the nation's future, white women's bodies are central to the project of nation building. However commonplace this idea may have become now, it is important to reiterate that *white womanhood in itself is an empty category*. It has no meaning outside of the relations that it secures and through which it is secured in a particular temporal context. White women, Radhika Mohanram (2007) reminds us, "become white through . . . their relationships with white men rather than from being intrinsically white in themselves" (p. xxiii). And the ideologies that structure these relationships are white femininity. White femininity is an ideological formation through which the bodies and desires of white and nonwhite women are regulated—a regulation that is always connected to the needs of patriarchal nationalism at any given time. How white femininity is scripted, mediated, and reproduced thus reveals larger patriarchal desires and enactments of the nation.

A contemporary highly charged example that might seemingly have nothing to do with white women but actually has everything to with white women will suffice to illustrate the point that the script of white femininity is intricately tied to the anxieties and desires of white national patriarchy. Consider the debate on the veil (the hijab) that has been going on in the United Kingdom (as well as in other parts of Europe). At the crux of this debate is not only the assumption that the veil is a sign of female oppression and Muslim incivility but also that the wearing of the veil, as ex-British Foreign Secretary Jack Straw stated in 2006, makes "communication" difficult. The veil thus is seen as a marker of separateness that manifests (seemingly) how ethnic traditional Muslim women refuse to assimilate to the civilities and communicative structures of Anglo nations that offer them hospitality. This debate on the hijab and headscarf, however, is only able to occur in the first place because the normalized narrative of femininity—that is owned and reproduced by white patriarchy—is already that of white femininity.

And given that the dominant script of white femininity is ultimately geared toward making white heterosexual men comfortable, the covered-up veiled woman, whose eyes we can barely see, constitutes a reversal of the visual relations (of the "gaze") that mark the power relations between white men and white women. The white heterosexual woman is always there to be looked at (and hence owned) by the white man; her sexual desire for the white man is necessary for the stability of white heterosexual masculinity. So, when Jack Straw stated that the veil makes communication difficult, what was unspoken is that it makes communication difficult for *white men* (Hall, 2006; see also Hall [in Adams], 2007).[8] So used to "owning the gaze" of women, the white man suddenly cannot "see," and therefore "control," or make sense of, female desire. His masculinity is unmoored and shaken under those dark sinister eyes (at least he perceives them that way) behind the veil. The dark sinister eyes peering out from behind the veil, while the rest of the body remains covered (and hence cannot be sexualized), produces an ambiguity, an angst, that cannot be resolved. The "male gaze" (Mulvey, 1975), so central to heterogendered "looking relations," cannot be performed in its usual way. The script of white femininity, although seemingly absent in discussions of the veiled Muslim woman, is actually *very much present,* as it forms the unspoken communicative structure governing a white nationalized man's relationship with women of the nation. This example illustrates how the visual display of the female body (that the Muslim woman's body refuses) is important in the production of hegemonic nationalized "ways of seeing" (Berger, 1972) femininity in the white West.

Given white femininity's role (overt or everyday) in securing various borders of national belonging, white femininity is a script filled with anxieties and tensions, for it is the site through which the nation can slip into various forms of unwanted Otherness—racial, sexual, classed, and global. The white woman's body thus is ironically a point of fear for the nation—and hence subject to regulation and control. It is a site of fear because any nontraditional deployments of the white female body (whether as a lesbian or by being in a sexual relationship with a man of color) can dangerously overturn the dominant structures of national desire and wreak havoc on the rigid logics of race, gender, sexuality, and globality through which various grids of national body politics are maintained in Anglo-dominated national contexts. The white female body, consequently, is also a location of resolution and hope because skillful and effective containment, regulation, and deployment of the white female body through scripts of white femininity enable the stabilization of racialized, gendered, sexualized, and global borders through which patriarchal Anglo-national hegemonies are maintained. White femininity, thus, is a site that constantly haunts and taunts the nation and reveals the (in)determinacy of its signification. It is that mark through which the nation struggles to hold on to its boundaries, and it is also that *trace* through which those very boundaries are in danger of slipping away from themselves. The location of white femininity, situated in the performance of boundaries, is characterized by a constant slippage through which we view, to borrow Homi Bhabha's (1990) words, "the unheimlich terror of the space or race of the Other" (p. 2). Consequently, white femininity is a modality through which the nation performs the *heimlich* comforts of (e)racing and negotiating that terror through stabilizing national meanings even as those very meanings may be undercut by forces that interrupt the national borders that white femininity is deployed to produce and secure at any given moment in the nation.

For instance, since the 1990s especially, Western nations have been confronting again what they see as the "Muslim problem" and reproducing new Orientalist logics to do so. In particular, the "Muslim man" has received a new lease on life in our contemporary times as a licentious, duplicitous, sexually depraved, and extremely dangerous Other who threatens the white patriarchal boundaries of Anglo modernity. As media images continually make visible, too often the vilification of the Muslim man occurs through references (explicit or implicit) to white women. White femininity as a structure then is often deployed in national discourses to contain and pathologize the Muslim man and render him a threat to the nation (and its domesticity). To that extent, the threat of "Muslim masculinity" is often constructed via white femininity. This book devotes an entire chapter to the mediated constructions of the Al Fayed family and many other prominent Muslim men (especially those perceived as Muslim "dictators") and how white femininity (including Diana) figures in them. This particular chapter demonstrates how the contemporary otherness of Muslim masculinity itself is an outcome of how the nation positions and imagines the white female body in relation to the Muslim man. A script of white femininity not only allows us glimpses into the desires of white patriarchy, it also allows us glimpses into the (Anglo) nation's productions and containment of non-Western masculinities via white femininity.

The centrality of white femininity in representing and negotiating national borders becomes especially visible during times of national crises and shifts. These are moments when the boundaries of national belonging become confused and slippery. At such times, national contradictions and ironies that interrupt, and erupt, in the nation become renegotiated by particular images of white women through which a fractured national landscape is sutured. A few months after 9-11, *Newsweek* published a cover page in one of its commemorative 9-11 issues (December 3, 2001) where the copy headline read "The

Spirit of America." This cover page was composed of a young white blond female child (probably no more than 3 years of age), looking up, waving a U.S. flag as she is being carried on the shoulders of men. Appearing a few weeks after 9-11, this image reproduced some very traditional ideologies of white femininity—white women as innocent, pure, and in need of protection (signified by the blond female cherubic child) and white women as a symbol of the nation's future captured by the title "The Spirit of America." What was remarkable is that while the image did show some men of color in the group (signifying a superficial multiculturalism) carrying the white female child, the very visual primacy of the white blond child waving a U.S. flag revealed the limits of that multiculturalism. The white blond female child, taking up most of the visual space in the image, symbolically negotiated and domesticated the terror of the Other.

An argument of this project is that white femininity is a mechanism for the distribution of national hope. Ghassan Hage (2003) has argued that "national identities work as a mechanism for the distribution of hope" (p. 13). But this distribution is not universal; that is, the nation at a given time, faced with particular challenges and desires, distributes *particular* kinds of hopes and not others. And whatever the content of that hope the nation distributes, it is always "a distribution that allows people to invest themselves in [a particular] social reality" (p. 12). In Anglo-dominant societies, white heterosexual women's bodies become central to this distribution given that the (white) female body is a site for the reproduction of (white) national future. The example of the white female child is an instance of such redistribution. A white female blond beautiful child signified hope and future for the nation at the very time that the nation was in danger of spiraling into hopelessness and saw itself as being violated by Others.

The Princess Diana phenomenon is also a powerful example of this. Diana's body, and what that body signified about New Britain in 1997, was a dominant narrative informing the Diana phenomenon (particularly the narratives that emerged after her death). Diana's body was framed as a body of hope, a hope for a new modernity, and new ways of being and belonging in Britain. Diana's body, following her death, became a body for distributing a new kind of post-imperial hope. Her body, so in our face all the time since the 1980s, taught us (in the 1990s) that reinventing the body to meet the challenges of the times is the ultimate responsibility of a citizen. The rationalities of neoliberalism that were endorsed by New Labor in the mid-1990s in Britain required a refashioning of cultural values and national identity. British feminist media scholar Rosalind Gill (2007) writes that the significance of neoliberalism for cultural analysis is the way in which its rationalities articulate individuals as "entrepreneurial actors" (p. 163) whose worth is measured by their capacity for self-care and reinvention (pp. 156–158). The symbol of Princess Diana, especially later Diana (of the mid-to-late 1990s), is an example *par excellance* of this neoliberal self. Diana's image became an instrument that was put into the service of rewriting the nation through neoliberal cultural rationalities central to the Blairite project of modernizing Britain.

Nonwhite Women and the Nation

To suggest the primacy of white womanhood in national scripts is not to claim that women of color have no relation to the nation. Quite the contrary. While in the past—even about 20 years ago—women of color rarely had any serious representations in the national imagination, today that is certainly changing. But that representational change has not necessarily resulted in changes in power distribution. Both in the United Kingdom and the United States today one sees images of nonwhite women on television screens—even as news anchors—in fashion magazines as models, and even as celebrities. Although disproportionately small, the presence of these images is significant. For instance, Michelle Obama, the first nonwhite First Lady has definitely made it more possible to see black women on national family screens in the United States today. But that acceptability only occurred after Michelle tamed her image. Branded at first as the angry black woman, who was unpatriotic and wrote an angry thesis on race in graduate school, Michelle was not a comfortable figure to the people at first. But by the time presidential candidate Senator Obama became a serious contender for the White House, and then moved into it, Michelle's image became more disciplined. Her image as a fashion icon and a mother committed to her children (without calling attention to the specific challenges of black motherhood) is dominant on screens and is comforting because it reflects scripts of nationalized femininity *that have already been naturalized by white femininity*. Her beautiful fashion style makes her even more palatable to the nation now. Further, her attention to the problem of (child) obesity and her campaigns promoting healthy eating (that rejects fast food) suggests an "in control"—disciplined—black female body. Although the script of white femininity through which Michelle is articulated sometimes ruptures—as in the images of Michelle doing pushups or dancing—images which have reportedly made some uncomfortable—for the most part Michelle's example illustrates how the norms of white femininity are what she has to negotiate to be acceptable. The (seeming) cosmopolitan postracialism that our current times, both in the United States as well as United Kingdom celebrate, is one where we value cultural difference as a sign of the nation but use it to suppress issues of systemic racial tensions. This is a postcolonial cosmopolitanism that offers new modes of selfhood in the West where we are solely encouraged to understand people of color in terms of meritocracy and the individual self instead of as human beings caught in a wider system of structural inequalities.

In the United Kingdom, too, it is not uncommon today to find nonwhite women as television anchors, fashion models, or gracing magazine pages— although it is still significantly disproportionate to representations of white women. When Diana died in 1997, there were indeed fewer nonwhite faces on national media screens than today. The images of Diana with babies and people of color from within and without the nation, or images of her wearing clothes typically worn by South Asian women were promising (seemingly) a new kind of cosmopolitan future for the nation. And the press and the public went overboard celebrating what they saw as the birth of a truly multicultural and cosmopolitan Britain. We all remember media shots of black and brown women weeping for Diana just as we remember cuts of crowds in candle-light vigils in places as far flung as Japan and South America. Repeatedly, the message that came through our mediated screens was that Diana was beyond race and that with her we saw the arrival of a cosmopolitan Britain—a cosmopolitanism that seemed to override or neutralize race.

Derek McGhee astutely observes that with the coming of New Labor we saw in Britain the rise of what he terms "compulsory cosmopolitanization" (2005, p. 175). Cosmopolitanism was encouraged and even pushed. But while cosmopolitanism was pushed and endorsed, multicultural "disorder" was policed as part of New Labor's "managed" migration and asylum strategies. The governmental strategy was one of ensuring "that the difficulties that arise in relation to culture, tradition and identity do not undermine the political necessity. . . . of building 'inclusive and democratic communities'" (p. 180). This kind of cosmopolitanism that encouraged multiple cultural communi-ties to succeed while at the same time containing cultural subversiveness was recently seen in the story of the first black British beauty queen. In 2009, Rachel Christie, a black British young woman became the first black Miss England. In her press interviews, Christie stated that she became Miss England to prove to blacks that blackness was not an excuse for failure: "if you come across as smart, if you dress nicely, it shouldn't make a differ-ence if you are black or white."[9] Underneath the comment in the *Daily Mail* online edition is a photo of Christie speed-running in a running track. The photo emphasizes her active, be-all-you-can-be entrepreneurial body. Yet, later in that same year, Ms. Christie was arrested on suspicion of assault in a nightclub. She subsequently relinquished her crown to focus on clearing her name. Christie is also the niece of former Olympic champion Linford Christie, who has frequently complained about institutionalized racism in

Britain and British sports. In this example of the Christies (especially Rachel Christie), we see both the terms of inclusion of black bodies in neoliberal racial imaginaries in the United Kingdom and the limits of that inclusion when those bodies become (seen as) disorderly.

The national script of white femininity that structures who counts as an appropriate female subject in the national imagination has implications for women of color, women of the Global South, non-Western women, lesbian women, and all Other women. How bodies of white women, especially white heterosexual women from North Atlantic nations (who constitute the dominant nationalized category of white femininity), are represented in national imaginations simultaneously reveals to us how bodies of nonwhite, lesbian, non-Western women may be viewed (or not) by the nation. How bodies of white women are imaginatively deployed by the nation reveals to us the racialized, gendered, sexualized, classed, and transnational circuits of power that make up the script of nonwhite femininity in a given moment. An exercise in the analysis of white femininity's functioning in national imaginations is not just about understanding white womanhood. It is about understanding also how white femininity is both a centripetal and centrifugal force that harnesses, and is harnessed by, relations of race, gender, sexuality, class, and the global in the constant making and remaking of itself in the service of the nation. Unpacking the script of white femininity is important because it may enable more white heterosexual women to see their implications in racialized patriarchal nationalist logics. Such a process of seeing involves charting the various scripts of white femininity that are normalized during times of national shifts, confusions, and tensions.

New Britain, New Labor: Rebranding Cool Britannia

To adequately contextualize the story of white femininity and national identity that this book charts, it is important to revisit in more detail the social and political context within which Diana's death occurred. Britain had just seen a major political shift—the victory of Labor Party in May 1997—after 18 years of Tory rule. This new Labor Party headed by Tony Blair marked itself through the signature of New Labor that promised a New Britain—a Britain that would eschew what Blair called the "get what you can" philosophy of Thatcherism. Modernization became the rhetorical cornerstone of this vision of a postcolonial Britain in which Britishness was to be rebranded as a democratic, exciting, young, forward-looking place that would move beyond its heritage image and attract investors and tourists from all over the world.

The Blair administration was the first administration to think of Britain overtly as a product, a national brand, to be marketed and packaged with catchy public relations slogans and careful image management in order to perform a makeover of British national identity. For instance, starting late in 1996, the British Tourist Authority, which received government support of about £35 million, began a major marketing campaign, based on focus groups and opinion polls (with many conducted overseas) to note international public perceptions about Britain in order to draw tourists. A British Tourist Authority spokesperson was described in the *Guardian* as noting that "Britain is being sold as 'modern, fashionable, and stylish'—with Morris dancers ditched in favor of Spice Girls . . . and fish and chips passed over in place of curry."[10] In the same year, the insides of British Airways were redone to connote a Middle Eastern decor and spicy Indian curry was nominated as a national dish in 1997. Consultancy Dragon International—a marketing research group that spent vast amounts of time and money exploring the power and appeal of concepts such as New Britain and Cool Britannia—concluded that

> New Britain is made up of big themes that won't go away, like female power, multiculturalism, openness, Europe and technology. . . . It symbolises a shift in aspirational, social and cultural values, as well as a shift in political priorities. For many the components of a new Britain may be aspirational but that no longer means they are unachievable.[11]

This idea that the image of Britain desperately needed a makeover, that the nation had to be repackaged in order to rewrite its identity internally and globally, was also asserted by a report published by *Demos*—a centrist Left think tank tied to the Blair administration—titled *Britain: Renewing Our Identity* (Leonard, 1997). The report justified this makeover approach by stating, "today, nations use new tools—logos and branding techniques, advertising campaigns and festivals, speeches and trade fairs—to project their identity to the outside world" (Leonard, 1997, p. 8). Thus, Britain became a visual product to be marketed worldwide through colorful exciting themes that would help promote an identity counter to its traditional imperial identity. In 1996, Blair defined this rebranding exercise as expressing

> a patriotism born not of nostalgia but of an understanding of the changing nature of the world. . . . A new Britain for a new world, finally breaking free of our imperial shadows. Strong in the world because we are cohesive at home . . . A new confidence in the world. Britain as one nation. Britain as a young country again. (Blair, 1996, p. 268)

One notes here Blair's careful dearticulation of patriotism from imperial nostalgia and its rearticulation to a new modernity and worldliness. One also notes the problematic suggestion that a clean break from the nation's history is possible as the nation moves toward a modern and cosmopolitan image of itself. Indeed, as Anne Marie Fortier (2008) has queried, "what is the role of the 'new' [i.e., in New Britain] as a way of writing history? What is it that the people are trying to recover, forget, or erase?" (2008, p. 27). One of Fortier's suggestions is that in wanting to look ahead and produce a new pride for a New Britain, there is a refusal of the "shame" of imperialism and a "refusal to interiorize" (p. 29) that shame as part of the national body.[12] In a different way, this has also been argued in Gilroy's (2004) work on postcolonial melancholia, especially his argument that we need to interrogate how the past atrocity of British imperialism is being managed, how it is being rendered as something that does not project its shadows in the present, and how it is being referenced in a manner that suggests that one can (apparently) break free of those imperial shadows.

Indeed, one logic underlying this management and rebranding of British national identity is that it was infused with a sentiment that refashioning the image of the nation is all that it takes to rewrite a postcolonial and postimperial identity. Fortier (2008) argues that one of the effects of this new politics of pride in a new Britain was

> to separate ethnic "others" into subjects who must be hailed as figures of the tolerant, multiracial Britain that many commentators "cherish." They constitute "our" diversity, which is what "we" are proud of. A *new visual referent* of what it means to be British . . . [was] surfacing. . . . (p. 31; emphasis added)

The implied logic was that "if the visual referent [of Britishness] changes, 'we' change" (Fortier, 2008, p. 36). But the fact that Britain has a history steeped deep in colonialism and racism, and that history continued to permeate the everyday lives of postcolonial citizens in Britain, and that structures of history cannot be overhauled simply by an image makeover, were matters left unsaid in this Blairite multicultural visuality of a new Britain. Perhaps Stuart Hall had the New Labor political pundits in mind when he sarcastically wrote in the *Observer* (October 14, 2000),

> Some commentators do suppose that Britain will obliterate all traces of its imperial history, devolve government, integrate with the global economy, play an active role in Europe, treat all minority peoples as equal citizens—and retain its self understanding intact since Magna Carta! This is not serious analysis, it is cloud-cuckoo land.

Even as Cool Britannia and New Britain became defining slogans in the mid-1990s, numerous racialized incidents continued to occur. On April 19, 1990, Norman Tebbit, the former chairman of the Conservative Party, stated that a large portion of Britain's Asian population fails the "cricket test" because they root for their home country teams in matches against England. Tebbit, at that time, was also leading a party revolt against the government's plans to admit up to 250,000 immigrants from Hong Kong. This same individual, a few years later on October 7, 1997, publicly decried multiculturalism, saying that it will lead to the breakup of Britain. On May 25, 1993, Conservative Member of Parliament Winston Churchill, grandson of the wartime leader, called for a crackdown on Asian immigrants because they were seen as destroying the British way of life. On June 10, 1995, the arrest of two Asian youths who had been subject to police brutality led to two days of massive rioting. Subsequent reports agreed that discrimination, poverty, and culture played a big part in sparking the riots. On December 9, 1997, the British Home Office (under the Blair administration) released a report, that was discussed in the *Times* on December 10. The report illustrated that racial attitudes among police were becoming entrenched. For every one stop-and-search procedure done for a white person, 4.4 blacks and 1.2 Asians were stopped. On May 15, 1998, according to the organizer of the notable Ethnic Minority Media Awards, only 1 in 100 media employees in Britain came from an ethnic minority (Ahuja, 1998). On April 13, 1998, a British government report *Ethnicity and Victimization* found that 30% of blacks, 27% of Indians, and 22% of Pakistanis avoided certain events such as football games because they were afraid they would be victims of racialized crime and harassment (Ford, 1998).

Perhaps one of the most publicized racial incidents of the 1990s was the murder of black teenager Stephen Lawrence in 1993 by a gang of white youths in London. A botched police investigation and a failure to bring Lawrence's killers to justice for several years resulted in massive public outcry throughout the country. Additionally, other hate crimes such as the two bombings in communities of color in April 1999—one in Brixton injuring 39 people, including a 23-month-old baby, and the other in a Bangladeshi neighborhood the following week by Combat 18, a neo-Nazi group, injuring 6 people—provided further evidence of the intense racism that marked local communities in Britain. Indeed, as someone who recently lived in Britain (London) for a couple of years, I must admit that I have been shocked at the intensity of overt racism in Britain. A report on contemporary racial relations, published by the Runnymede Commission in 2000 and headed by the Asian scholar and activist Bhiku Parekh, noted that despite some changes, larger racial problems and attitudes still plagued the nation. When these facts are considered, the Cool Britannia rhetoric of New Labor revealed a hollowness that was neither able to address, nor was even serious about addressing, the real effects of present and past colonial structures on the nation's marginalized populations.

In fact, the New Labor political culture, while spouting a rhetoric of modernization and newness, did not, in substance, signal a radical break from the Conservatives and Thatcherism. For example, while arguing for a more inclusive society, New Labor's economic policies did not return society to public ownership (an approach that basically distinguishes the Left from the Right) guaranteeing *redistribution* of wealth as well as a redistribution of the *outcome* of wealth creation. Rather, the policies continued to support free market economy, wealth creation, and entrepreneurship because these were seen as central to the creation of opportunities. As Driver and Martell (1998) have suggested, whether "opportunity for all" (p. 49) necessarily translated into equality of effect was not an issue that was addressed by the Blair agenda. In fact, the "newness" through which New Labor became a hegemonic ideology in the late 1990s had to do with carefully distinguishing its position from the hard "old" labor with its explicit Leftist agenda. New Labor claimed that that agenda of Old Labor was irrelevant for the "new" times. What it claimed new about itself was a refusal of both the outdated (as it saw it) hard Left and the Right. Instead, New Labor presented itself as offering a "third way" that would embrace certain democratic principles such as community and society, without overhauling many of the traditional economic and social structures. Sarah Franklin (2000) notes that

> by focusing on community and individual agency, where people in families and communities share responsibility with government agencies for social exclusion, there has been a tendency to disregard the significance of wider social and economic forces and inequalities they produce. Individuals are encouraged to take the opportunities offered to them by the Government, and if they fail to do so, they become, in effect, responsible for their own inequality. (p. 139)

In a scathing critique in the *Observer* in 1997, Martin Jacques and Stuart Hall described the political culture of the Blairite 1990s as signifying knee-jerk and shallow liberalism that refused to take any radical positions. In an article titled *"Blair: Is He the Greatest Tory Since Thatcher?"* they noted that

> Blair embodies the ultimate pessimism, that there is only one version of modernity, the one elaborated by the Conservatives over the last 18 years. He represents the historic defeat of the Left, the abandonment of any serious notion that the Left has something distinctive to offer. This is not just a rupture with the past but a rejection of it. It is a break with any serious commitment to any form of social democracy. . . . There is no question that the world has changed irreversibly over the last three decades. But any reforming party worth its name must address these changes in a radical spirit and invent new ways of addressing these challenges. . . .

The Struggle and Confusion over Britishness

The rhetoric of Cool Britannia through which a national makeover was being staged by New Labor in the 1990s cannot be written off merely as an "image campaign" or reduced to Blairite politics. Rather, it needs to be situated in a larger anxious discourse about what being British meant at the millennium. The Blairite national image makeover was merely one symptom of this anxiety. This anxiety was an outcome of major tectonic shifts that were unsettling the national landscape such as the push for devolution of Scotland and Wales; an increased presence of several postcolonial populations within the citizenry who disrupted the ideology of "one nation, one politics"; massive economic disparities brought about by Thatcherism since the 1980s; the fall of the Conservatives in 1997 after 18 years; the federalization of Europe and what that meant for Britain's relationship with the world and Europe; the handover of Hong Kong—the last British colony; a monarchy rocked by divorces and embarrassing exposés of its young generation; and a decreased global presence and power. These situations produced a context in which what it meant to be British became a major focus of public discussion. (Often these discussions revealed an anxiety particularly over Englishness [given England's projected cultural superiority] in relation to other parts of the United Kingdom.)

For example, the *Guardian,* in early 2000s, ran a special online report "What Is Britain?" The report comprised a collection of articles published in the newspaper over a few months on this topic. The logo on top of the web page carried a silhouette of an individual (whose race, gender, and ethnicity cannot be determined) standing against the Union Jack. The shadowy silhouette, unmarked in its race, gender, and ethnicity, captures the confusion about Englishness that characterized the times. A particular entry in this report was a quiz on "how English are you?"[13]

The quiz ran a headline copy that stated, "Home Secretary Jack Straw has spoken of a 'rising sense of Englishness.' But do you possess the endearing traits of England's island race?" The questions in the quiz alluded to rather staunch characteristics of traditional Englishness, ranging from cricket, to weather, to football—almost as if it was testing whether these markers of Englishness, so in danger of slipping away, were still remembered and embraced by the public. Another entry in this same report included an article about the relevance of the Union Jack as a symbol of the United Kingdom. The article queried: "At the start of the 21st century what does the Union Jack represent? Indeed, in an era of devolution and internationalism . . . [does] it have any tangible meaning at all?"

While discussions such as these reflected a strong confusion about Englishness, and Britishness at large, there were other commentaries that were more overtly reactive to the changes going on in the country. On July 27, 1997, an article in the *Observer* despairingly commented that

> to talk of English national identity is to invite immediate denunciation on the grounds of racism, elitism or xenophobia. [. . .] Despite the National Curriculum, too much history sets out to teach everything but of British or English history, on the grounds that it is racist and exclusivist to teach national culture because the histories of England and Britain (which appear to have begun with the British empire) are racist and exclusivist.

Similarly, the *Daily Telegraph* ran an article in 1999 with the headline "The Englishness That Dare Not Speak Its Name."[14] The article commented,

> For centuries being English needed no definition or examination; it simply was. . . . Yet, suddenly, astonishingly quickly, the idea has come under threat [. . .] [T]here has been a determined exploitation of post-imperial guilt among people, who in truth are entitled to feel proud to be English.

The article resentfully asserted "we live in an atmosphere of appeasement and nicey nice-ness and immense pressure only to say what is acceptable." Despite its strong conservative reactions, this commentary is right in noting that the 1990s was the first time that national identity was so overtly marked and so forcefully debated in the public sphere.

Such confusion, and even overt reaction to changes in the national landscape, revealed that while a superficial political correctness might have become the rhetorical order of the day, beneath it still prevailed staunch traditional reactions to a perceived dissolution of (white) Britishness. Stuart Hall (2000), in a special report on *What Is Britain?* in the *Observer*, noted that unless ethnic minorities become "an integral part of the national culture," Britain will be "a multi-ethnic, mono-cultural society, which is a contradiction in terms." Hall's comment taps right into the essence of the problem of the New Britain rhetoric—in which inclusion was emphasized but the larger systemic logic of nationhood was still white. Historian Catherine Hall (2000) summed up the dilemma of British national identity in the 1990s with these words:

> If the nation is no longer an empire, what is it? If Englishness is no longer a hegemonic identity, defining the national characteristics of all those who claim belonging in Britain, then what does it mean to be British? When the "fantasy of ethnological unity"—one people, one nation—can no longer be maintained, what kind of nation is left? (p. 2)

This is the core question that characterized the political and social anxieties of the times, the central issue that had to be negotiated—one way or
another—if "belonging" to the nation was to be rethought, both for whites
and minorities. The Princess Diana phenomenon provided a cultural and
popular space through which one such negotiation occurred—a negotiation
that, as this book argues, carefully maintained a logic of white nationhood
into which "difference" was accommodated—and even embraced—in a spirit
of superficial liberalism.

Diana and New Britain

It is within such a context that this book explores popular discourses about
Diana in order to address how Diana's body became a site of articulation
through which racialized, sexualized, gendered, and global relations were
rewritten in the performance of a postcolonial neoliberal British identity
during the turn of the century. Many of the media discourses that emerged
in the wake of Diana's death explicitly linked her to the nation and its "new
spirit." For example, the *Sunday Mirror*, explaining the outpouring of grief
in the wake of Diana's death stated,

> After decades when the people of this country seemed to be losing their na-
> tional identity, we have found one . . . It is about Diana and what she meant to
> our country—hers and ours . . . It is the new British spirit. The spirit of Diana
> proclaimed loud and proudly throughout the land. Since she died, *the people
> have spoken*. (p. 11; emphasis mine)[15]

At the time of her death, NBC reported that the "Diana story" broke records in the history of print media.[16] In the British press, 35% of space was
devoted to Diana, whereas 27% of space had been devoted to key events of
WWII taken collectively.[17] *Time* reported that compared to an average of
181,591 weekly newsstand sales, there were over 850,000 sales of the "Death
of a Princess" issue.[18] Elton John's special version of "Candle in the Wind"
reached a world record figure for the sale of a single, of 3.5 million copies in
just one week.[19] Major television stations in the United States also reported
ratings matched by very few events. Nielsen reported that the combined funeral coverage of Diana on ABC, CBS, NBC, Fox, CNN, MSNBC, Fox News,
and E-Channel reached about 82% of households in the United States.[20]

William Hutton, the editor of the *Observer*, commented in the September
14, 1997 issue that "she was seen as the modern against the traditional. That's
at the heart of it. I think the country is moving into a modern phase." Leading
politicians too cast Diana as the new face of England. For example, the new

Labor Prime Minister, Tony Blair framed the legacy of Diana as a challenge that faced the future of Britain: "Let her legacy be compassion. Let's be a better, more compassionate Britain."[21] The *Daily Telegraph* on September 3, 1997, made the following comment about Blair's use of "the people" in his famous "people's princess" speech. The comment highlighted how his rhetorical move reflected New Labor's dominant rhetorical structure in which "the people" were everywhere.

> We are to have a People's funeral, to go with the People's Wimbledon, the People's opera, the People's Question Time and all other innovations of the People's party. "She was the people's princess. And that is how she will stay, how she will remain in our hearts and memories—for ever." So spoke Tony Blair . . . It [the speech] is like the ingenious party conference speech that echoed the song of the football terraces, "Labour's coming home . . .". (Johnson, 1997, p. 22)

Many commentators even went so far as to describe the public response to Diana's death as a modern revolution. The *Evening Standard* on October 24, 1997, stated that with this kind of public response to Diana's death "we are seeing a modern day equivalent of the Italian Renaissance of the 15th century" (Handy, 1997, p. 21). Phrases such as the "people's revolution," "Diana revolution," the "New Renaissance" were routinely thrown around in the media. Such phrases revealed the extent to which the affective investment that the people were making in Diana's death was ultimately an investment in a feeling about being modern, about a new mode of belonging in the nation and new ways of imagining the national body and one's own self in relation to it.

The Approach of This Book

This book primarily focuses on media materials and narratives about Diana through which larger logics of New Britain were being enacted at the turn of the century. Many of these media materials emerged, or were recirculated from earlier times, in the wake of Diana's death in 1997. Given that the mediated assemblage that we call Diana seems to have no end—that is, it is constantly produced and reproduced and constantly shored up with new stories and fragments every day—it is clearly impossible to analyze all representations about Diana. This is not just because that would not be feasible but also because that would result in a loss of a particular contextuality that is the focus of this project. I have limited my materials and analytical focus primarily to the years in (and around) Blairite New Britain in which a huge modernizing wave intersected with the 1990s representations of Diana. Most of my analysis illustrates how the representations of Diana and other white iconic women of the late 20th and early 21st centuries reflect a larger neoliberal recrafting of national identity in North Atlantic nations such as the United Kingdom (and the United States) In particular, I have focused my analysis on topics such as motherhood, global humanitarianism, multicultural fashion, relations between white women and Muslim men, and non-Western healing and inner wellness practices that mark late-20th- and early-21st-century cultural logics These topics embody not just the larger logics of individualization that Blair's neoliberal agenda called for but also many millennial logics of citizenship that have been sweeping North Atlantic democracies since the 1990s.

To engage in a manageable study, I have limited my focus primarily to Western media materials. There are reasons for this. First, as I kept collecting materials for this study, I became struck by the dominance of Western media in producing the Diana phenomenon—such that, most of the time, it was the same image of Diana captured by a Western photographer, magazine, or newspaper that would show up and circulate in media in other parts of the world. Second, in keeping with the goals of this project, it seemed more pertinent to focus on the highly interlocking British and American media coverage of Diana. This is not to deny that other media approaches to studying Diana would not be useful—such as how her representations were negotiated in local contexts of several non-Western nations or what she meant to non-Western nations and populations. But these questions, while being important avenues for future research, are beyond the goals of this project.

The media materials that form the basis of analysis in this book constitute everyday popular cultural materials. Such materials reflect "the waste materials of everyday communication in the national public sphere" and constitute "pivotal documents in the construction, experience, and rhetoric" of national identity (Berlant, 1997, p. 12). In other words, the materials on which this study is based deliberately avoid "high culture" constructions of Diana. For instance, I have deliberately stayed away from representations of Diana by the monarchy—for example, in royal portraits of Diana or the images of her in royal biographies or royal websites. I am more interested in exploring the everyday and even seemingly banal media forces through which Diana's construction eddies and swirls in the public sphere—for it is in the everyday materials of the popular, materials that may even seem trivial, silly, or insignificant, that the culture of a nation is secured (Berlant, 1997; Billig, 1995). The fantasy of national identification arises in and through the everyday taken-for-granted-ness of the popular. To this end, newspapers, television clips, magazines, tabloids, videos, and special commemorative books and items have constituted the main empirical materials for this book.

Although this book situates the discussion of white femininity and national modernity in the New Labor cultural scape of 1997, it does not suggest that the Diana phenomenon can be directly read off Blairism or reduced to it. Nor does it suggest that there is a direct one-to-one correspondence between the struggles over Englishness/Britishness and representations of Diana. Media discourses do not work in such simple and neat ways. In fact, while a lot about the representations of Diana worked to reinforce dominant racialized national boundaries, there were also aspects of her representation that were more complex and ambivalent and that did contain the possibility for at least imagining more progressive articulations.

While it may be obvious, I still wish to clarify that this project is not interested in the "real" Diana. I say this because I have often been asked by people about what Diana thought about this or that. My focus is on Diana the image, the media text, the spectacle, and the signifier. So, when I refer to Diana, I am referring to an image, a constantly shifting text, a simulacrum of white femininity that went by (and still goes by) the name Diana. From the time of her entry on the public screen, Diana had always been a product of the media. She was actively screened by the media just as she actively worked to project the image she wanted to have screened. The media and Diana were not separate entities; they were one and the same. As Richard Wilding (1997) astutely notes, "Diana existed in the frame of an after image. To be Diana was to be caught in this frame" (pp. 145–148). Indeed, Diana was an ultimate simulacrum of our times that was actively involved in the production of a national and global public for 16 years. The production continues even today as I indicated earlier. With the Diana phenomenon, we have an unique case study where a white woman was not only hyperspectacularized by the media, but she herself was also well aware of her power as a spectacle and what worked and did not work for "the people." She performed a script of white femininity, just as she was performed upon by it; she offered herself to be viewed, just as she was relentlessly viewed through; she presented herself as an active image, just as she was actively imaged upon. To that extent, it is even inconsequential to ask at what point the spectacle was directed by Diana and at what point it was just the media at work. With someone like Diana, the boundaries blur. In the end, what matters is the mediation that we call Diana and the complex postcolonial script of white femininity that it forged.

Although this book focuses on popular media materials about Diana, it is not a book about public memory—although no doubt the arguments offered will have implications for understanding how public memory functions. There is also quite a bit of work already on public memory in relation to the Diana phenomenon. In simple terms, all this book attempts is an investigation, through the Diana phenomenon and beyond, of some of the specific articulations through which the script of white femininity remains linked to the production of a national modern.

Organization of Chapters

The Diana phenomenon, as a script of white femininity, is so expansive that it is difficult to do justice to every aspect of its signification. Each chapter in the book examines one significant articulation between Diana/white femininity and the nation in the context of New Britain. The chapters also draw on numerous related examples of other white privileged women in popular culture in order to signal how the Diana phenomenon speaks to a larger racial formation of white femininity at the turn of the century that has significance beyond the specificities of New Britain.

In Chapter 2, I focus on how ideologies of white motherhood function as sites through which shifts in a nation's sense of the modern is enabled. In particular, I locate the Diana phenomenon in the social context of the 1990s Britain, when motherhood became a site that was heavily regulated in response to perceived "moral panics" about dysfunctional families and out-of-control children (especially boys). Further, visions of "bad motherhood"—mothers who were dependent on the state for their needs and did not take responsibility for their own children—became articulated to Blairite policies of cutting welfare for poor families and lone mothers on benefits. Illustrating how representations of Diana's motherhood (as well as many other [white] mothers in popular culture in 1990s and early 2000s) signal a neoliberal logic of motherhood, I explore the racial implications of such logics. Specifically, I contrast such white maternal (neoliberal) logics with the conditions of black mothers in Britain at this same time. The analysis in this chapter further addresses how the representational politics of Diana's (white heterosexual single) modern motherhood (producing modern men) additionally gained significance through contrasts with images of the queen's "out of touch" imperial style of maternity. I discuss how this reveals how the nation reproduces its modernities through larger struggles over temporalities that are often embodied by the body of the (white) mother.

Chapter 3 examines the relationships among fashion, white femininity, and the nation—an area that has not been explored much in critical race studies and fashion studies. How does a "fashionable" white female body come to signify a nation's modernity given the link between fashion and newness? How do shifts in dominant fashion styles signify shifts in a nation's temporality? Through a focus on Princess Diana's changing fashion style, I address how (white) female fashion functions as a site through which shifting spatiotemporalities of the nation are narrated. Relatedly, this chapter addresses how nonwhite female bodies rarely enter the logic of the modern in Western imaginaries. A significant aspect of this chapter addresses how white female fashion today functions as a vehicle for mediating, negotiating, co-opting, and even containing the fashion aesthetics of global multiculturalism(s) as they travel into the West. In particular, I discuss how Diana, as well as many other white female celebrities, embraced South Asian fashion and through that contributed to an image of a multicultural Asian-friendly Britain that was being promised by the incoming Blair administration. I address how elements of Asian fashion become dishistoricized and how this dehistoricization ironically enabled white women's embrace of Asian fashion. Issues related to the complex politics of transnational cultural translations are also discussed here.

Chapter 4 examines how contemporary global intimacies are imagined through the white female nationalized body. Examining contemporary discourse of global humanitarianism—especially the emerging Western-driven discourse of what I term *global motherhood* in which celebrity white women are increasingly positioned as mothers to children of underprivileged parts of the world—this chapter addresses how the discourse of global motherhood, embodied in the figure of the white celebrity woman such as Diana and others, functions as a tool for a cosmopolitan renationalization of the national self. Such renationalization obscures the geopolitical violences and neoliberal policies that result in children being abandoned or deprived in the Global South. Particular attention is paid to the discourse of international adoption.

Chapter 5 continues the exploration of a transnational politics of white (national) femininity by focusing on the relationship between white (national) femininity and transnational masculinities—in particular Muslim men. Given white femininity's role in guarding and preserving racialized borders of the nation, threats to that role—especially in relation to white women's associations with nonwhite men, or with men of non-Western nations—produce all kinds of racialized and nationalized anxieties. How does the nation manage these anxieties? Although much has been written about the intersecting politics of race, gender, and sexuality in narratives of miscegenation, there is not much on representations of white women in relation to men of color from the non-West and specifically Middle Eastern Muslim men.[22] Academic work on Western representations of Muslim cultures has largely focused on images of Muslim women, but little has been discussed about mediated images of Muslim masculinity and how those images are often secured in relation to images of white women. Attempting to correct this gap, this chapter maps the ways in which the Fayeds were represented in the media and situates these representations in the anti-Muslim climate in Britain in the 1990s and beyond. The chapter also explores Western media's representations of other Muslim men and "dictators" such as Saddam Hussein, Colonel Gadaffi, the Fort Hood, Texas psychiatrist Colonel Hassan, and recent films such as *Sex and the City 2*. I argue that one of the ways in which contemporary visual structures in the West often give meaning to Muslim men is through the structure of white femininity—that is, it is often in relation to white women that we in the West visualize and construct subject positions for Muslim males and then treat them accordingly.

The final chapter addresses what I call the "spiritual fix" of white femininity. I suggest that spirituality is increasingly functioning as cultural capital and a site of consumption through which a new kind of gendered white national transcendence is being imagined today in popular and consumer culture. I argue that many Anglo nations are writing their modernity through a logic of healing and spirituality that comes to be located in the white female body and enables the performance of a spiritualized cosmopolitanism in which the nation, signified by the white female body, positions itself as transcending materiality and hence historical accountability. From cultural practices of yoga, to healing retreats, to spiritual spas and meditation, to wellness programs in the West—most of which are targeted toward middle- and upper-middle-class white women—the white female body in contemporary times reflects a turn toward the interior. In the process, it offers that interior as a new site through which to reimagine the (white) national self. Focusing on representations of later Diana, as well as other prominent white women of the millennium who embraced (and continue to follow) alternative and particularly Asian-based healing techniques, I explore what such an engagement with inner wellness by privileged white female bodies means for understanding new formations of whiteness in the late 20th and early 21st centuries.

One important issue will be clear throughout my discussion. Each chapter illustrates how white femininity is a *dependent* formation; its privilege is constantly dependent on the cancellation or negation not just of the nonwhite female body but also of women from the Global South. This is important to highlight in order to better understand how bodies of national and global women of color continually underlie (whether visible or not, whether acknowledged or not) the performance of white national womanhood in a given context in North Atlantic nations as well as many other western nations.

On the Relevance of Critical Whiteness Studies

A few comments must be made about the relevance of critical whiteness studies within which this project positions itself. While critical whiteness studies broke new ground in race studies in the 1990s, a concern sometimes expressed in this literature is whether in focusing on whiteness, we run the risk of reprivileging whiteness or offering new (seemingly) antiracist positions for white people to occupy, which may then result in whiteness being shored up in new ways. For instance, the goal of the controversial 1990s journal *Race Traitors* was to declare that it is not enough to interpret whiteness but to abolish it. Scholars then questioned whether it is even possible to abolish whiteness and whether such a goal might ultimately be unrealistic and even romantic in an odd sort of way. Similarly, concerns have also been raised about whether, as seen in some strands of critical whiteness studies, the goal to produce a positive antiracist identity of whiteness ends up, in effect, offering one more subject position of power for whites to take on (Ware, 2001). This strand, for instance, has been seen in works such as *White Reign* (1998) where the editors note that the goal is to produce "a positive, proud, attractive, *antiracis*t white identity that is empowered to travel in and out of various racial/ethnic circles with confidence and empathy" (Kincheloe & Steinberg, 1998, p. 12; emphasis added). As Ware (2001) notes, "one of the problems with this type of approach is that it is in danger of reifying the idea of race as a reliable index of human difference . . ." (p. 6). Ware argues that "it is vital that the impulse to identify, mark, and analyze whiteness does not lead into the trap of reifying the very concept 'race' that it intends to question" (p. 29). Similarly, Wiegman (2012) argues that the "massive hope invested in a white subject who can produce the right kind of agency to bring down his own political overordination" (p. 29) may be "inspiring but hardly predicts a future in which white-on-white preoccupations are deferred" (p. 29) (see also, Hill, 2004). What Wiegman means is that it is not as though the moment we get white people to "see" whiteness through our studies that they will bring down whiteness. So the implied question in her statement is: Why are we then doing whiteness studies?

I share all of these concerns. They, indeed, prompt a serious reflexivity in the project that is called whiteness studies. And along with scholars like

Ware (2001), Cherniavsky (2006), and Wiegman (2012), I am certainly not comfortable with the notion that critical whiteness studies should aim to produce antiracist understandings of whiteness, or that in rupturing whiteness in our academic ventures, we can somehow always bring forth more antiracist ways of being white. For whiteness, after all, is a matter of power structures, and white people cannot suddenly be without white privilege, or suddenly be outside the power structures of whiteness (as whiteness is less a matter of intent and more of structural positioning). Does this mean then that it is pointless to engage in investigations of whiteness?

While I do agree that we need to be very cognizant of the goals of engaging in critical whiteness studies, I am not willing to say that examining whiteness is ultimately problematic and hopeless. If anything, I would assert, along with many colleagues and scholars who continue to produce important interventions into whiteness studies, that critical whiteness studies in general has opened up a very different and much needed way of studying racial dominance and racial formations. And while the field should be seen very much as part of the larger field of critical race studies, the major benefit of critical whiteness studies is to enable *both nonwhites and whites* to recognize the specific techniques through which whiteness sustains and reinvents itself and in the process continually produces new contours of racial dominance that are situated in particular national needs and desires. This, to me, is still important. And while recognizing the operations of whiteness may not always change one's relation to it (for some will simply want to function in ways that maintain the white system because the system benefits them, despite their awareness of the moral violence of that system), one still has to hope—and must hope I would say (for why else engage in any kind cultural criticism in the first place)—that recognizing one's implication in whiteness can also provoke serious ethical reflections about the societies in which we live. For along with whites, even many nonwhites—socialized as they are within the power structures of whiteness—do not always recognize the specificities of the operations of whiteness in a particular context and moment. While the caution expressed by scholars such as Wiegman (2012) must be heard and reflected upon, that caution cannot result in closed doors. Critical engagements with formations of whiteness (as part of larger racial formations) must continue to remain an important and urgent political project for our times.

Whiteness indeed matters as *a current of racism*. As the racial mappings of the 21st century become more complex—on the one hand seemingly more diverse, on the other plagued by all forms of white nationalisms—it seems important to continually mark how everyday forms of whiteness navigate this diversity. How does whiteness accommodate itself to diversity without really giving up its power? What new forms and shapes of whiteness do these accommodations need and require? What are the cultural vehicles—and the media is a central one in our times—that enable this? Such questions complicate our engagement with racial power structures. They also invite us to move beyond a nation-bound analysis of whiteness (i.e., inward looking, insular) to one that attempts to grasp how national formations of racism are informed by transnational relations.

In a comprehensive review of the future of whiteness studies in the journal *Ethnic and Racial Studies*, Twine and Gallagher (2008) frame the current wave of whiteness studies as the "third wave" (p. 4). They suggest that this third wave of whiteness studies has moved beyond "voyeuristic ethnographic accounts and personal narratives" (p. 5) to examinations of how white privilege is maintained even as the "prerogatives" of whiteness are "*challenged by the new interracial social movements, progressive social policies, democratization projects and multiculturalism*" (p. 5; emphasis added). This project is situated within this emphasis. It seeks to understand a nationalized whiteness that claims democratization, progressiveness, and multiculturalism at the same time that it rewrites its privileges and produces new racial formations.

But here I also want to offer a caveat. I want to suggest that it is important to be always mindful of *why* we are engaging in the study of various assemblages of whiteness. It is far less to understand whiteness and more, as Les Back (2010) puts it, to understand whiteness as a *structure* of racism in a particular context. Thus, the reader will note that throughout this project, while marking whiteness, I have constantly situated my analysis in specific contexts of race (in Britain in particular). Back (2010) writes that the study of whiteness needs to be "sociable" (p. 445) and "outward looking" (p. 466) (instead of narcissistic) so as to produce ways of interpreting how "white actions, definitions and understanding are implicated within cultures of racism" (p. 445). Whiteness is ultimately not about whiteness, but about racism. And that racism is simultaneously about larger national and global relations.

I think back to Stuart Hall's (2007) reminder as to why we do cultural studies (or I would say any critical study) in his plenary lecture at the Cultural Studies Now Conference at University of East London:

> No study of *Big Brother*, no study of *The Sopranos*, no study of television programmes or any other particular instance of culture is in my view properly Cultural Studies unless, in the end, it is haunted by the question—"*But what does this have to do with everything else?*" (Hall, 2007; emphasis added)

Indeed, what does a particular study of whiteness have to do with other things, what does it tell us about many of the other social relations that make up a context in a particular moment? This project seeks to address this important question in relation to the Diana phenomenon by exploring how it expressed particular formations of whiteness in the late-20th- and early-21st-century Britain that were needed to write larger neoliberal logics of national belonging. While this is not a perfect or even a comprehensive project by any means, at the end as at the beginning, it has been haunted by the questions: Why did the particular version of white femininity that Diana signified work so well in Britain in the late 20th and early 21st centuries? And what did that have do with everything else?

2. Racialized Maternalisms

White Motherhood and National Modernity

This chapter focuses on how white motherhood functions as a site through which the nation reproduces its modernity. Perhaps one of the most problematic narrativizations of Princess Diana as a postimperial white female subject in the 1990s—and especially after her death—was the mediated production of her as a modern mother. Although a later chapter discusses the production of Diana (and many other contemporary white female icons) as a global mother, this chapter remains concerned with a particular model of (white upper-/ middle-class) motherhood that the Diana phenomenon validated under the guise of a modern national subject. It is a model that became articulated to a 1990s social formation (on both sides of the Atlantic) of an idealization, and vilification, of particular types of motherhood (independent, hands-on, and active on the one hand, and working-class, single, lesbian, and nonwhite on the other) that drove debates about crime, family values, parenting, and welfare programs. The scrutiny of the family was an outcome of the neoliberal reworkings of the economy under Blair whereby social benefits were cut as part of a policy to reprogram welfare. Blair called for "compassion with a hard edge"[1] and "welfare to workfare" (similar to Clinton's promise to "end welfare as we know it"). As state subsidies to poor families were reduced, motherhood—especially single motherhood—became a targeted topic in this economic restructuring. Val Gillies (2007) argues that "family relationships" that were traditionally seen as "immune from state intervention" were now regularly "transgressed in an explicit and determined effort to mould and regulate individual subjectivity and citizenship at the level of the family" (pp. 1–2). Kiernan, Land, and Lewis (1998) further note that single mothers (read: working-class, poor, or ethnic mothers on welfare) were "seen primarily as

a drain on public expenditure and as a threat to the stability and order associated with the two-parent family" (p. 2).

Discussing the politics of motherhood in Western democracies in the
1980s and 1990s, Annelise Orleck (1997) notes that the "much-reviled 'bad
mothers' are the same in many parts of the world" and especially in Western
democracies (p. 225). "They are women 'tainted' by feminism, women who
insist on the right to use birth control," "poor mothers of color and lesbian
mothers," and teen mothers (p. 225) (see also, Ladd-Taylor & Umanksy, 1998).
While not all these categories reflect the British landscape in the 1990s, many
do—especially the categories of working-class mothers, teen mothers, and
mothers of color who too often signified "bad mothers." Powerful narratives
of bad mothers dominated popular culture in Britain in the 1990s and early
21st century. For instance, BBC News in 2001 (cited in Gillies, 2007, p. 4)
argued that

> tips on good parenting should be printed on the back of cereal packets and
> milk cartons, posted on buses and shown on television. . . . And the government
> should introduce "beacon" parents, the naming and shaming of bad parents,
> parent achievement awards, a system of fines for parents who failed to meet
> their targets and child benefit bonuses for those who performed well.

While such arguments about evaluating parenting through a rewards-
punishment system were gripping the national consciousness, one of the most
famous incidents of the times occurred. And it constituted a prime example
of a "crisis in family" rhetoric. The incident was the murder of 2-year-old
(white boy) Jamie Bolger in 1993. Jamie Bolger had been abducted and killed
by two young (white) boys who were around 10 years of age. As the case received national attention, the focus closed in on the mothers of the two boys
who kidnapped Jamie Bolger. In press reports, these mothers were turned
into symbols of irresponsible motherhood that creates "brutalized children
of the wasteland" (Coward, 1999b, p. 55). The *Guardian* noted (on October
31, 2000) that "to many, these two women (the boys' fathers seem somehow
to have been absolved of blame) were ultimately responsible" for the death
of little Jamie.[2] It discussed how Ann Thompson (one of the mothers) was
being portrayed in the media as an alcoholic while Susan Venebles, the other
mother, (separated from her husband) was portrayed as a "loose woman"
with many men friends. The report further stated,

> A narrative emerged of two childhoods influenced . . . by the environment in
> which these boys lived, a world of social and economic deprivation, of trashy
> television and cultural poverty, inadequate social services, failed schooling

and general confusion. It was a place that left a *moral vacuum* for two children who would go on to kill and leave the unanswered question: why did they do it? (emphasis added)

As Blake Morrison, who was initially hired to cover the trial for *New Yorker* magazine (and then wrote a book on the subject), noted in the *Guardian* in 2003, the Bolger murder "came to symbolize a moral panic about children—the threat of other people's, the defencelessness of our own." Motherhood became a sign of a crime-ridden and dysfunctional community, of a larger "moral vacuum." Hence, it had to be regulated and remobilized in order to reinvigorate the community and the family. Tony Blair, in the mid-1990s, had run his election campaign by linking bad motherhood to crime. He had stated, "the break-up of family and community bonds is intimately linked to the breakdown in law and order" (in Fairclough, 2000, p. 42).

The Bolger murder case also drew attention to a prevailing discourse of "crisis in masculinity" and "bad behavior" of young men that was dominating Britain in the 1990s. The case especially called attention to the relation between *white motherhood* and the nation. In particular, it revealed that the nation's engagement with white motherhood is intimately tied to narratives of appropriate masculinity that the mother is charged with producing. The (white) mothers in the Bolger murder case were seen as having failed to perform this duty.

What is also interesting is that when white mothers are unable to produce "successful" men who can serve the nation, then it is the mother instead of the men she has produced who is demonized. The *Guardian,* in October 2000, noted (through the words of someone who had interviewed Ann Thompson) that "Ann lives in terror of being discovered . . . by anyone who might recognize her when she is out . . . It is as if she thinks of herself walking around with a sign above her head: Mother of Bulger Murderer."[3] We saw this also with Nancy Lanza, the mother of Adam Lanza (the Newtown, Connecticut shooter). Reports called attention to her own troubled family, which seemingly impacted her childhood. They raised questions about why she had so many guns in her basement and taught her son to shoot. A *Daily Mail* report, for example, ran a headline that emphasized her dysfunctionality: "She would get very upset that he wouldn't let her hug him: *Dysfunctional relationship of Sandy Hook gunman and his mother*" (emphasis added).[4]

Similarly, the mother of John Walker Lindh (the American Taliban) had also recalled receiving anonymous threats such as "great parenting job" and "you should be shot with the same gun used to shoot your soon."[5] Reports on Lindh highlighted that his parents were separated and that the father had "declared himself gay" (note the feminization of fatherhood here) while the mother "wandered into New Age." The description evokes an image of the mother as an irresponsible hippie wandering aimlessly through life.[6] Unlike representations of damaged, broken, nonwhite families—where the damage is usually seen as a symptom of the culture itself—in white mother-son relationships gone wrong, the media scrutiny usually takes an individualized form. The individual white mother is criticized for her individual personality or background flaws. But those flaws do not stand in for a deficit in white people in general. In contrast, black mothers, for example, are seen as reproducing a form of racial or cultural "degeneracy" (Roberts, 1999, p. 9). Thus, when something goes wrong with their children, it becomes seen as evidence of the racially degenerate body of the black mother, and hence the black culture, itself.

This time period in Britain was also marked by American sociologist Charles Murray's extraordinary influence on British culture in which he famously identified an "underclass" in Britain. And one aspect of this underclass rhetoric was a preoccupation with "'illegitimacy,' marriage and the state of British family" (Lister, 1996, p. 1). Another American thinker who influenced New Labor policies with his ideas of family and community was Amitai Etzioni. An influential concept advanced by Etzioni was "parenting deficit" from which he saw British society suffering. The other concept he advanced was "children as a moral act," which is the title of a chapter in his book *The Parenting Deficit* (1993) published by Demos, a New Labor think tank. He stated in that book that "making a child is a moral act. It obligates the community to the parents. But it also obligates the parents to the community. For we all live with the consequences of children who are not brought up properly" (p. 4). As Simon Prideaux writes about Etzioni's exceptional influence on New Labor, "quite simply it is this communitarian emphasis on family, community, social discipline, obligation and responsibility—as opposed to an indiscriminate conferral of rights—that lies behind New Labour's search for a 'Third way'" (2004, p. 128).

In light of this political context in the United Kingdom in the mid-1990s and beyond, this chapter argues that of all the myths of white femininity that the Diana phenomenon stabilized, perfect motherhood was the one most dangerous. It was dangerous because it was impossible to achieve. Yet, it prominently intersected with New Labor's vision of new modes of parenting that were based on self-governing, active, and responsible citizens. In fact, we remember how the rhetoric of Diana being a good mother devoted to the upbringing of her boys, despite troubles in her own life, had functioned as some kind of an alibi for her morality, character, and national service. Indeed, after her death, as the rhetoric of motherhood took center stage in how the people were being invited to remember Diana, Tony Blair himself played a role in centralizing the maternal metaphor. Blair's office (reportedly) found the queen's speech to the nation, which was submitted prior to being delivered, cold and impersonal. Blair reportedly had one of his aides insert personal elements such as "as a grandmother" or "I say from the heart" and add that the queen respected Diana for her "devotion" to her sons. In utilizing a maternal and grand-maternal rhetorical framework, Blair mobilized a national public and reconstructed the nation through a logic of maternity. The Diana phenomenon, like so many other nationalist mother narratives, illustrates how during times of national change, "nationalism reduces women to their motherhood. Nowhere in the iconography of nations is there space for women as sisters, as a sisterhood" (Eisenstein, 1996, p. 41). It also reveals how national revision is often invoked through *white* family dramas—or what Ann McClintock (1993) terms "family feuds" (p. 61). As we will see later, the familial tension between Queen Elizabeth and Diana, which has been the focus of so many television programs and tabloid trash, produced contesting visions of the national mother.

The myth of motherhood invoked in the Diana phenomenon embodied what Susan Douglas and Meredith Michaels (2004) have termed "new momism": "a highly romanticized and yet demanding view of motherhood in which the standards for success are impossible to meet" (p. 4). In its production of a halo around motherhood—that was often visually enhanced through photographic techniques as in many images of Diana with William and Harry where they almost radiate light; and in its injection of a supermom-like quality to motherhood—where the mother balances everything to raise perfect good men for the nation—this myth of motherhood valorized qualities that would be unrealistic for any mother to meet who is not white, upper or upper-middle class, able-bodied, and a citizen. As a myth, it rewrote responsible motherhood as something that is individualized (i.e., an individual mother's duty without support from community/state). As a myth it was so elevated and so sacred that, despite being situated in the specific national politics of 1990s Britain, it validated mothering as a universal practice of what Sharon Hays (1996) has termed "intensive mothering" (p. 6) in which child rearing becomes the central function of the mother who spends inordinate amounts of time, energy, and emotional labor to organize all her activities around her children.

What is interesting about the Diana phenomenon is that the image of Diana entered the national screens as a caretaker for young children and exited those same screens as "Mummy" (as Prince Harry's card on her coffin defined her). Thus, maternal subjectivity was her point of entry into and exit from the nation. Every talk show, magazine, newspaper, video documentary, and web page that commemorated Diana made motherhood a central focus.

Labels such as "Hands-on Mum" ("The Diana years," *People's Weekly* [Com-memorative Edition], 1997, p. 119), "The devoted mother" (*Reader's Digest* commemorative tribute, Owen, 1997, p. 48), "Diana's darlings," (*Ladies Home Journal*, February 1990, p. 107), and "Children's Favorite" (*Diana: The People's Princess*, Wood, 1998) have been voluminously attached to her. After Diana's death, the numerous women (and men) who were interviewed by journalists stated how they admired the way she brought up her sons, and how they thought she was a great mother. Indeed, we all remember this Madonna-like script of an ideal mother gaining momentum in the days following her death, and casting a glow on the very (patriarchal and patriotic) meaning of motherhood that Diana embodied—a meaning in which raising good white modern national men is the prime duty of the mother.

Such glorification of motherhood through Diana in the 1990s was simul-taneously reinforced in the popular culture of the times through images of several white celebrity moms (for example, Claudia Schiffer, Uma Thur-man, Elle McPherson, Demi Moore, Madonna, Posh Spice [now Victoria Beckham], Cherie Blair, and many others—all white privileged women). Many of these representations contracted motherhood into a narrow white upper-middle-class heterosexual national space. For instance, Demi Moore's now-famous and controversial 1991 nude image of her pregnant body in the August issue of *Vanity Fair* shot by photographer Annie Leibovitz can hardly be erased from our minds. Although the image was controversial, it reflected the idealization and glorification of pregnancy and motherhood. The lighting in the image is especially significant: Moore's body and pregnant stomach glow against the deliberately chosen dark background. The lighting casts a halo around the body. Moore frames her pregnant stomach with her two hands—almost as though it is something to be revered. The two diamond pieces—a big ring on her right hand and ear studs—position her body as a white upper-class body.[7] Similarly, *People* magazine's cover page in May 1997 (see Figure 2.1) screamed "New Sexy Moms" (with images of celebrity moms).[8] The subcopy read: "Finally, Hollywood discovers a woman can be a mother and a hot number." The celebrities displayed are Niki Taylor, Pamela Lee, Demi Moore, Debbe Dunning, and Madonna. Niki Taylor, the primary photo, in the cover page is carrying two toddlers on her back and beaming a big smile. She reflects the active mother (always happy) that will be discussed later in this chapter. Every celebrity mom represented is also white, upper class, and heterosexually identified. Similarly, bad girl Madonna appeared on the cover of *People* in 1996 as "Mama Madonna."[9] And in a later issue of *People*, Madonna, again on the cover, was quoted as saying "I'm going to be the mother I never had."[10]

Figure 2.1. Cover page of the May 26, 1997, issue of *People*. (*People* © 1997 Time Inc. All rights reserved. Reproduced with permission.)

This chapter examines the relationship between white motherhood and nation in relation to this popular idealization of a particular type of motherhood that was going on in the 1990s in the United Kingdom and beyond. The chapter suggests that whenever the nation undergoes a shift, experiences "moral panics," and stages new visions of the national family, it also stages new images of ideal motherhood (which is almost always white and upper or middle class) through which new national futures can be imagined (see also Cherniavsky, 1995; Davin, 1997; Feldstein, 2000; Glenn, Chang, & Forcey, 1994; Hill Collins, 1999; Jolly, 1998; Ram & Jolly 1998). And often such visions of the ideal mother are "produced through motherhood's *abandonment* of a myriad of 'bad mothers'" (Trimble, 2008, p. 179; emphasis added). My goal in this chapter is to trouble the various logics of whiteness through which the Diana script (as well as scripts of so many other celebrity moms) became a model of revered motherhood in late-20th-century Britain and beyond. It was a model that shifted the care of children primarily to mothers and produced new logics of "can do" instead of "at-risk" mothers dependent on state support.[11] It was also a script based on Western liberal logics of parental care that marginalize or render invisible non-Western, ethnic, immigrant minority maternal experiences that are so present, yet ignored, in Western national landscapes. Consequently, such mothers and their children are rendered as being outside frames of national recognition (Hill Collins, 1994, 1999; Kaplan, 1992; Phoenix, 1996; Reynolds, 2005; Roberts, 1999; Wong, 1994). They can never be "national mothers."

The Active (White) Mother

Perhaps the most dominant theme through which Diana was remembered as a maternal subject, especially after her death, is that of the active mother. We constantly saw images of her in active and visible maternal positions illustrating her 24/7 involvement with her children. Some now-famous images include Diana throwing baby William in the air, sliding down a water ride with the princes, walking her sons to kindergarten, running a mother's race at the children's school (see Figure 2.2), or being covered with sand on a beach by the boys. In such images of active maternity, there is frequently an element of theatricality.[12] Whether flinging her arms wide open as she rushes to greet her sons, or sliding down a water slide with Prince Harry and cheering with both her hands up in the air, or breathlessly running with other mothers at a school race with her body racing toward the finishing

Figure 2.2. Diana running a mother's race at the children's school. (Anwar Hussein/Getty Images. Reproduced with permission.)

line, Diana's body is always in action suggesting a fit can-do maternal body. This can-do maternal body is enterprising, always on the move, confident, and never relies on anyone else (especially the state) for the development of her children. *Doesn't say (rely not rely) or no state?*

Associated with this model of active maternity is also the emphasis on Diana's tactility. Tactility has been significantly associated with Diana. How Diana loved to "touch" people has been the subject of many discussions. For instance, a commemorative book by the *Daily Mail*, *Diana: The Untold Story* (Kay & Levy, 1998) devoted an entire chapter to Diana's mothering style. The chapter reproduced an image of Diana with her boys that had been taken by photographer John Swannell in 1996 during a photo shoot for a Christmas card (see Figure 2.3). The photographer is discussed in the book as saying that the shoot took a long time because the boys would playfully mess up Diana's hair. "I thought at the time: 'what a wonderful relationship she has with them'" (p. 64). This is one of the many images of tactile mother-son bonding through which Diana's maternal position has been visualized in media narratives.

The copy, framing the image in the book that tells us that the shoot took twice as long for the boys were being playful with their mother's hair, is a highly unnecessary detail indeed. However, it seems to deliberately function to buttress the visual logic of loving playfulness that Diana's tactility evokes in the image. Later we are given a discussion of Diana stating, "I feed them love and affection—it's so important" (p. 66). This particular photograph by Swanell, as it was reproduced in the book, takes up approximately one and a quarter pages. Diana is casually dressed. The image shows them laughing together. Her body is leaning back in laughter toward William, while she is

Figure 2.3. This is the original image by the photographer John Swannell that was reproduced in Kay and Levy (1998), *Diana: The Untold Story*, pp. 64–65. (John Swannell, Reproduced with permission.)

looking down at Harry with an expression that combines joyous mirth and maternal devotion. Both sons have one arm touching the mother in a gesture of connectedness.

The affects of happiness and joy associated with Diana's white motherhood are often sentimentalized through visual techniques of lighting that Richard Dyer (1997) has discussed as a mode through which white women are signified as pure. In many images of Diana with William and Harry, Diana often glows as the lighting illuminates her. Anthony Holden's *Diana: Her Life and Legacy* (1997) is one of the most popular commemorative books produced on Diana. The book, along with brief commentaries, comprises beautiful photos from various parts of Diana's life. A series of black and white photos of Diana with her children are also included. This series is striking for the way lighting organizes the images. In one particular image (p. 72), Diana's hair and upper body are lucent. Along with William and Harry, she glows as she literally radiates light. In another highly circulated image of Diana with Prince Harry as a baby, we see similar visual techniques (see Figure 2.4). The dark background contrasts with the light on Diana and Harry and heightens the lighting effect. Although in a later chapter I will offer a detailed discussion of lighting in relation to white maternity, here I simply want to note that the glow in such images seems to stand in for the white mother's happy bonding with her children.

In contrast, I have yet to see nonwhite mothers lit up like this in popular culture. Michelle Obama—the "mom-in-chief"—perhaps remains the only exception from our times. Figure 2.5 is the cover page of *US Weekly* (February 9, 2009). Michelle and the children look radiant in the image. A subcopy states, "keeping it real: Pottery Barn décor, no nanny, J. Crew fashion, romantic dinners."

Figure 2.4. Diana with Prince Harry as a child. Both glow. (Reuters/Stringer Spain. Reproduced with permission.)

Figure 2.5. Cover page of the February 9, 2009, issue of *US Weekly*. (US Weekly LLC © 2009. All rights reserved. Reprinted by permission.)

The message here is that although they are in the White House, this is a typical middle-class mother with her children. The problem is that such a radiant black family, which actually reflects white upper-/middle-class happy familial logics, misrepresents the struggles of black families in contemporary America, as many have noted. Research continually suggests that black men still experience high rates of incarceration, while black women are often rendered husbandless and struggle to bring up children on their own. Black mothers, for instance, have to continually worry about their sons on the streets (Trayvon Martin being a recent example in the United States). My argument is not that black families cannot be happy. Rather, it is that the kind of production of a (upper-/middle-class) black family narrative that has been occurring through the Obamas solidifies a logic that diminishes the realities of class and race that impact black families.

The issue of white heterosexual women being made to glow through lighting techniques is clearly not new. As noted earlier, Dyer (1997) had brilliantly dissected the racialization functions that photographic lighting performs. What I want to add, in the context of the Diana phenomenon, is this: While looking up literally hundreds of images of Diana in magazines, newspapers, documentaries, interviews, and so on, questions (among many others) that

I was interested in examining are these: In what kinds of contexts do we see Diana as a white female body glowing? In what kinds of contexts do we see that kind of lighting that Dyer has talked about casting a purifying and halolike glow? I have noticed that frequently it is when Diana is positioned as maternal figure that she is made to glow. In contrast, surprisingly, she does not seem to radiate light as much when she is represented as a fashion icon (as one might expect). In such representations, then, the lighting becomes a metaphor for all that her maternal body cannot verbalize: joy, happiness, exuberance, and so on. This is important to note for when we ask what it is about the representations of Diana's motherhood that so seduced us into believing that she was the best mother the world has ever seen, the model we all should follow, we realize how the visualities organizing her image (and particularly the lighting techniques) played an important role in enabling us to embrace the universal myth of "Mother Di."

Taken together, such representations narrate a story of a motherhood whose features are worth noting, if only for the ways they contradict many of the realities of motherhood on the ground in late 1990s Britain (and beyond). First, as noted, we see the maternal position being represented as an active position. And this is very much in line with the "active citizen who was put forward [by New Labor] as an alternative to the welfare state" (Yuval-Davis, 1997b, p. 16). This active mother is also very visible. She publicly displays affection for her children. National domesticity in Blairite "new times" required visible signs of (apparently) healthy parenting. Given that "absent" (and therefore not seen) and negligent mothers (also frequently framed as "single mothers") were targets of attack in the New Labor discourse, the image of a maternal body visibly performing parental love became an important logic in staging a new vision of national motherhood. The maternal body of Diana was always seen as doing the work of producing the national family and nurturing the national children (i.e., the national future). In fact, since the late 1990s, visible mothering has become a hallmark of mothering in Western nations that constantly calls attention to itself. Indeed, it would not be unreasonable to argue that with the Diana phenomenon, we witnessed the first glimpses of a neoliberal reorganization of the meaning of motherhood, where motherhood was celebrated as being at once public (you have to be visible and seen as doing things with your children) and private (it is your personal responsibility, not the state's, to raise your children).

Second, the logic of motherhood that the Diana phenomenon represents—along with images of so many celebrity moms who graced popular screens in the 1990s—are racialized through particular themes. For one, it assumes the mother always has a safe space from which to engage in mothering activities. Yet, as feminists of color have noted, for mothers of color—especially in the working class and below—there is often a lack of safety—physical, emotional, social, and interpersonal—in their communities and homes (Hill Collins, 1994). The very act of mothering occurs in an environment where poor nonwhite fathers (or sons) may have been thrown in prison, or killed in violence, or where the mother may have been separated from her children by social services for not being able to attend to them (as working-class mothers of color often work multiple jobs). Or they may have been separated for not having the wherewithal to take care of their children's needs, including material needs. Patricia Hill Collins (1994) has reminded us that "motherhood occurs in specific historical situations framed by interlocking structures of race, class and gender, where the sons and daughters of white mothers have 'every opportunity and protection,' and that the 'colored' daughters and sons of racial ethnic mothers *know not their fate*'" (p. 45; emphasis added).[13] White heterosexual (and particularly middle-class and upper-middle-class) mothers engage in mothering through an *affirming* relation with the nation-state. In contrast, mothers of color—especially working-class or poor mothers of color—have historically, and even today in most Anglo-dominated nations, engaged in mothering *against* the dominant norms of the nation-state (Roberts, 1997).

Doreen Lawrence: The Black Mother

One of the most powerful examples of the trials of nonwhite motherhood in 1990s Britain, which contrasts with the white national motherhood of Diana and other white celebrity mothers of the times, is the experience of Doreen Lawrence, the mother of Stephen Lawrence—a young black boy who was killed in a racist attack in 1993. The Stephen Lawrence case became national and international news. It resulted in New Labor Home Secretary Jack Straw ordering an official investigation into the murder and the handling of the case by the police that finally in 1999—six years after Lawrence's murder—produced the famous Macpherson report. The report pointed to widespread institutional racism in the police force. In her book, *And Still I Rise* (2006), Doreen Lawrence documented how the murder split and broke her entire family. Her husband separated from her and later left for Jamaica. She remained alone in Britain with her remaining children to fight for Stephen's justice. For the longest time, justice was evaded. The family was continually told by the police that there was not sufficient evidence to try the case. It is only in 2012 that the Lawrence case saw justice. Doreen Lawrence stated how she was so filled with anger, frustration, and pain that she "physically hurt all the time" in those years immediately following Stephen's death.[14] In the first few weeks after Stephen's murder, there was hardly any national attention given to the case. It is only after Nelson Mandela visited the Lawrence family in 1993 and stated, "I know what it means to parents to lose a child under such tragic circumstances" for "such brutality was all too common in South Africa 'where black lives are cheap'" (quoted in Stone, 2013, p. 10) that the case received national attention.

While researching the social context of Britain for this chapter—and reading up on the plight of many working-class and nonwhite mothers in Britain—I was drawn to Doreen Lawrence's book. When all the national fuss was going on about good motherhood and single motherhood in the 1990s, here was a case of a perfectly normal family being splintered by the murder of their son, and the mother being rendered a "single" mother by such violence. Doreen's single motherhood status—when her husband left Britain unable to cope with the injustice—ironically was delivered by the state (which for the longest time denied the existence of any evidence of wrong doing in Stephen's case). In the case of Diana (or other privileged white mothers like her), in contrast, the model of motherhood she reflects works with the state. For the likes of Doreen in 1990s Britain, there was no happiness in being a mother to a black son. In fact, it is important to note that while the Stephen Lawrence case received national press attention, around this same time numerous other racially motivated attacks and killings, which received far less attention, also occurred. Some of these are the racist murders of 15-year-old Rolan Adams in Greenwich, South London (1991); 15-year-old Navid Sadiq in Southwark, London (1992); 15-year-old Rohit Duggal in Eltham, London (1992); 15-year-old Manish Patel (1997) in Harrow, London; 24-year-old Ruhullah Aramesh in South London (1992); 18-year-old Imran Khan in Glasgow (1998), as well as many others that space does not permit me to bring into discussion. I name these youths deliberately to refuse the "data" logic through which they are often referred. The fight for Stephen's justice was ultimately about more than Stephen; it was a fight against such racist attacks on nonwhite youth (which continues even today) in Britain. Similarly, Doreen's anguish was not just the anguish of Stephen's mother. It was and is the emotional landscape of every nonwhite mother in the United Kingdom and beyond who has lost a son, or a daughter, or has lived in fear of losing them to racist violence.

Doreen—the black mother—had to work against the state for almost two decades, hiring her own private prosecution when the crown repeatedly failed her and messed up the investigation. She launched a fund-raising campaign for Stephen's justice and later initiated many race-awareness campaigns for the safety of black families. Doreen Lawrence thus poignantly began the preface of her book (2011 [2006]) with these lines: "Two lives ended one chilly April night thirteen years ago. One was the life of my eldest son. You don't have to be a mother to understand what that means. . . ." Perhaps Doreen should have said, "you don't have to be a *black mother* to understand what that means." She went on to say that "the second life that ended was the life I thought was mine. Since my son Stephen was killed with such arrogance and contempt I've had a different life, one that I can hardly recognise as my own."[15]

The discourses of Doreen and Diana in this same period evoke two very different frameworks of motherhood. "It's a lonely place—I wouldn't wish it on anyone," Doreen had once stated while describing her emotional situation following Stephen's death.[16] This statement could very well be elevated to the experiences of so many black mothers or nonwhite mothers—especially with a working-class or poor background. Indeed, it is a lonely place. It is a lonely place when your son has been lost to racism or other forms of state violence; when your husband has been gunned down by the state, or removed to prison by a racially biased law and order system; and when, despite not courting single motherhood, single mother is what the state turns you into—through its policies, racism, and negligence—and then comes at you with guns blazing for being a single "welfare" black mother.

In contrast, Diana's statements about motherhood that were constantly replayed in the media after her death were often about how she was happiest being a mother. Unlike the black mother, the white mother bonds with her children through happiness and joy—in other words, safety and security. In contrast, black mothers often have to bond with their children through completely opposite affects—fear and terror. The Diana phenomenon, like so many other popular white motherhood narratives, associates motherhood solely with affects of joy and happiness. In the process, it normalizes those emotions as the desirable affects of a (national) mother, a good mother. In doing so, such narratives end up pathologizing or even criminalizing those affects of nonwhite motherhood—that a white middle- or upper-class woman will not experience—of fear, terror, and anger (at society) that ironically also become evidence of "bad motherhood." As far as I know, there is little work on the racialized affects through which motherhood is given meanings, through which motherhood of various types are produced, and through which one type of motherhood is sentimentalized over others in a given national context.

The contrasts between Diana (a white national mother) and Doreen (a black mother) in millennium Britain also reveal a larger politics of death and life through which motherhood remains linked to the nation. In both these cases of motherhood, death (and thus life) was very much a discourse framing the context. But death played out differently in the two cases that reveal

important differences in the relations between white or nonwhite motherhood and the nation. The differences also remind us of Mbembe's (2003)
discussion of necropolitics—that the "expression of sovereignty resides, to a
larger degree, in the power and the capacity to dictate who may live and who
must die" (p. 1). When Diana (the white national mother) physically died,
there was a literal death. But her death in effect produced more life-giving
and life-nurturing narratives—narratives of hope and future for the nation.
As the nation witnessed young Princes William and Harry looking shattered,
it (i.e., we the spectators at the funeral) vowed to protect the boys. In doing
so, the entire nation was articulated into a (white) maternal position. Thus,
although the white mother died, the national public symbolically stepped in
to become the national mother who would make sure that William and Harry
(the nation's future) could grow up "open" the way their white mother had
wanted—a sentiment consistent with New Labor's rhetoric of "opening" up
Britain. One remembers images of so many women at the funeral reaching
out to William and Harry as they walked by. We saw such instances of the
nation being turned into a mother in another famous case as well. When we
saw 4-year-old John John jutting out his chest and raising his hand to salute
JFK's coffin, the Kennedy children, as Jay Mulvaney, the author of the popular
book *Diana and Jackie* stated, "became America's children" (Mulvaney, 2002,
p. 169). In such moments of death, the nation turns not just into a mother
but a white mother. And although this is unspoken, when Mulvaney refers
to the children as "America's children," the nation that flashes before our eyes
does so in the image of a good white mother (and not an ethnic mother).
We, the national public, become articulated to the nation as a "white" mother
through which our relationship to such national children (and thus national
future) are forged. This is what we witnessed again after the Newtown, Connecticut, shootings (2012) and the Columbine school shootings (1999). The
white mother never dies; she cannot die. She is the very symbolic structure
through and upon which a racialized patriarchal national order continually
writes its shifting visions.[17]

All this illustrates the leveling power of white heterosexual middle- and
upper-middle-class maternity—its ideological power to articulate diverse
groups into some kind of national community during times of national crises
under the logic of the maternal. An especially interesting aspect of white
(national) maternity during Diana's funeral is how frequently the images
of people of color, including black women crying at Diana's funeral, were
articulated into a larger (white) maternal gendering of the national public.
And in the process, the specificity of the black maternal position was erased,
and absorbed, by the overarching symbolism of white national maternity that

[handwritten margin note: Is this a universal spectator?]

framed the events following Diana's death. Late liberal accommodationist logics of the nation such as these constitute what may be termed *enlightened nationalism*.[18] This is a mode of nationalism where minority positions are articulated into patriotic discourses through logics (visual or nonvisual) that suggest that everyone has an equal place in the national polity being imagined.[19] We saw this also after 9-11 when people of color were consciously represented in the image of America that splashed on so many television screens. Nationalism, in such instances, instead of being seen for what it is—a complex structure of feelings and belongings that distributes identities unequally in the nation-state—becomes presented as a progressive enlightened structure that can mobilize diverse people through (apparently) equal logics of recognition into a polity especially when that polity is under crisis.

Let me return to Doreen Lawrence (the nation's black mother). Doreen's relationship to her son was also marked by death. And his too was not just a physical death. It was a death born out of larger social deaths within which black lives negotiate and navigate their subjectivities. There is no "life" narrative here (as there is in abundance in white middle- and upper-class familial spaces). There are only death narratives (whether a literal death or a fear of death visiting anytime) in black lower-class spaces of the nation. A death like Stephen's only produces more fear of black deaths. Thus, while both the contexts of Diana and Doreen were written by a literal death, and within four years of each other, in one case (of white motherhood), the death simply rose to articulate new (white masculinist) national lives and futures—represented primarily through images of young William and Harry. In the other case, the dead black (male) body (of Stephen) and the (living) black maternal body (of Doreen) both became what Abdul Jan Mohammed (2005) has termed "the death-bound subject": the subject who lives under the "threat of death" and where death "penetrate[s] into the very capillary structures of [its] subjectivity" (p. 4).[20]

I bring up this issue of death because a mother's prime responsibility is to provide safety for her children—the nation's children. But this narrative of safety that we attach to motherhood is not so simple. What it means to engage in mothering under conditions of death (literal, material, and social) is an important question that troubles the equations among life, mothering, and the nation, and it reveals the role of whiteness in naturalizing motherhood as always being a "life" narrative. Sharon Holland (2000), for instance, has asked, when "'hell' is a condition arising from encounters with whites" and "when 'living' is something to be achieved and not experienced . . . how do people of color gain a sense of empowerment?" (p. 16; emphasis in original). All this further leads us to inquire what we mean by a child's "life" and which children's lives we see as lives worth weaving into our national narratives of renewal and hope. For instance, the nation will usually not hesitate to weep for little middle- or upper-class white boys (or girls) who have either experienced violence toward their bodies from shootouts or who have been killed (think Sandy Hook or Columbine). In such moments, these little beings are turned into heavenlike creatures in media coverage. They become angels for whom we weep. And in weeping for them, we end up occupying (if only temporarily) a national maternal position. Jamie Bolger's story, for instance, became a story of national innocence betrayed. On November 28, 1993, the *Independent* described the Bolger case as expressing "the death of innocence."[21] Yet, one hardly finds images of little nonwhite boys or girls being elevated to angelic figures for whom we can and should weep. To weep for someone is to first *recognize* them. Then after recognizing them, we have to see them as equals, as humans with worth, as part of us and our polity. Indeed, as Judith Butler (2012) notes, "if only certain populations are deemed grievable and others are not, then open grieving for one set of losses becomes the instrument through which another set of losses are denied" (p. 21). Weeping for little white children and being articulated as (white) national mothers during national grieving function as affective instruments through which the losses of nonwhite mothers are denied. National grieving is never racially innocent.

The Can-Do Mother

Long before the term *postfeminist* entered academic and public vocabularies in 1990s, *People* magazine in October 1989 declared Diana as the "first postfeminist princess."[22] A prominent feature of Diana's postfeminism was described by the magazine in these terms: "After producing an heir (William) and a spare (Harry) Diana took on another '80s role: *Working Mom . . .* Between cutting ribbons, accepting posies from bashful children, waving and smiling from banner-decked balconies and cuddling young hospital patients. . . . [she involved] herself with *gusto* in the day-to-day drama of runny noses and tiny tantrums" (emphasis added). Here, we see the first glimpses of the can-do mother who would dominate popular culture imaginations from the mid-1990s and well into the first decade of the 2000s in the United Kingdom (and beyond). The can-do mother would also be upheld to demonize working-class mothers on benefits and state welfare (see also Douglas & Michaels, 2004; McRobbie, 2009; Nash, 2012; Tyler, 2008).

This neoliberal theme of can-do through which contemporary female subjectivity has been imagined in popular culture has been critiqued by feminist scholars such as Angela McRobbie, Susan Douglas, Rosalind Gill, Diane Negra, and Yvonne Tasker, among others. This concept of can-do—initially a phrase used by Body Shop to evoke girl power—has been particularly utilized in girlhood studies—and Anita Harris's (2004) work remains prominent here—to explore consumerist neoliberal constructions of girlhood. In this chapter, however, as indicated earlier, I utilize this concept to discuss how late 1990s and early 21st-century representations of motherhood in popular culture have also been constructed through this can-do logic. As Imogen Tyler (2011) states, "whilst it has been claimed that girls are the 'privileged' subjects of neoliberalism," this time period was "also the era of 'maternal femininities'" (p. 22), which manifested many of the can-do attitudes of turn-of-the-century femininity. Although in the mid- to late 1990s many popular figures such as Victoria Beckham (Posh Spice), Cherie Blair, Kate Moss, and Hilary Clinton (in the United States) seemingly balanced work and motherhood to perfection, the first glimpses of this logic of motherhood was found in representations of Diana or were certainly attributed to her. For instance, a few days after Diana's death, the *Spice Girls* epitomized Diana as one of the ultimate symbols of "girl power" at the New York MTV awards. Ginger Spice Geri Halliwell said, "I think what we are really about is what Lady Diana had—real girl power." Wearing black armbands, the Spice Girls sang "Say you'll be there"—a song they dedicated to Diana.[23]

A prominent feature of Diana's life that enabled so many, like the Spice Girls, to attribute to her such can-do status was her simultaneous dealing with motherhood and the outside world—(what is today known as work-life balance and is increasingly a logic that defines citizenship in the 21st century). Narrations of how Diana insisted that baby William accompany her on her first public tour of Australia or that despite her heavy work schedule, the children were to never be ignored are well known. Such narrations received a boost during the numerous commemorations of Diana in 1997 when she was being upheld as an exemplar of a new Britain that did things in a modern way.

An especially significant representation of Diana's motherhood was its very middle-class construction (see also, Douglas & Michaels, 2004). Instead of being seen as a royal mother, Diana's modern approach to her children was frequently framed in the media through a middle-class logic that constructed her motherhood as something to which everyone could relate. This is important to note given the war on single (poor) mothers that was going on in Britain in the 1990s. In 2007—the 10th anniversary of Diana's death—a book *Diana: The Portrait* was released. It was authorized by Diana's estate and the Princess of Wales Memorial Fund. It was written and put together by Rosalind Coward. *The Portrait* is a legacy summing up Diana's life. It draws from numerous famous incidents from Diana's life as remembered by people who knew or met her. In the section titled "Motherhood," we are provided details such as her attempt to "combine motherhood with a public role" and that it put her in touch with "what many women were going through in *that era*" (p. 59; emphasis added). Such details emphasize Diana's seeming ability to connect with all mothers of that era. A quotation from Diana's own father is also provided: "In my day, the royals had one job a day. My Diana sometimes does two or three. She loves it, but I am worried she is working too hard" (p. 59). In this description, Diana's royal functions are simply reduced to a job at which she, like regular middle-class people, works "too hard." We learn in *The Portrait* book that "she would drive them to school herself in the mornings in jeans and her canvases" and her "day was exactly like many mothers of that *social class*. She'd arrive at school in the morning in a track suit, no make-up, drop the kids off, say 'hello' to other children" (p. 60; emphasis added). We also learn how sometimes other mothers would casually let Diana know that William was coming by their house to play, to which she would say, just like any regular mother, "that's fine" as though William was just a regular boy whose presence at a playmate's house simply required a casual last-minute letting his mother know. We further learn things like how she would "join in parents' activities with other mothers" (Wood, 1998, p. 19) or how "dressed in jeans and sneakers the boys went with her to theme parks and to see the latest movies" (p. 19).

What we have is an image of a typical 1990s (white) middle-class woman successfully juggling work and children. McRobbie (2011), in her discussion of 1990s "postfeminist masquerade" (p. 4), notes that one technology of the postfeminist masquerade is the "working girl/woman" rhetoric in which the working girl/woman maintains "high achievement in work" but also exemplifies success in motherhood (p. 5). McRobbie notes how this individualization logic reflects a "new sexual contract" in which "there is no prospect of a feminist politics of the household or of childcare" and which required that the mother (or working girl/woman) "jostles and juggles" (p. 5). Diana constituted one of the early images of this kind of new femininity/ motherhood that could do and balance everything. But she was not the only popular figure manifesting this individualizing logic.

Many other figures in the mid- to late 1990s in Britain also shored up a growing formation that was rewriting femininity and motherhood through a logic of individual female success. When Cherie Blair became pregnant with baby Leo in 1999, Ros Coward wrote in the *Guardian* (November 1999) that "Cherie's pregnancy is being offered as the vision of a female afterlife in the 21st century. Women no longer have to face a living death as their families grow up . . . Now they can have it all: work, motherhood, and even a second crack at a family, defying ageing and the end of fertility." The *Los Angeles Times* in that same month noted how Cherie's pregnancy provided a big political boost for Blair. It certainly did as it solidified many of the logics underlying Blair's policies around family and parenting (Miller, 1999). The *Los Angeles Times* article, like so many reports at that time, emphasized that "as for Cherie Blair—a lawyer and judge who uses her maiden name, Booth, and whose salary is nearly twice her husband's—'she has been a good role model for women, happy in her family and at work.'"[24]

Another powerful can-do mother figure was Victoria Beckham (Posh Spice). Popular commentators have often coded Beckham as one of the earliest examples of the "yummy mummy" phenomenon that was to become powerful in the late 1990s and the early 2000s (Jenkins, 2009). An especially interesting example reported in the media and meant to highlight Victoria Beckham's can-do attitude is a story of how someone once tried to snatch baby Brooklyn—her first born—in 1999, but she chased him away. The *Guardian* (1999) reported an onlooker stating that: "The guy tried to grab Brooklyn. Victoria did what any mother would do and hit him. She knocked him over and managed to stop him," while David Beckham held on to the child on his chest (McIntyre, 1999). Here is the can-do mother at her (seeming) best overshadowing even the mega-athlete football star Beckham in the pursuit of the baby snatcher. Clearly, the new female subject position of maternity that Diana offered in the 1990s was part of a larger social re-formation of maternity through which logics of the self-governing female subject/mother were being enacted (McRobbie, 2009, pp. 57–58). The *Observer* in an article in September 2000, labeled this self-governing, active, and can-do maternal subject as the *e-mother* (emphasis added). The e-mother stands for the everything-mother "who must demonstrate her commitment to the maternal role by looking after her children herself, while doing everything else as well [. . .]. The e-mother orthodoxy holds that it is cruel and heartless to hand your baby to someone else" (Turner, 2000).

When we place these can-do mother images of the times against New Labor's attacks on working-class single mothers, we see how such hyperefficient models of motherhood by implication position working-class mothers in "fragile and restricted positions" that suggest that the "working-class self must be regulated, corrected or left behind" (Allen & Osgood, 2009, p. 2). Thus, when Blair came into office, within a short period, he offered the controversial The New Deal on lone motherhood (1997), which caused a revolt in his own party. The New Deal was a policy initiative that required mothers on benefits to seek employment, to come in for compulsory interviews (or run the risk of losing all benefits), and to embrace trainings that were being offered by the government. However, often the work that was available simply would not meet the standards necessary for lone mothers to get off benefits or provide sufficient care for their children. Further, if these mothers wanted to pursue college to improve their professional skills—and hence upgrade their lives—they would lose their income support and end up being reliant on student loans. Such problems were rarely reflected in the press that only reinforced the perception of "welfare scroungers." For example, on September 20, 1993, the BBC's *Panorama* ran an entire program with the title "Babies on Benefit." On July 28, 1996, the *Sunday Times* ran a feature on lone mothers titled, "Public Enemy or Backbone of Britain? The Truth About Single Mothers." This attack on lone motherhood continues even today in Britain. In recent times, there has been an emergence of the stereotype of *Chav Mums*—a term that designates white working-class and poor mothers (Tyler, 2008). Indeed, it is worth mentioning that the United Kingdom's percentage of single mothers is one of the highest in supposedly "advanced" nations, and the highest in relation to any European Union nation.[25]

Where logics of whiteness and the nation are concerned, several issues are to be noted in this gendered formation of the can-do mother of the Blairite "new times." First, such a formation of maternity produces new logics of white universality. In being able to manage a successful career and being actively involved in her children's life, the white mother presents a vision of a normative mother/female subject who can be everywhere and anywhere. And as this becomes presented as the gold standard for millennial mothering, what is overlooked is that many such white upper- and middle-class women choose to engage in e-mothering and that choice itself is an outcome of white upper- and middle-class privilege. In contrast, nonwhite mothers and working-class mothers throughout history have always engaged in e-mothering, not out of choice, but out of needs that keep increasing as the state cuts family support. For instance, many black working-class mothers (often in lieu of an actively present father in the house) perform all the duties in and out of the house necessary to maintain the family. They also have to perform acts that white mothers would never have to perform: such as the acts of constantly protecting their sons and daughters from state and community violence. Yet, this kind of incredible e-mothering is rarely celebrated or recognized as e-mothering or ideal mothering or even as active mothering. As many black feminists have noted, it has rather yielded stereotypes of the Strong Black Woman who can bear anything. This is a stereotype whose logic has also served to desexualize black women/mothers.

Second, the individualizing logic of can-do motherhood celebrated through the Diana phenomenon, and images of many other celebrities of the 1990s and beyond, valorizes not only a tight reductive nuclear family framework but also neglects the differing kinship patterns of nonwhite, non-Western origin families that live in the United Kingdom (Phoenix, 1996; Reynolds, 2005). British sociologist Forna (2000) explains how welfare policies regarding lone mothers both in the United Kingdom and the United States have been based on the assumption of a lone mother being with her children by herself: "the rules regarding welfare have contributed to the fragmentation of families, particularly Black families, by enabling a mother to live alone with her children and penalizing her if she chooses to live as part of a household, with relatives or a partner" (p. 397). Furthermore, black and Asian mothers in Britain (and elsewhere) often operate in a social context of shared parenting where friends and family members will frequently look after the children while the mother is attending to other things (Reynolds, 2005). There is often a larger communal parenting toward the child. Yet, compared to the individualized maternal logic of white Western cultures, such culturally differing paradigms of parenting, by default, end up being seen as deviant and negligent, and thus a threat to the (white) nation and its familial structures.

A notable trend presently on the rise is Western media's fascination with the "Tiger mum." A direct spin off from "tiger economies," which referred to the economic growth in Asian countries such as China in the 1990s, tiger mums are represented as strict overambitious Asian—and particularly Chinese—parents living in the West. The term was made popular by Amy Chua's controversial international bestseller (2011) *Battle Hymn of the Tiger Mother.* Amazon.com, in its bookseller description, described the book as having "ignited a global parenting debate" for its strong criticism of Western models of parenting. A January 2011 article in the *Telegraph* described the tiger mum as follows:

> Be afraid, be very afraid. After Pushy Mum, that Ghenghis Khan of secondary-school applications, here comes Tiger Mother. Tiger Mother is Chinese with a fearsome outboard-motor of ambition for her offspring. By the age of four, Tiger Mother's baby is reading Sartre, but thinks that, on balance, Balzac is the better prose stylist. Tiger Mother's children are never allowed to watch television, play computer games or go to sleepovers, which are a time-wasting invention of indulgent Western parents who are too lazy to put in the hours needed to raise a genius. Tiger Mother rarely sleeps herself. Why would she? Sleep prevents you shouting at your child to practice her violin![26]

In that very same month (on January 31, 2011), *Time* magazine's cover image visually presented the Tiger Mum. We see her body shoulder down—the face is cut off (note the dehumanization)—wearing a drab gray skirt, brown schoolmarmish low-heeled shoes, and a dull blue shirt. In front of her, in visually diminished size, is a little Asian girl (probably Chinese one speculates from the preceding excerpt) playing the violin and looking up at the Tiger Mum, who visually towers over her. The child playing the violin evokes the stereotype that all young Chinese people excel at the violin (or some classical musical instrument). The little girl is wearing a dark gray dress—over a blouse or shirt—that looks like a school uniform, black stockings, and black conservative shoes. The child's clothing contrasts with the (seeming) casual individuality of the informal clothes of North American children. The Tiger Mum in the image emerges as someone fearful and whose strict parenting borders on the abusive (for she even shouts at her child as the *Telegraph* tells us). Such an image of a Tiger Mum also resurrects the age-old "dragon lady" image of the cruel heartless Asian woman that has dominated Hollywood screens.

What is going on here is not just a marking of cultural difference by the media but a displacement of larger contemporary Western geopolitical anxieties about Asia, and China in particular, onto the terrain of motherhood itself—in this case, the Asian mother (and thus the Asian family and Asian nations). The racialization of this geopolitical anxiety becomes particularly evident when we consider that when the can-do white mother, as an active entrepreneurial citizen, involves her child in so many things, without turning to the state for help, she becomes the ideal mother of the late 20th and early 21st centuries. Yet, when an Asian mother, through different cultural norms around parenting becomes overambitious for the future of her children, she is reduced to a fearful tiger mum—a caricature of a tiger (Asian) nation—trying to groom her "cubs" to compete fiercely in the global marketplace and probably eat us (the West) alive.

The parenting patterns of white motherhood are thus never marked. But maternal patterns of any other culture symbolize that culture (and its [seeming] deficit) itself. Additionally, the hyperefficient can-do mothers of the late 20th and early 21st centuries such as Diana or Victoria Beckham (and others), despite their can-do attitude to mothering, always manage to look beautiful and attractive (Allen & Osgood, 2009; McRobbie, 2006; Nash, 2012; Tyler, 2008). As the *People* magazine cover discussed earlier confirmed through its images of white celebrity mothers, one can (apparently) be a great mother and a sexy "hot number." In contrast, the overactive nonwhite or non-Western mother rarely looks physically attractive in popular culture (and thus she is not really a can-do mother). The tiger mom in the *Time* image is certainly not fashionable; she wears dreary clothes that desexualize her. And we do not even know how she looks for her face is cut off. These examples reveal how motherhood frequently becomes a terrain in which larger battles over national modernities occur. And given the West's present anxiety over the "rise of Asia," we see how that anxiety is being displaced on to the gendered body of the Asian woman once again. I say "once again" because historically this has been the case, as the influential documentary *Slaying the Dragon* (Gee, 1988) and its sequel *Slaying the Dragon: Reloaded* (Kim, 2011) as well as scholarship in Asian and Asian American studies have documented well (Espiritu, 2008; Feng, 2002; Ma, 2000; Ono & Pham, 2009; Shah, 1997).

Oppositional Scripts of White Motherhood

Scholars in whiteness studies have often argued that whiteness stages itself in contrast to what it is not—the nonwhite other. While this is indeed true, it is also the case that in any given political moment, whiteness also stages its hegemonic status in contrast to other forms of whiteness that it may variously code as undesirable in a particular national context. This is especially the case given that not all forms of whiteness become hegemonic in a given national moment. Whiteness is not a monolithic formation. Competing versions and visions of whiteness struggle in relation to each other in particular national moments to gain ascendancy. In the politics of motherhood staged through the Diana phenomenon, we see this occurring. Constructions of Diana's maternity that reflect a touchy-feely culture of intimacy that characterized the Blairite new times acquired meaning through constant contrasts made with the queen and her (failed) maternal performances. In commemorative media narratives, for instance, as Diana came to signify the loving, caring, maternal body of the emerging modern postimperial Britain, the queen became a signifier of the cold and uncaring imperial domesticity that had to be left behind to regain Britain's value in the world. The queen signified motherhood modeled on prewar years. And that model of imperial motherhood had to be jettisoned to produce a motherhood of "the people."

Such contrasts between two models of national maternity—imperial and postcolonial—through which the queen and Diana were oppositionally constructed were emphasized in numerous journalistic texts, especially after Diana's death when her model of motherhood was being upheld as a sign for these new times. A particular image that has been replayed in several videos captures this opposition well. The image is from an old black and white newsreel of the queen from the early 1950s. We see the queen stepping out from a train, returning home after a long foreign tour. The Queen Mother and little Charles—probably about six—are waiting on the station platform to greet her. The queen, followed by the duke, first goes toward her mother. As they lightly embrace, we see little Charles, left outside of this circle of imperial embrace, looking away, distracted by something that is outside the frame of the image. The queen then bends toward Charles and lightly shakes his hand. There is no warm hug, no tight maternal embrace, and no spontaneous show of affection. After this brief and formal greeting, she moves Charles out of the way to make room to greet another woman—probably a lady-in-waiting. Little Charles, appearing both confused and left out, looks up at his mother with an expression that suggests that he clearly wants more attention.

This particular image has been used in several commemorative programs after Diana's death to highlight the difference in a similar scene of Diana greeting her sons on the Royal Britannica, after being briefly separated from them. The image captures Diana in a red and white checked skirt suit, rushing toward her sons, her arms wide open, her expression bursting with maternal love. The color scheme and the visual framework in the two images heighten the narrative contrast between the maternal coldness and distance of the queen and the warmth and spontaneity of Diana. The color photograph of Diana in a chic red and white suit evokes a vibrancy and intimacy lacking in the bland black and white newsreel featuring the queen in a stiff knee-length overcoat. Further, in the photo of Diana, the image has been clicked exactly at the moment in which she flings her arms wide open. In the image of the queen, the camera is at a distance heightening our (the viewer's) distance from the queen. The point at which the camera does close in is when little Charles looks up at his mother, thus inviting the audience to identify with his sense of neglect and confusion.

Such visual contrasts between the loving, intimate, active, and modern maternity of Diana, and the distant, aloof, and "old world" maternity of the queen are further heightened by numerous journalistic comments that construct Charles as a dysfunctional and confused product of a cold and uncaring mother. For instance, in January 2002, less than five years after Diana's death—a death that itself had called into question the queen's "cold" style of motherhood, the *Telegraph* published a two-part series on the queen, "The Real Elizabeth II," written by its feature writer Graham Turner. This series critiqued the queen's parenting style and included comments from interviewees in the royal household. Comments on her parenting style included statements such as "it had been formed pre-war—It was really a complete *time warp*" (emphasis added) or "The Queen's character, like that of the upper class as a whole, was moulded for an imperial role. 'She's one of those people deeply unemotional'" or "'she shied away from responsibility for the family all the time'" (as stated by a courtier) or "the dramatic death of Diana in 1997 pitched the Queen into a crisis which, for a few feverish days, sent the monarchy reeling."[27] Comments in other journalistic reports also included similar statements:

Diana did not want her boys to suffer the same traumas [as Charles resulting from parental neglect]. (Kay & Levy, 1998, p. 64)

. . . she viewed with horror the possibility of them being "hidden upstairs with the governess." Charles seldom saw his mother when he was a boy.

Diana's approach was to "hug my children to death." (Kay & Levy 1998, p. 66)

It fired her with an unshakeable determination to make sure that her children did not suffer from the same family remoteness and resulting unhappy childhood as their father. (Kay & Levy, 1998, p. 64)

Diana had seen the results of the Windsors' child-rearing tradition in her husband and his siblings [and] she fought harder than ever to mix the contemporary with the traditional, to bring a modern perspective to an ancient practice. (Mulvaney, 2002, p. 157)

Such contrasting representations of Diana and the queen reveal several complex relations between white motherhood and the nation. We find that two different imaginations of white motherhood—one imperial and traditional, and the other, modern and postimperial—being staged through Diana and the queen, in which one functions as a critique of the other. And in this relay race between tradition and modernity, in this contest between two visions of national domesticity—one old and damaged, and the other modern and emerging—the very body of the white mother functions as a technology for staging a shift in the reimagination of the national future. Relatedly, we see how the white maternal body constitutes a site of a split: in this case, a split between an imperial past (or imperial whiteness) so vigorously being jettisoned, and a liberal and modern present (so enthusiastically being embraced by New Britain and its cool atmosphere). In Jolly's (1998) words, "the embodied maternal subject is pervaded by a profound tension . . . as the mother is sundered in contests between 'tradition' and 'modernity'" (p. 1). The (modern) nation and the (past) empire are pitted against each other in the staging of new maternal domesticities.

These examples reveal white femininity's ambiguous relation to the nation. White femininity is never completely of the nation; it is merely the staging ground of its fantasies and, simultaneously, the site of its denials and forgetting (jettisoning the old model of prewar motherhood allows for a forgetting that is dangerous). White femininity works for the nation as long as it can be put in the service of certain national hegemonies. When that hegemony shifts, new formations of white femininity are needed, and the old formations often begin to symbolize the "problems" against which new white national hegemonies emerge. In the politics of motherhood staged through the Princess Diana phenomenon, we see this occurring where white motherhood—as the site for the production of the national family—becomes the grounds upon which different visions of the white nation struggle against each other.[28]

But what might such evocations of different national temporalities through the figure of the white mother really reveal about the relationship between nation, time, and white femininity—and in particular white motherhood? Homi Bhabha (2004 [1994]) has discussed the nation in terms of a "double narrative movement" (p. 208). On the one hand, as Neil Larsen (2001) explaining Bhabha puts it, the nation is something that is "narratED (original emphasis) to its 'subjects'—as a pedagogical object—the nation remains constant. . . . through a 'continuous empty time,' punctuating this time itself as both its origin and its telos" (p. 40). Yet, on the other hand, the nation also has to enact "the people" as a constant performance. And it is here that the "nation enters a different time" (Larsen, 2001, p. 41). For "the people" to "retell or 'perform' the story of the nation" (p. 41) and for the nation to remain vibrant and evolving, it has to be a living and changing principle. The brilliance of Bhabha's argument lies in recognizing the enactment of national time in terms of both constancy and change, stasis and movement. And it is this that, for Bhabha, reveals the very ambivalence of the nation as narration.

While Bhabha does not address gender in his discussion, I want to suggest that in Anglo modernities, the figure of the white woman, and the white mother in particular, reveals this ambivalent double movement of national time. I bring up this matter here because the constant contrast between the queen and Diana—which has been a fulcrum of the Diana phenomenon—expresses a larger ambivalence in the construct of white femininity where the white mother is both the nation's site of constancy (reminding us of the permanent desirability of white reproductive boundaries) and the grounds of its shift (reminding us that different formations of whiteness are valued in different times). The white mother functions both as a sign of national change—of the nation's progress—and the limits of that change. The queen and Diana are at one level the same—they make up the body of the generic white mother who is always present in the nation, always doing the work of producing and reproducing it. The queen and Diana are also not the same—they signify different familial formations of whiteness that collide against each other in writing changing "white mythologies" of the nation.[29]

Conclusion

The topic of white motherhood is of immense significance. As demographic landscapes of Anglo-dominant nations change and as alternative cultural frameworks of mothering permeate our landscapes, what happens or is happening to the framework of white motherhood becomes an important question, surely. While there is little evidence to suggest that the white maternal framework underlying national domesticity is about to change dramatically—given that whiteness seems to find new ways to fortify itself against challenges posed by multiculturalism and globalism—it is important to continually look at how white motherhood is recrafted to fit contemporary national needs and desires (including liberal multicultural desires). The Diana phenomenon is indeed contextually specific. Its performance of motherhood was linked to the specific performance of New Labor's new times. But where the phenomenon provides insights that have a broader significance are in these following matters that I have discussed in this chapter but summarize here. The Diana phenomenon illustrates (a) how white motherhood is not homogeneous but a constant site of tension through which shifting national hegemonies are enacted; (b) that during times of national shifts, differing versions of white motherhood frequently collide against each other; (c) that the white mother in the nation never dies, while an individual white mother may die, the symbolic white mother is always there, underlying every landscape of national domesticity; (d) that models of white motherhood constantly contradict nonwhite motherhood, rendering it deviant and dysfunctional; and (e) that white motherhood exists not for itself but to perform new (patriarchal) national hopes. The topic of motherhood will be picked up again through a different slant in Chapter 4. There we will see how the national white mother's body becomes global. What new formations of whiteness are managed through that particular global positioning of white maternity is the subject of that investigation.

3. Fashioning the Nation

The Citizenly Body, Multiculturalism, and Transnational Designs

Chapter 2 addressed how images of a new kind of (white) mother are often needed by the nation to produce a vision of a modern family. Continuing with the focus on how the body of the white woman functions as a site through which a racialized national modernity is staged, this chapter examines fashion, and the (white) fashionable female body, as being another site through which the nation manages its "newness" and expresses new logics of national belonging. The Diana phenomenon especially lends itself to such a discussion. Diana's body was overwhelmingly associated with style and glamour—as captured in labels such as "fashion princess," "princess of style," "fashion icon," "fashion ambassador," "new age Diana," and so on. Additionally, there has been a plethora of magazines, videos, television documentaries, and special newspaper supplements devoted solely to Diana's fashion and her continuously evolving sartorial style. As noted in Chapter 1, numerous exhibitions on both sides of the Atlantic continue to display Diana's clothes today, and people pay significant admissions fees to view them.

Fashion journalists have noted that Diana herself had been very aware of the power of fashion through which to endear herself to the people. A detailed reading of numerous fashion books, magazines, and videos on Diana's fashion reveals that for the princess, her clothes, style, and body were not simply decorative items. They were sites of struggles—her struggle with the royal establishment and her desire (especially in the 1990s) to mark herself as being of "the people," of being seen as ordinary instead of extraordinary. Reports frequently note that Diana had recognized full well that her clothes, looks, and body were instruments through which she was going to ally herself with a new Britain, a young Britain—a Britain that wanted to be flexible and global. Fashion journalist, Georgina Howell (1998) noted that fashion was a terrain through which "the Princess was able to act out the heartfelt phases and turning points of the sixteen difficult years that followed her wedding" (p. 14). Indeed we saw this in the famous Christie's auction in New York, in which Diana got rid of her billowing gowns and skirts from 1980s and traded the earlier utopian romantic look for a more civic and urbane look.

After her death, journalists explicitly linked changes in Diana's clothes, looks, and style to shifts in the nation's own temporality. For instance, in a television/video program by the *Daily Mail* titled *Diana: A Life in Fashion* (1997), Liz Tilberis, the editor of *Vogue* stated that at first Diana courted the English country look, the "Chelsea" look, and that it served her well "to look very conservative, very sort of English, English rose, country sort of person." According to Tilberis, this style made sense, for Diana was trying to reflect the romantic movement of the early 1980s when the nation was trying to recover from the "winter of despair." There are numerous media images in which Diana's early body is situated in country landscapes and her clothes—tweeds, Wellingtons, felt hats, and plain corduroys—evoke countryside rurality. Her body in such images is without much makeup. Her looks and clothes mesh with the country landscape. Such images became articulated to a new Britain rhetoric that enabled the staging of a contrast between the "new" urban cool Britain signified by the mid-1990s clothes of Diana and the earlier repressive, insular Britain, signified by the early 1980s weighty clothes.

The 1980s was a time when "heritage," under Thatcherism, became a prevailing concept. Andrew Higson's (2006 [1993]) well-known work on British national cinema during Thatcherism has discussed the emergence of a whole host of heritage films during the decade of the 1980s that recreated the past and exhibited a pastoral quality. John Corner and Sylvia Harvey (1991) have noted that the concept of *heritage*—pastness and national pride—during the Thatcher years became cleverly wedded to the concept of "enterprise." As the reorganization of British capitalism (and increasing privatizing) within an international economy occurred during the Thatcher years, resulting in various kinds of fragmentations and destabilization in society, a "resurgent nationalism" (p. 46) emerged that remobilized the notion of heritage (seen especially in popular culture) to offer a sense of (an imagined) continuity and stability of national identity. In addition, this decade saw the National Heritage Acts of 1980 and 1983, which were committed to the preservation of heritage properties and buildings. Thus, country, nature, pride in past Britain, and heritage became cultural signatures of the 1980s decade. The early images of Diana, where her gowns looked more like costumes, and where we often saw her in the country dressed as a country girl (in tweeds and corduroys) thus reflected the 1980s heritage reconstruction of the nation. In fact, fashion journalists who link Diana's changing fashion to an emerging new Britain often talk of

CHAPTER 3

her unsophisticated style of the early years in which the true potential of her body (read: the national body) had not yet emerged. Her early dress style is referenced through terms such as "raw material,"[1] "fuddy duddy clothes,"[2] "frumpy outfits,"[3] "girly,"[4] or "childlike." In such references, the yet to emerge (and "grown up") modern national body of 1990s is seen as being awkward and trying to find itself. It is unable to express itself under the weight of the frumpy and bulky clothes it was made to wear in the 1980s, in contrast to the later edgy cool clothes and pared-down style that were to "free up" the body. In the *Daily Mail* program *Diana: A Life in Fashion*, we are told by one of Diana's designers, Victor Edelstein, that in the 1990s, as she became more free of royalty (read: the traditional nation), she felt less "obliged to wear British fashion. [. . .]. *She became in a sense more global*" (emphasis mine). Similarly, noted photographer Tim Graham and fashion editor Tasmin Blanchard (1998) in their book *Dressing Diana* note that the "Diana of the nineties" left "behind the shackles and constraints of the Establishment" as she became "sleeker and more streamlined" (p. 134). Numerous photos of Diana of the mid-1990s emphasize her "freed up" gym-toned body and her pared-down style of dressing (see Figure 3.1, which has been reproduced in many magazines and books).

Figure 3.1. Diana's "freed up" gym-toned body and her pared-down style of dressing. (Photograph by Theodore Wood/Camera Press London. Reproduced with permission.)

Alternatively, many fashion rhetorics celebrating Diana's changing fashion (especially after her death) call attention to her growing Americanized style in the late 1980s. For instance, a well-circulated image of Diana in a white sweatshirt (with the word USA on it) and running half pants calls attention to her (and the nation's) growing reorientation toward the United States in the 1990s. Thus, from the Chelsea look to the global look, Diana's fashion has been frequently framed in the media as reflecting shifts in a national temporality where we were invited to view her body—the national body—moving from a bounded British geography (in the 1980s) to a cosmopolitan "worldliness" that was necessary to resignify British-ness in the 1990s.

However, it was not just the temporality of her body and clothes that make the textility of the Diana phenomenon so powerful as a case study for analyzing the relations among white femininity, nation, and fashion. It was also the *spatiality* of her body. In many media narratives, Diana's body literally functions as a spatial metaphor through which national space was reimagined as moving from the country to the city and then to a cosmopolitan/global world. This was best captured in PBS's *Newshour* with Jim Lehrer (September 1, 1997) on "Remembering Diana." In this show, *Newsweek* reporter Michael Elliot stated,

> By the time she died on Sunday morning, she had become what . . . the new Brits thought, epitomized themselves at their best, cosmopolitan *hating the country but loving the city*, absolutely at ease in different societies, and in different settings, unhung up by people's sexual orientation or ethnic background . . . I think the secret is that they saw her grow and change as the country grew and changed (italics added).[6]

In this excerpt, that emphasizes the spatiotemporal shifts in Diana's body, we are invited to see the fashioning of a national community that is (seemingly) "unhung up" by relations of race, class, sexuality, and globality—that is, relations of difference. Later in the chapter, we will see how Diana's fashion incorporates transnational geographies and their material flows and how her body becomes a site through which new (and seemingly cosmopolitan) transnational connections are staged.

The 1990s was also an important time for the solidification of neoliberal relations (which would dominate Blairite policies) in which, as Giddens (1991, p. 102) noted, "we" were to become "responsible for the design of our own bodies." The body was to become an "accessory" (Hancock et al., 2000, p. 3) constantly making itself over. Diana was one of the first visible and visual signifiers through which we saw an ethos of a neoliberal postimperial British body take shape. Studying Diana's fashion enables us to glimpse into the larger neoliberal reworkings of the national body that was going in Britain (and the North Atlantic West at large) in 1990s and beyond.

In this chapter, my focus is primarily on the global and multicultural phase of Diana's fashion—when we begin to see Diana take on Asian fashion, especially Indian/Pakistani clothes such as the salwar kameez. This was an important cultural moment reflecting the emergence of a white-driven multiculturalism in Britain that also speaks to a larger contemporary trend of white upper-class women wearing "Asian" (especially South Asian) fashion. In examining this trend, I will particularly address the transnational racial politics of sartorial *translations* and how that enables us to witness new national formations of gendered whiteness that are situated in a neoliberal logic of reinvention and absorption of "difference." I will suggest that the white female (upper-) class body becomes a tool for the management of the contradictions between a global (multi)culturalism and the underlying material and racial inequalities of globality.

However, before turning to these issues, a few reflections on the relation between nation, whiteness, and fashion are first necessary. Following this, I will describe how fashion became a citizenly discourse in Britain from the mid-1990s and address the emergence of the phenomenon of Asian kool—when Indian/Asian-inspired multiculturalism was heavily in vogue. This background will enable us to better comprehend the transnational transracial politics of white upper-class British women—such as Diana, Cherie Blair, Jemima Khan, Liz Hurley, and many others who embraced Indian-inspired clothing in the 1990s. Further, this background enables us also to inquire about the following in our analysis: What kinds of shifts in national subject positions were being promised (yet contained) by the white (upper-class) female body as it adopted the salwar kameez or the sari or other related South Asian aesthetics as evidence of its new—1990s—love for India and South Asia more broadly? And what does that reveal about the ways in which the white (upper-class) female body often functions to mediate the challenges of global multiculturalism in the (Anglo) national imaginary?

Fashion, Nation, and Cultural Politics

The relationship between fashion and cultural politics is not a new area of investigation. Until a few years ago, fashion was not seen as a site of worthy scholarship, but now there is a recognition that fashion is more than just a specific garment (McRobbie, 1998). It is centrally about what the dressed or re-dressed body communicates about the anxieties and dreams, desires and despairs of modernity (Barnard, 2002; Craik, 1994; Wilson, 1985). Influential works of scholars such as Valerie Steele, Roland Barthes, Dorrine Kondo, Angela McRobbie, Elizabeth Wilson, Gilles Lipovetsky, Jennifer Craik, Malcolm

Barnard, Louise Crewe, and Alison Goodrum, among many others, as well as of the young journal *Fashion Theory*, have now taught us that the seeming "shallowness" of fashion—that scholars until very recently avoided—conceals and reveals intense (and often unarticulated) social longings and belongings. As Roger Griffin (2002) notes, "what people wear to conceal and expose their persons can take the historian to the core of complex social and political processes of stability and change, conformism and challenge to status quo" (p. 225). Chen and Zamperini (2003) argue that fashion is a "fabrication" that mobilizes "multivalent discourses, practices, and power relations to express simultaneously, although not necessarily in a complementary manner, individual, local, national and international notions of self " (p. 265).

Fashion trends constitute macro racial, gendered, sexual, classed, geopolitical, and global statements about the body in relation to which we define, distance, or confirm our sense of "belonging" to society (whatever that may be—a nation, a region, a culture, and so on) at any given moment. Fashion is a situated bodily practice (Entwistle, 2000). And because situated bodily practices are specifically situated in national formations and geographies, "only *certain* bodies can corporealize the state" (Parkins, 2002, p. 5; original emphasis). It bears mentioning that although there can be numerous fashion trends in a national habitus in a particular time (for example, subcultural fashion, alternative street fashion) not all necessarily function as expressions of a nation's civility or its desires. Some styles deliberately function as antifashion (especially subcultural styles) that may critique and mock the "proper" modes of conduct and bodily appearance desired by the nation-state. Others—especially high-end fashion, or fashion worn by celebrities, the elite, the affluent, and so on—tend to function as signifiers of a nation's desired "look." It is this kind of fashion—of stars and celebrities—that I am interesting in addressing.

While much has been written about fashion, especially fashion's connection with modernity, there is little work on whiteness and fashion, just as there is limited work on fashion and nation (for some exceptions see Goodrum, 2005; Lipovetsky, 1994; Parkins, 2002). In particular, there is little on the intersections between nation, whiteness, class, gender/sexuality, and fashion. Further, our very coding of fashion is Eurocentric (Craik, 2009, Niessen, 2011). Sondra Niessen's work (2011) has challenged fashion studies arguing that "fashion has been defined a priori as a Western phenomenon" and that "non-fashion" usually refers to "indigenous/local Asian dress forms" (p. 151) (although this should be expanded to all non-Western dress styles). Indeed, fashion styles in and from Africa or Asia are seen more as exotic than as fashion. And when they are embraced in or by the West (as for instance Indo-chic) they are often seen as migrations of exotica, or migrations of "culture" into the West manifesting what Tony Bennett (1995) calls the "exhibitionary complex" (p. 73).

While there have been some important works on ethnicity and fashion (Bhachu, 2004; Crang, 2010; Dwyer & Crang, 2002; Dwyer, 2010; Kondo, 1997; Puwar, 2002), these works have not specifically theorized whiteness (and its intersections with nation and the transnational). If whiteness is centrally imbricated in regimes of seeing, then it makes sense to understand fashion, with its constant association with change and "newness" (Craik, 1994), as a regime through which to view constant reinvents of whiteness in the nation. Similarly, if fashion is about the relationship between the body and its lived milieus, and if national identity is a central expression of that relationship, then fashion is always imbricated in national-looking relations. Fashion is a citizenly discourse—whether it is affirming, contesting, or negotiating dominant national relations of bodily being and becoming.

Although as noted earlier, scholars have theorized the linkage between fashion and modernity, it is the assertion of this chapter that fashion is not just a site through which we witness the staging of modernity. More specifically, we witness the staging of white racialized modernities and their underlying civilities. And this is usually expressed through the figure of a white (upper-class) woman given her naturalized association with beauty, glamour, style, and sophistication. (Although this is beyond the scope of this project, it is worth noting that until recently, men were not seen as having much to do with fashion. That is changing, however.) Fashion is a modality through which whiteness announces itself as cultural capital and distinguishes itself from all other populations (for example, nonwhites, the working class including white working class) who can never be fully modern.

Because fashion enacts racialized modernities and civilities that are attributed to white (upper-class) women, it is significant to note then how black supermodels and celebrities, even in this day and age, are often visualized through a jungle narrative (i.e., nonmodern, barbaric). In September 2009, *Harper's Bazaar* ran a series of images titled "Wild Things" with Naomi Campbell as the model. The photographer is Jean Paul Goude. The images depict Campbell in various animalistic positions in an African-inspired background. In one image, Campbell is outrunning a cheetah and consequently becomes more animalistic than the cheetah. Her clothes are animal prints and her hanging animal tail, which is part of her animal print garb, has turned her into an animal. In an image such as this, we see an animal that has blended with the cheetah. In other photographs in the series, she is jumping ropes with wild monkeys, again, wearing animal print clothing, riding a crocodile in a swamp, and sitting on top of a wild elephant that has big tusks (and,

again, in animal print clothes). I requested, but did not receive permission
to reproduce these images (perhaps because I also submitted the context
within which I would reference them in the book). I invite the reader to access these images online for they are rather striking in what they still evoke
about a black (female) body in the 21st century.

There is also the fascinating case of the first black African (Somalian) Muslim supermodel Iman who hit the Western fashion scene in the 1970s. Iman
was discovered by photographer Beard in Somalia in the late 1970s. However,
to bring her to the United States and have her pursue a modeling career, he
spun a deliberate fiction in the United States. The fiction is that Iman was a
beautiful tribal goatherd whom he discovered in Africa and who spoke no
English. This story became the story of Iman's background in Africa. The
fiction reinforced the stereotype of the tribal African exotic woman. And it
sold in fashion circles in New York. The reality, however, is that Iman was a
highly qualified university student, who spoke five languages. Her father was
a diplomat and her mother a gynecologist. In Western imaginations, these
are features of modernity and civility. But in this same Western imaginary, an
African woman cannot be modern—she will not "sell." Thus, it is the exotic
fiction of a beautiful Somali goatherd spun by a white male U.S. American
photographer, who then also (seemingly) rescues her from her surroundings,
that captured the imagination and interest of the New York fashion world and
resulted in Iman coming to the United States for a modeling career. Iman's
black body could travel from Somalia to New York only through the fiction
of African exotica and tribal primitivity.

If invocations of race (and blackness in particular) in fashion narratives often
rely on barbaric, animal-like visualities, then where class is concerned, one of
the interesting things we notice is how class is often invoked to produce oppositional scripts of whiteness—or white antibodies. That is, in fashion narratives,
we often witness struggles over different versions of whiteness that are expressive of larger struggles over class (where class is not just economic deprivation
but lack of cultural capital, that is, of civility and respectability). The heavily
classed aspect of fashion played out in the difference in the representations of
Diana and Sarah. Although the contrasts between Diana and Sarah are not the
primary focus of this chapter, a few words are in order here given the promi-
nence of Sarah in British public life at this same time. Throughout the mediated
career of Diana, Ferguson often represented the anti (white female) body of
the nation and Diana's opposite. This was particularly articulated through their
differing dress sense. Diana was always seen as elegant and classy, whereas
Sarah, despite donning expensive clothes and trendy outfits, could never escape being framed as "loose," "crass," and with a money-chasing attitude. A

March 17, 1997, *People* magazine's cover displayed images of Diana and Sarah with the headline "Class versus Cash." This copy said it all. Fashion magazines frequently emphasized Sarah's unbecoming body, her clumsy dress styles, her loud prints that highlighted her "fat" figure, and large behind, all of which are signifiers of being lower class (Sweeney, 1997; Tyler, 2008). Additionally, she acquired the label that never quite left her—"Duchess of Pork." Beyond its association with fat, pork (originating from pig) represented Sarah as unclean (again a class metaphor). Sarah's body was not tight, lean, and "in place." And given that cameras often focused on her behind, her body was visually classed as a lower form of body (Kipnis, 1997). Further, Sarah's body functioned in the 1990s as a metaphor for Britain's obsession with fat. As British sociologist Skeggs notes, the "loud, white, excessive, drunk, fat, vulgar, disgusting, hen-partying woman" in the 1990s embodied "all the moral obsessions historically associated with the working class now contained in one body," which was a "body beyond governance" (2005, p. 965).

In contrast to the framing of Sarah's body as big and "in your face," images of Diana's body (especially the gym-toned body of the later years) frequently drew attention to the body's stature and power, often producing a sense of worship toward it. In the final analysis, Diana's was a story of a body that transcended into godliness. Many of the images from the last months of her life frame her body through a rhetoric of transcendence in which the body became a site of worship—for example, images of her buried in an island at Althrop surrounded by a lake or surrounded by dying swans in a Swan Lake performance. This is the classed rhetoric of an elevated whiteness that will also be addressed in Chapter 6. In contrast, Sarah's was a story of a body that was always struggling with and against itself (weight and looks). Her relation to her body brought her *down* to, and sometimes even below, the level of "the people" as she frequently used her body as a site of commerce (for example, she was the commercial face of Weight Watchers, or, more recently, she promised to give access to Prince Andrew for a sum of money). Diana's relation to her body moved her *up* to a deity kind of figure. Sweeney (1997) suggests that distance is that quality of unknowability that is always attached to identities deemed socially superior. Pure whiteness finally is beyond and above the body, and while the body may be a physical expression of it, it does not reside *in* the body nor is it fully defined by it (Dyer, 1997; Redmond, 2007). In contrast, impure whiteness (of the "white trash" kind symbolized by Sarah) can never transcend the body; it is the body and its crass physical drives.

If Sarah's was a grotesque, loud, and classed body (in contrast to Diana's elegant and later transcendental white body), then Camilla Parker Bowles (in the 1990s and earlier) was the rural, country-oriented, unfashionable hag, who was out of sync with the spirit of Cool Britannia. Where Diana's body represented edgy cosmopolitanism, Camilla's signified an insular nationalism found in the English countryside. Where Diana's body always mutated—to reflect changing times of the nation—Camilla's body and dress style (until very recently) remained resistant to change. Hers was a dumpy and old-looking body. In the words of a *People* magazine article in 1992, Camilla was a "jodhpurs-and-wellies sort whose hair usually looks as if she's spent the day on a damp racecourse" and who (in the words of a friend quoted in this same article) is "happiest 'hunting for grouse in the howling wind.'"[7] Similarly, the *New York Times* in a 2005 article described Camilla as a "woman who usually looks as if she would be more comfortable walking through fields in mud-spattered Wellington boots than trussed into an evening gown or be-jeweled stiletto heels."[8] Camilla signified the insular country "heritage" ethos of the 1980s. And while Camilla, unlike Sarah, did not signify an excessive, out-of-control body, she did signify a body resistant to change and that was happiest in country wilds.

These contrasting representations among Diana's, Sarah's, and Camilla's fashion (and bodies) in numerous media narratives of the 1990s call attention, once again, to a point made in the previous chapter: that Anglo-national modernities frequently exhibit oppositional scripts of white femininity in which one cancels or negates the other(s) in order to tell us what kinds of white women a nation desires at a particular time. Not all scripts of white womanhood are articulated or legitimized by the nation in a given moment. Some scripts are disarticulated, as we see here. Like all hegemonic formations, white femininity is an assemblage of power that has built into it its own moments of contradictions. Yesterday's script (of white femininity) becomes disarticulated from the nation today, while today's script might be disarticulated from or rearticulated to new national formations tomorrow. This is why the slowly, but surely evolving narrative of Kate Middleton's white womanhood—in the postrecession "austerity" era of 21st-century Britain (that under Cameron seems to call for a retreat to traditional British values)—becomes interesting to observe. By serving as (fashion) foils to Diana, Sarah's and Camilla's images threw into relief quite explicitly what kind of script and body of white femininity the nation desired and rejected in the mid and late 1990s.

Fashion as Citizenly Discourse in New Britain

Fashion, as part of the national renewal of British culture, became central to the project of re-envisioning New Britain and expressing Cool Britannia. Demos, the Blairite think tank, emphasized this in 1997 when it stated,

Britain has a new spring in its step. National success in creative industries like music, design and architecture has combined with steady economic growth to dispel much of the introversion and pessimism of recent decades. Cool Britannia sets the pace in everything from food to *fashion*. (Leonard cited in Crewe & Goodrum, 2000, p. 25; emphasis added)

In the late 1990s, the topics of fashion, design, and branding dominated newspapers that frequently carried discussions about Britain being dominated by style. Media reports noted that there is a "designer-led revolution" going on in which Britain is at the forefront.[9] The European editor of *Vanity Fair* declared in 1997, "London is once again a city on the international fashion agenda that sets the pace of what is style" (Talley, 1997, p. 127). In March 1997, *Vanity Fair* screamed, "London Swings! Again" and declared that the "British capital is a cultural trailblazer, teeming with new and youthful icons of art, pop music, fashion, food and film. Even its politicians are cool. Or well, coolish."[10] As O'Bryne (2009) argues, such comments really referred to the

revamped Labor party, which, with Tony Blair at its head, would soon win the British General election of May 1997. The Conservative Party had run the country since 1979 and though the national economy had since recovered from recession, the outgoing Prime Minister John Major—represented on television satire *Spitting Image* as *a grey faced man in grey clothing who ate grey peas off a grey plate*—symbolized a tired regime that had long run its course. (p. 210; emphasis added)

Such thinking was in accord with Tony Blair's "call me Tony" "sofa cabinet" decision-making style (i.e., sitting casually on sofas instead of dark meeting rooms with men in suits) and wearing open necked shirts and chinos at work.

This was also a time when the works of British fashion designers were being packaged and exported abroad by the *British Council* as a sign of the vitality of contemporary British culture. The chairman of Saks Fifth Avenue stated in the *New York Times* at this time that "we were going to the London markets and saw a lot of newness and vitality that we hadn't seen in recent years" (in O'Bryne, 2009, p. 205). Such comments from heads of major U.S. fashion stores led to a revival of interest in British fashion in the New York market. Indeed, "fashion with all its spectacle and glamour" was being "heralded as the lifeline for a flagging national image" in the United Kingdom (Goodrum, 2005, p. 17). Fashion became part of the government's emphasis on *creative industries*—a concept that, like "the third way" concept—became intimately linked to New Labor's agenda of revitalizing the cultural industries, including the arts, fashion, architecture, music, food, and more. A British Council Creative and Cultural Economy Series report (2010) offers a detailed discussion of the emergence of creative industries in Britain. It states that the "concept [creative industry] [as it emerged in the late 1990s] was an attempt to change the terms of the debate about the value of arts and culture" (p. 15).[11] Arts and culture were not just to be limited to theater and music but were also to embrace things such as advertising, architecture, designer fashion, design, crafts, film, television, and radio, for example. Therefore, there was a conscious attempt to move from high culture (as a marker of Britishness) to popular culture. In its first mapping document in 1998, the Department for Culture, Media, and Sport—that was created by the incoming Blair administration and whose first initiatives were to set up a Creative Industries Task Force—designated design, fashion, architecture, and film (along with some other areas) as "creative industries."[12] And as an integral part of the creative industries, fashion became seen as a citizenly discourse—one through which new-looking relations in Britain, and toward Britain, were to be forged.

This new ethos understandably emphasized the body as a site of national renewal (Morley & Robbins, 2001). The body had to be reworked to mirror these exciting cultural changes being imagined for New Britain. For example, in the 1990s, the culture of gyms, fitness centers, and spas became a national rage. The *Times* reported in February 1997 that Cherie Booth (not yet then the first lady but wife of then Opposition Party head Tony Blair) works out at a health club that "invites its members to 'worship at the *temple of fitness*'" (emphasis added).[13] A religious trope, temple is co-opted here such that the body becomes a "temple"—the ultimate site of worship. If the body is a temple, then the body is ascribed a morality wherein it becomes a means to access and encase a new national spirit. The body thus became a site of renationalization. Further, this was a body that was to produce itself as a spectacle—for underlying the logic of building up and training the body in gyms and health clubs was a logic of spectacularization and "self spectacularization" (During, 1994, p. 64). The body was not only to be on display as evidence of a changing national self; it was constantly to be subject to self-surveillance and self-regulation. Diana was the ultimate example of such spectacularization of the body. One of her designers noted that whenever Diana discussed clothes with him, "'part of it was always': 'what message will I be giving out if I wear this?' For her, that became the real language of clothes" (in Howell, 1998, p. 14).

The centralization of the body as a means through which to fashion and communicate a better national self was also seen in the coverage of politicians at this time. In June 1997 (a month after Blair came into power), Tony Blair, in the June 1997 Amsterdam summit, which he attended with EU partners to finalize work on the Amsterdam treaty, received wide attention through the lens of body and fitness. Commenting on a sporting event in which EU leaders participated, British newspapers noted that Prime Minister Blair won the bicycle race against fellow European leaders. The *Evening Standard* underscored that "the feat allowed them [spin doctors] to get pictures . . . showing our lean and brisk new leader."[14] This particular report added that this feat allowed Blair to exhibit to the EU leaders "a trim pair of thighs and exquisite sense of balance." Blair's "lean," "trim," and "active" body signified some kind of proof of an emerging new Britain's ability to outdo other nations in the EU. The body thus directly became linked to national power and change.

Cool Britannia's highly visual body politics thus resurrected a logic of individualism in which the body was constantly displayed as a source of national capital. Diana's life story became a perfect metaphor for this logic in which social responsibility for the body shifts from the state to the individual. The body becomes privatized. Instead of seeing the body in the country, in the 1990s, we see the body move indoors—built up in gyms, trained through technology, and trimmed through diet regimes. As I illustrate in Chapter 6, this was also a body of "wellness" that ultimately reflected the privileges of a white middle- and upper-class ethos. Indeed, the story of Diana that emerges in media narratives is of a woman who built herself up, fought her oppressive personal conditions, and endeared herself to the people—domestic and global—through the glamour and style of her body. We forget the cost of other people's labor that went into producing this body; we forget the material and menial labor that Diana never had to do. Consider this image (Figure 3.2) from a later stage of her life

Diana: A Life In Fashion

Diana was proud of her figure and she wasn't afraid to show it off. And each gorgeous gown declared: 'I am a survivor'

Figure 3.2. From the *Daily Mail's* special supplement *Diana: A Life in Fashion* (1997, part 5, p. 90). (Daily Mail/Solo Syndication, Alpha Press, UK Press via Antony Jones/Getty Images. Reproduced with permission.)

that was published in a special supplement of *Daily Mail* (in 1998) on Diana's fashion. The image centrally celebrates Diana's toned, strong, and fit body. The small inset at the bottom corner shoots Diana's body from the back to call attention to her firm, muscular, and toned back. And the copy explicitly positions her body in the realm of individualism as its states: "Diana was proud of her figure and she wasn't afraid to show it off. And each gorgeous gown declared, 'I am a survivor.'"

Heat and Dust

As noted earlier in the book, multiculturalism and cosmopolitanism were important logics through which the British national body of the 1990s new times was being rewritten.[15] In an effort to integrate ethnicity into the postcolonial British national imagination and attract global finance, part of the campaign of rebranding Britain was to multiculturalize its looks and logics of belonging. And a significant aspect of that multiculturalism expressed itself through an explosion of things Asian and, more particularly, Indian or Indian-inspired. A big part of this also had to do with liberalization and deregulation of the Indian economy since 1991, which positioned the Indian state to attract global finance and weaken foreign trade barriers. This was also a time when Britain saw a new demand for equality from a generation of South Asians who were born and raised in Britain (unlike their earlier generations) and who were fighting, through numerous creative ventures (such as music, dance, arts, fashion), to resignify Britishness through expressions of South Asian culture. For instance, the music of artistes such as Bally Sagoo, Apache Indian, DJ Talvin Singh or groups such as Cornershop or Asian Dub Foundation acquired significant presence in the mainstream music industry. Sony Records actively chased such crossover stars as Bally Sagoo. The 1997 single "Brimful of Asha" by Cornershop reached #60 on the U.K. singles chart in 1997 and #1 when rereleased in 1998. When it was re-released, it pushed Celine Dion's *My Heart Will Go On* out of the #1 slot. At the *Anokha* nightclub in London in the late 1990s, white women on the dance floor moved to the music of "Brimful of Asha" in trouser-saris. This music scene and its aesthetics have been documented well by scholars (Banerjea, 2000; Gopinath, 2005; Hutnyk, 1998; Hyder, 2004; Karla & Hutnyk, 1998; Sharma, Hutnyk, & Sharma, 1996; Shukla, 2003; Zuberi, 2001) and its elaboration is beyond the scope of my argument.

In 1998, the unofficial World Cup anthem was "Vindaloo" (referring to the red hot curry dish). In that year, the magazine *India Abroad* noted that three out of four Britons cook Indian food (in Bhachu, 2004, p. 26), and curry became a national dish in Britain. Upmarket Indian restaurants, catering to a sophisticated clientele, mushroomed in many of the glitzier parts of London in the mid-1990s. In fact, since the 1990s, one could walk into a British pub in London and see curry listed on the menu along with other traditional British food. This was also the time when Indian cuisine became a formal area of study. Thames Valley University launched a series of courses in Indian food (Suri, 1998). Referring to this "Indian kool" phenomenon Sharma et al. (1996) note that "finally it appears that the 'coolie' has become cool" (p. 1). Journalist Sanjay Suri stated in *Outlook* (1998) that though India has always "lived" in England, it is now "stepping into that middle England of beer, beef and football. Admittedly, a little, but that's a lot. Not exotic India, not ghetto Indianness, but as just a fact of everyday life, a factor in everyday living." The Asian weekly newspaper *Eastern Eye* came into being at this time. It was first published by the English newspaper the *Guardian* in 1989, although later the *Guardian* sold it. It is now part of the Asian Media and Marketing Group. The BBC2 comedy *Goodness Gracious Me*, based on Indian culture in the United Kingdom, first aired in 1998 and continued until 2001. The famous Andrew Lloyd Webber production *Bombay Dreams* opened in London in 2002.

In the realm of fashion, too, South Asia and particularly India was significantly "in." Kiki Siddiqui, manager of Ritu Kumar (whose clothes Diana frequently bought) near Oxford Street, London, stated in a 1998 report that the store was seeing an increasing number of working women who did not want to go out in the little black dress any more: "'Most of our clients are Europeans' and 'women who have the confidence to wear something different'" (in Suri, 1998). Another Indian designer Anokhi also set up shop in London at this time. The British fashion week in 1998 saw the "Indian look" everywhere. Pashmina shawls, Kundan jewelry, the *nuth* (nose ring), and the *bindi* were everywhere. Although rare, we once saw Diana too in the red dot that was probably put on her forehead during a visit to an Indian temple—Shri Swaminarayan Mandir—in Neasden, North London, in 1997. In this case, it was a religious marking (that you receive when you go to a temple) on her forehead. Whether put on her forehead by the members of the Indian temple community or not, the press made sure that image of Diana with a red mark on her forehead circulated everywhere. *Outlook* noted in 1998 that the "biggest sellout at the London fashion week was an Australian designer selling skirts and dresses embroidered in Delhi" (Suri, 1998). It was also at the London Fashion week that British heiress and socialite Jemima Khan, then married to Pakistani cricketer/politician Imran Khan, unveiled her fashion business. Her clothes comprised traditional rich embroidery done by Pakistani women in villages. In the 1999 James Bond movie *The World Is Not Enough,* we saw the French actress Sophie Merceau in a gold salwar kameez ensemble. In 2002, the store Selfridges staged a month-long exhibition of Bollywood-inspired clothes that included Bollywood costumes, interiors fashioned by the beautiful Bollywood icon Dimple Kapadia, and fashion shows exhibiting the works of haute couture Indian designers such as Tarun Tahiliani.[16] In fact, this late-20th century trend of embracing Indian fashion styles has continued today in Britain where we have seen Camilla Parker Bowles in a *ghaghra*—an Indian-style long skirt with a jacket and a salwar kameez—or Miriam Clegg (wife of Nick Clegg, who is actually Spanish) in a bright pink sari at an Asian Women's Achievement dinner in 2011. Clegg was photographed along with Home Secretary Theresa May and Shadow Minister for Olympics Teresa Jowell, both of them in Indian garments.[17] We have also seen in the last few years Dame Judi Dench, Sarah Ferguson, Camilla Parker Bowles, Helen Mirren, and Liz Hurley in saris or salwar kameez.

One of the ultimate endorsements of Indian fashion in Cool Britannia occurred when Cherie Blair commissioned British Indian African designer Babs Mahil (from the East End of London) for a sari for a 1998 mega event: a business dinner with 200 rich Asian businesspersons. This was an important event for the Blairs. It saw Tony Blair as the new premier going over the top wooing Indians, for he recognized full well that since the mid-1990s, India's arc was only rising, as India had just liberalized its economy following a massive foreign exchange crisis. After this event, Mahil took charge of all of Cherie's Asian wardrobe and in the process made the salwar kameez and sari regular fashion items in Downing Street. In 1998, Mahil reported that at least 40% of her clients were Western women. In 2002 when the Blairs visited India, Tony Blair became the first foreign prime minister/leader to wear a Nehru jacket (the smart jacket style inaugurated by the first postindependence prime minister of India—Jawaharlal Nehru) which too was created by Mahil. British South Asian cultural studies scholar Rajinder Dudrah (2010) notes that if in the earlier decades "brown was the difficult and un-absorbable signifier in mainstream British culture," then in the millennium years, brown found a new "confidence" (p. 143).

From the mid-to-late 1990s, thus, Asian kool (and particularly Indian kool) became an important trend through which we saw British Asians demanding specific attention to their transnational racial politics. It also reflected an important political moment because for the first time, British politicians became keenly aware of the need to court India in a changing global economy, which would soon be looking eastward. And the fact that all this was occurring during the 1990s when culture and creative industries were receiving a new push from the Blair government only provided a vehicle for such new expressions of British and Indian identity.

This moment was further important for rethinking race politics in Britain. Tariq Modood (1994, 1998, 2005) has noted that one of the limitations of much of race and cultural studies work in the United Kingdom is the slim attention given to the particularities of Asian race politics. Especially after the 1976 Race Relations Act, a consensus evolved around the term *blackness* as an overall signifier for communities of color. However, British Asians have often resisted the term because it primarily connotes blacks of Caribbean or African origin and erases the particularities of Asian histories in the United Kingdom. Modood has argued that radical race activists and scholars in the United Kingdom have normalized the equation between blackness and all communities of color. Indeed, the otherwise influential works of scholars such as Paul Gilroy (who Modood takes to task) and Stuart Hall reflect this trend. In much of their work, theorizations of race in the United Kingdom— that is, "black Britain"—occur primarily through an emphasis on blacks of Caribbean or African descent (Hutnyk, 2000; Miles, 1999; Modood, 1994, 1998, 2005; Sharma, 1996). To be fair, however, Hall himself had noted in his famous discussion (1997) of old and new ethnicities that "the question of Black, in Britain, also has its silences. It had a certain way of silencing the very specific experiences of Asian people" (p. 56). It is only in the last decade or so that work on Asian cultures has begun to emerge in a significant way that is intimately tied to all these changes that were taking place since the 1990s.

This "heat and dust" moment that made Indian/South Asian culture suddenly so prominent, however, prompts a larger question (that continues to be relevant even today as the West becomes more obsessed with India): Were (are) we seeing a serious visibility or a further invisibility, masked by a hypervisibility, of Indian (and broadly South Asian) culture in Britain in the 1990s? (Durham, 2001; Hutnyk, 1998, 2000; Karla & Hutnyk, 1998; Puwar, 2002; Sharma et al., 1996). Peggy Phelan (1993) has argued that there is no correlation between "increased visibility" and "increased power."

> While there is a deeply ethical appeal in the desire for a more inclusive representational landscape and certainly under-represented communities can be empowered by an enhanced visibility, *the terms of this visibility often enervate the putative power of these identities.* (p. 7; emphasis added)

Passage to "India": The White Female Body in Salwar Kameez and Sari

It is within such a national logic of multicultural (and Asian-inflected) new times that I situate the engagement of Diana's body (as well as the body of other white national women such as Cherie Blair) with Asian and particu-

larly Indian fashion. The reader will note that India in the heading above is
within quotation marks. This is because there is a particular construction of
"India" (or even Pakistan) that occurs in these representations, as the India
(or Pakistan) that we glimpse through white female multicultural Indian/
South Asian aesthetics does not necessarily stand in for the everyday life of
these regions. Additionally, given the intertwined history of India and Pakistan, it is, unfortunately, often the case that India and Pakistan are blended
in Western narratives especially when cultural issues such as food, fashion,
arts, and so on are concerned. The main issue I focus on is how Indian/South
Asian fashion aesthetics are mediated by the upper-class white female national body (of the West) in order to perform a sanitized and dehistoricized
global multiculturalism that enables the (Western) nation to secure a new
cosmopolitan subject position, while containing the subversive potential
and possibilities of that cosmopolitanism/multiculturalism. In fact, if we
look at contemporary multicultural landscapes today in nations such as the
United Kingdom, the United States, or Canada, we see a hunger for things
Asian—cuisine, healing arts, music, paintings, babies (dealt with in Chapter
4), architectural styles (doing up your indoors through Asian motifs), and so
on. This hunger, however, is often expressed by white privileged woman (and
less by men or by women of color—although as I suggest later, consumption
of Asian fashion by privileged nonwhite women is beginning to be visible).
Asian multiculturalism, embraced by the white female body today, often
functions as a kind of "soft power" (Nye, 2005) for the (Anglo) nation and
ironically also for many Asian nations. (In the following chapters, this will
become even more clear as we examine the white female body engaging with
Asian-inflected healing practices or adopting babies from Asia or Africa.)
The white female body in such contexts functions both as a cultural wall
that will not allow critical and historical otherness to interrupt the global
multiculturalism that its nation performs through its body, and a (seemingly)
transparent screen through which we are invited to celebrate the nation's
engagement with a multicultural globality. Anne Marie-Fortier (2008) has
described such a multicultural logic as expressing a "double process of *rap-
prochement* and distancing, of embracing and repelling" (p. 10). This dual
process positions the white female body (and not any other ethnic female
body), again, as a boundary marker in such multicultural national narratives.

Some of the questions that frame the following discussion are: What meanings, scripts, and histories of Indian fashion and India or South Asia (more
broadly) *cannot* be captured by the white female body as it engages Indian
fashion? What does such transnational engagement with Indian fashion enable the white female body—for example, the body and image of Diana—to

do for the nation at that particular juncture in the late 20th (and early 21st) century? And what does such "doing" reveal about the limits of white femininity's translation of the transnational—in particular Indian fashion and the corresponding histories that are written into the styles of such fashion? Although the matter of South Asian fashion—specifically Indo-chic—being taken up in Western metropolitan sites has been addressed by scholars (such as Bhachu, 2004; Durham, 2001; Maira, 2002; Mannur & Sahni, 2011; Moorti, 2007; Puwar, 2002, 2003), my focus is on what it tells us about new national formations of white femininity and their imbrications in transnational logics of Asia (and South Asia in particular here).

We first prominently saw Diana in salwar kameez in Pakistan, Lahore, in 1996, when she was visiting her friends Imran Khan (world renowned ex-Pakistani cricketer turned politician) and Jemima Khan (the famous British socialite who married Imran Khan although is now divorced from him) to help raise funds for Khan's free-of-cost cancer hospital. Consider these two images from that famous trip (Figures 3.3 and 3.4). In both these images,

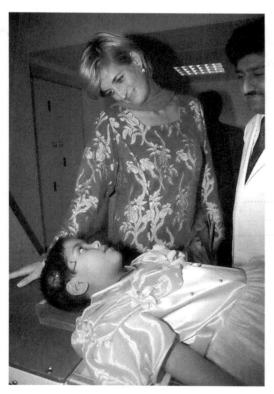

Figure 3.3. Diana, Princess of Wales, meets a cancer patient at the Shaukat Khanum Memorial Cancer Hospital in Lahore. (PA Photos/Stefan Rousseau. Reproduced with permission.)

Figure 3.4. Diana with Jemima Khan in Pakistan. A sick cancer patient/child sits on her lap (1996). (Anwar Hussein/Getty Images. Reproduced with permission.)

Diana is in a rather domestic maternal position. In the first image (Figure 3.3), she is in a blue, printed-silk salwar suit. She is looking down tenderly at a Pakistani child—a cancer patient—in the Shaukat Khanum Memorial Cancer Hospital. Her body draped in the salwar suit towers over the child in the bed and takes up visual space in the image. The blue and white floral salwar suit, while beautiful, is quite unremarkable—nothing very gaudy or fancy in style. While surely very expensive (as Diana usually wore suits made by high-end Indian designer Ritu Kumar), it does have a rather homely look. Any Pakistani, or Punjabi, or North Indian woman could have worn this straight and simple style on a regular day. In the second image (Figure 3.4), Diana is wearing a light blue chiffon salwar suit. She is at a gathering or function with Jemima Khan—also in salwar suit—watching a show that has been put up by patients at Imran Khan's cancer hospital. On her lap sits a young cancer patient. Diana's face conveys compassion.

I stated earlier, it is important to interrogate what the wearing of Asian fashion—in this case the salwar kameez—enables the white female (national) body to do at a particular juncture (here the mid-to-late 1990s). I want to suggest that in these images the salwar kameez attempts to mediate the cultural and global distance between Diana—a white British national woman—and the sick brown poor children of Pakistan. The salwar kameez functions as a tool of cultural translation. I use the term *translation* not to refer to a transfer from a seeming "original" to a "copy" (Apter, 2001; Liu, 1999; Spivak, 2001), but to suggest a repositioning of a subject (or object) in a different cultural circuit (and thus often a different power regime) than what is generally associated with it (Apter, 2006). The salwar kameez functions as a tool of translation through which the white British privileged woman recodes her body through the performance of an/other femininity and symbolically enters the domestic space of that other femininity—the space of (Pakistani) maternity. The salwar kameez stages what Grewal (2005) elsewhere has called a "transnational connectivity" (p. 3). This is a connectivity where the text(ility) of the salwar kameez sutures the historical, geopolitical, economic, and cultural gaps in this fabric(ation) of global caring. We see this even in the rhetorical framing in *Hello!* magazine's March 2, 1996 cover image (see Figure 3.5). Visually calling attention to Diana and Jemima in their salwar kameez, the headline states, "Two women working for the welfare of others." The importance of that welfare work seems to be signified by these white women's desire to wear the salwar suits, which suggests that their caring has now entered the structure of *local* domesticity (signified by local clothes). They are not strangers to the cultures they seek to heal and care for. They have become the women they are there to help.

✗ *Transnational Connectivity*

Figure 3.5. Cover page of the March 2, 1996, issue of *Hello!* magazine. (Copyright *Hello!* Magazine. Reproduced with permission.)

Imagine how different the meaning of these images would have been had we seen Diana in an expensive Chanel day suit, hugging a brown cancer-ridden baby in Pakistan. The Chanel suit—a signifier of high Western modern fashion—would have symbolically suggested a distance between the brown sick babies and the performance of white maternal love. However, here, the salwar suit draping the white female body in a cancer-ridden site in Pakistan, allows that body to tell another story about itself: "I am you; we are all the same; we dress the same; we look the same." The salwar kameez adorning the globally mobile white female body of Diana enables a liberal production of sameness and proximity that was integral to the kind of multicultural nationalism endorsed by Blairite Britain and that, since the 1990s, has become a signature of neoliberal multiculturalism in the (North Atlantic) West (Melamed, 2006). Yet, as Gayatri Spivak's work has taught us, sameness is not equality. Proximity (including of the sartorial kind) too is not equality, nor intimacy, nor community.

While the issue of translation is significant in cultural globalization, translation is never about equivalence, or a neat transfer of meanings and subject positions. Lydia Liu (1999) writes that a critical attention to translation enables us to think about "how *reciprocity* becomes thinkable and *contestable* as a problem in translingual and transcultural exchanges when predominantly unequal forms of global exchange characterize the material and intellectual conditions of that exchange" (p. 4; emphasis added). In these images, the white female body performs a cultural translation of a (Pakistani) maternal subject position through the material and symbolic aesthetics of the salwar kameez. But, as it does so, it also calls attention to the *impossibility* of (the "other" women's) "reciprocity" in this global context. A Pakistani woman/mother cannot just visually occupy the position of a white mother, hug white babies, wear fashionable Western clothes, have her image splashed across global screens, and then be celebrated as a symbol of global motherhood. This is a point that I take up in greater detail in Chapter 4.

If we expand our analysis of the performance of this kind transnational sartorial intimacy (performed by Diana) to images of other British white women of the late 1990s (and beyond) who have adorned Indian/Asian fashion aesthetics, we see some larger logics at work. For instance, we see that white women adorn Asian clothing primarily when they have to engage (and attract) the Asian community or have to signify their own bodies as being multicultural. One will probably not see white women in salwar kameez or sari going for a regular meal at a restaurant, going to work, or attending church on Sunday. This is important to mark. It tells us that for the white woman the salwar suit or the sari is consciously deployed in particular settings (and not others). There is thus a spectacle at work. For instance, after the Blairs entered Downing Street in 1997, Tony Blair consciously worked to attract Asians who traditionally had been attracted to Tories and had viewed Labor as interfering with their business goals. In high-profile dinner gatherings with Indians, fashion craft and state-craft frequently merged on the white female national body of Cheri Blair. For instance, when the Blairs attended the British Indian Golden Jubilee Banquet in 1997 (as this marked 50 years of Indian independence from British rule), Cherie appeared in a red and green sari. She was applauded all the way to her table (Suri, 1997). *Outlook India* called the event an example of "Cherie's Sari diplomacy" (Suri, 1997).

> British and Indian flavors blended with unusual ease. The Bishop of London read the Grace in Sanskrit. Scottish bagpipers blended with the tabla, the san-toor, the sarangi—there wasn't a false note in this evening of fusion. . . . *Every-thing was saying what the sari [referring to Cherie's sari] had said.* (emphasis added)

Red and green are very auspicious colors in India. Red signifies fertility and passion (and is traditionally worn by new brides), and green is the color of life. Originally, the Indian flag had red, green, and white as its colors, although now saffron replaces red. Cherie's wearing of the sari then is not just a regular everyday multicultural fashion choice. It reflects statecraft and fashioncraft coming together to recode the national body as being open and hospitable to Indians. Similarly, in an other instance—namely a dinner gathering of 200 rich Asian businessmen in March 1998 that I referenced earlier—the *Daily Mail* stated that "Mrs. Blair was particularly keen to look the part."[18] The comment is about Cherie's $800 Babs Mahil saree. The performative is emphasized by the word *part*—a role-playing of diversity and cultural inti-macy in a gathering of super rich Indians. Or, again, in a 1999 high-profile Diwali bash at Alexandra Palace (North London) thrown by the powerful Hindujas who billed the event as "tolerance and multi-cultural understand-ing in the new millennium," Cherie wore an extremely expensive off-white salwar kameez with glittering embroidery on it.[19]

Yet, while Cherie's Indian clothes (seemingly) "said everything" as the *Outlook* report noted, and Diana's high-end Ritu Kumar salwar suits also (seemingly) "said everything" about her welfare and caring for cancer-ridden children in Lahore, there is a clear distance that exists—that is not simply linear—between a Diana's or a Cherie's body adorned in sari or salwar suit and the bodies of cancer-ridden Pakistani children and Indian/Pakistani women as well as the Muslim and Hindu bodies of these nations.

Gayatri Spivak (2003) has argued that as cultural and international borders are crossed (and usually from metropolitan nations) in neoliberal globalization,

Figure 3.6. Cherie Blair in salwar kameez. (Rex USA. Reproduced with permission.)

"the everyday cultural detail, condition and effect of sedimented cultural idiom" does not "come up into satellite country" (p. 16). Suggesting that globalization is very much a metropolitan and mediated phenomenon (hence her use of the term *satellite country*), Spivak's point is that the very local, cultural, and historical dynamics and despairs (for instance, village workers in remote parts of the world whose lives may be used as statistical data in global narratives but whose despairs do not reach up to metropolitan-mediated screens) cannot be accessed by the circuits that enable globalization. Cherie's Babs Mahil saris and Diana's hyperexpensive Ritu suits cannot be afforded by most people in India or Pakistan, or for that matter even by many Indians, Pakistanis, and white working- or middle-class women in Britain and elsewhere. In 2002, when Cherie and Tony went to India (with Tony wearing for the first time a Nehru jacket), Cherie wore an embroidered salwar kameez that was made by workers in India earning 36 pence an hour.[20] Many of Mahil's creations sell for over £2,000. When questioned, Mahil refused to comment on the payment made to workers in India. "Although these factories are working for us, they are not our factories," she said. "We don't pay the workers. We don't get involved in that side of things." This is a classic instance that reveals what Soyini Madison (2013), in her discussion of the appropriative travel and consumption of African products to the United States, has described as "separating the product from its processes of production or the production of meaning from the production of the object" (p. 225).

Furthermore, while Tony and Cherie, in their multicultural/Indian garb, were falling all over rich Asians in their New Britain, and Tony was promising the Asian/Indian community that "be in no doubt that we will not tolerate racial harassment," the case of Satpal Ram hung like a dark colonial cloud over New Britain.[21] Satpal Ram is an Indian man who became the victim of unprovoked racist violence in an Indian restaurant in Birmingham in 1987. He was attacked with broken glass by a white man, Clark Pearce. In self-defense, Ram fought back, which resulted later in Pearce dying. Ram was convicted for an act of self-defense against an unprovoked racist attack and imprisoned for 16 years. In this time, he was moved from prison to prison, 74 in all.[22] He faced abuse and intense periods of solitary confinement. Activists and artists (including the Asian Dub Foundation) campaigned strongly for his release and against unfair prison treatment. In fact, in 2000, it was the Blair administration, and more specifically Home Secretary Jack Straw, who overturned the parole board's 1999 decision to release Satpal. Finally, in 2002, following a ruling of the European Court of Human Rights, which overturned Jack Straw's 2000 decision and ruled that the home secretary had acted unlawfully, Ram was released from prison.[23] When released, Ram stated in an interview with the *Socialist Worker*, "New Labor—New Right." Further, when the Blairs were engaging in Indian intimacy with the 200 rich Asians at the dinner mentioned earlier, Suresh Grover, of the Southall Monitoring Group, stated that "while there is no doubt there are some success stories we have to ask the question at what price?"[24] Indeed, most Asian businesses in Britain are in food and textiles, where there is very little job security and workers are poorly paid. Given the long history of South Asians in Britain, it is still the case that one will find South Asians mainly in low-end grocery stores and restaurants. Writing critically about the contemporary embrace of South Asian aesthetics by whites in Britain, Puwar (2002) points to the rage on the ground by marginalized South Asians in Britain because of such multicultural fashioning of the white female body through South Asian aesthetics.

> This rage carries memories of another history, of another type of Western gaze when similar items are worn by what are labelled as "traditional" Asians, who are in fact more hybrid in their tastes and everyday cultures than any of the women who flip their pashmino scarves over their shoulder, and hold their

studded nose in the air, while they jostle with the slippery mojay (shoes) with the backs folded down in Hampstead High Street (an upper-middle-class leafy neighbourhood in North London). (pp. 73–74)

This rage, she goes on,

> is the memory of violence, the familiar looks of revulsion (the greasy "Paki") that rush back when one sees cut and paste versions of sarees and jeans *on* white bodies that can create an unease. It is the power of whiteness to play with items it had only yesterday almost literally spat at, that lies at the core of this specific rage. (p. 75)

Perhaps one of the ultimate suturing functions performed by the representations of the salwar kameez on white female upper-class British bodies—especially that of Diana—was evident in the September 13, 1997, issue of *Hello* magazine. This is a coveted issue—devoted to the funeral of Diana. It has become an important memorabilia item. The issue is filled with beautiful images from Diana's funeral. Among several photos of this very British event, there is a double-page spread image of Diana in salwar kameez against the Union Jack. On the top left-hand corner is printed some text from Elton John's "Goodbye England's Rose" song. The presence of this image in relation to others in this issue seems highly unusual. The salwar kameez–wearing Diana positioned against the British flag, when seen in the context of numerous other images in the issue—such as the five royal men following the casket, or shots of the insides of the abbey, or images of crowds crying, or images of William and Harry accepting flowers from the crowds—seems visually out of place. Yet, its very quiet insertion into this issue—with Diana in a salwar kameez against the Union Jack, and being framed as "England's rose" by the copy on the top left side—repositions a multicultural/global Diana in South Asian clothing seamlessly into a larger nationalist subjectivity constructed in the *Hello* issue. It is almost as though there is no break, no rupture, between this particular image and the images preceding and following it in this magazine issue. What is also interesting is that this image is actually from a 1996 June trip made by Diana to Pakistan for Imran Khan's cancer hospital (see figure 3.7). The image is from a public gathering that Diana along with Jemima and Imran attended. There were many Pakistanis and children in that event. The background drape in the sitting area had a Union Jack pinned on it (possibly to welcome Diana). It is this image from Pakistan that was compressed in the *Hello* magazine reproduction of the image where this broader context disappears and all we have is Diana looking pensive in her Indian/Pakistani clothing against the British flag. Although I have not been able to secure the absolute exact

Figure 3.7. Diana in front of the Union Jack. (Reuters/Russell Boyce. Reproduced with permission.)

image as it appeared in *Hello* magazine (where text of Elton John's song appears on the picture), what is presented here (Figure 3.7) is an almost identical image—the only difference being that Diana's head in this image is lowered a little more than in the *Hello* magazine image.

[I deliberately wanted to present this image because it is symbolic of what this chapter is attempting to do: illustrate the renationalization of the white woman as she takes on clothing such as the salwar kameez and blends it easily with the desires of the Union Jack. And yet, between the salwar kameez and the Union Jack is a vast sea of difference, violence, and inequality that is covered over by the suturing function of the salwar kameez.

Much also hid under Diana's salwar kameez that were celebrated in so many media images in the mid-1990s. In Figure 3.8, she is wearing a gaudy embroidered rich silk kameez (the top part) with the salwar (that is closer to loose straight pants). According to reports, it was encrusted with pearls (note again the distance between her salwar kameez and that of regular Indian/Pakistani women and their quotidian practices). This image is of her entering a fundraising event for Imran Khan's cancer hospital at the luxurious Dorchester Hotel in London in 1996. Like the images discussed earlier, this image too has become iconic as a sign of the later "free" and "multicultural" Diana.

What is hidden by Diana's salwar kameez, however, is its underlying history and relations with British colonialism.[25] The salwar kameez entered India (when Pakistan, Bangladesh, and current-day India together made up India or the British Raj) as early as 12th century through Mughal (Muslim) invasions from Central and West Asia. India and Pakistan have a strong Persian influence. Until before India's independence from the British, it is Muslim

Figure 3.8. Diana in salwar kameez entering Dorchester Hotel in 1996. (Rex USA. Reproduced with permission.)

women (and men) in the then British Raj (the term used to refer to India before independence) who primarily wore the salwar kameez, although there were gender and regional variations in style. After Pakistan/Indian independence from the British, the salwar kameez became an everyday clothing item especially for North Indian women (including Sikh women, although Sikhs are not Muslims) and Pakistani women because the influence of Muslim culture was the strongest in Pakistan and North India around the time of independence. Although today many Indian women will wear salwar kameez, as it has been transformed into an everyday garment for working career-oriented women, not all women will wear the salwar kameez. People of my grandmother's generation—in Eastern India (Bengal)—would often look down on the salwar suit because it was associated with what they saw as the "uncultured" Muslims. For their generation of Hindus, the salwar suit evoked the context of violent Hindu-Muslim relations in India around the time of independence that were an outcome of the horrors unleashed by the division of the country by the British when they departed. When the British left, they choreographed a violent and cruel process of national division along religious lines that in 1947 led to the birth of Pakistan (Muslim-dominated) and today's India (Hindu-dominated). This division led to one of the biggest diasporic migrations in world history when Hindus from Muslim-dominant parts of preindependence India came to the new India, and Muslims from Hindu-dominant parts of preindependence India went to the newly born Pakistan state (Muslim-dominant). And those who did not move, whether Hindus in the new Pakistan or Muslims in the new India, become a minority in those respective nations and were targets of violent attacks from the dominant cultures of those newly formed nations. My grandmother's generation had been a witness to this horror of Muslims and Hindus butchering each other when many Hindus migrated from today's Bangladesh into today's India (although at that time they were all part of the same country). This history of British-choreographed violent division of India, that today continues to fan the flames of anti-Muslim sentiments in India, as well as the rich Mugal (Islamic) culture from which the salwar kameez emerged, however, is blithely obscured as white British women such as Diana and Cherie recode their bodies for a multicultural statecraft.

While I do not want to descend into a history lesson, I do want to note that this Muslim (Hindu) history—so written into the salwar kameez within which the British culture is intimately situated—is erased in this tactile (as the salwar kameez touches your body) and textile transnational intimacy of white femininity. Western white national women chase the salwar kameez at the same time that their nations hunt Muslims worldwide and suppress Muslim histories from even being taught in educational institutions. In stating this, I am not calling for a return to "origins" (i.e., only people associated with the origins of the salwar kameez can wear it). However, there is history—present and past. Dick Hebdige (1987, p. 10) writes, "there is no such thing as a pure point of origin . . . but that doesn't mean that there isn't history." And when there is an inequality in power relations of global exchange and movement, those histories are important to be aware of because "we" (in this case Britain and its intimate historical linkages with Muslim-Hindu relations in India/Pakistan) are implicated in that history. What we see then is the white female body in a salwar suit compressing, and unifying, multiple histories (and their violences in which that white female British body is fully implicated) into one singular linear temporality of multiculturalism and national "progress."

In fact, where the 1990s New Britain was concerned, this point is especially important to emphasize. After the First Gulf War in 1991, and then the Oklahoma City bombing, hatred for Muslims simply skyrocketed in Britain. The Rushdie affair in the late 1980s also enabled the media to construct Muslims as intolerant, uncivil, and irrational. The "Honeyford affair" in the mid-1980s (in which Muslims in Britain demanded the removal of a right-wing racist headmaster in a largely Muslim/Asian school in Bradford) equally illustrated the deep hatred and hostility that Muslims experienced in Britain. Further, the global developments regarding a so-called rising Islamic fundamentalism that were fueled by the First Gulf War, the bombing of U.S. embassies, and numerous mosque disputes raging in Britain in the 1990s, exacerbated anti-Muslim sentiments. This prejudice toward Muslims in Britain was explicitly acknowledged in the watershed 1997 Runnymede Trust report, which formally recognized "Islamophobia" in Britain and offered policy recommendations. However, the Blair government did not see the need to institute separate laws against religious discrimination. It was felt that the existing race discrimination laws would take care of religious discrimination (which is not possible as Muslims are targeted because they are Muslims, not just because some of them may look "different" although many do not). This was also the time—the 1990s—when Muslim women in Britain and elsewhere were targeted for covering their faces and heads. In a more traditional Muslim sartorial style, the dupatta (the scarf) of the salwar kameez exists often to cover the face or head as a mark of respect to elders (and not oppression) or in front of male strangers. Yet, while Muslims were being targeted for various reasons, including for their clothes, a dehistoricized salwar kameez began draping hypernational white female British bodies. The very empty universality of the white female subject (Frankenberg, 1993) is ironically limited. Whiteness's universality is lateral, but it cannot (and will not) cross borders in a downward vertical movement into the layers of hidden histories—for instance, the histories that stitch the salwar kameez (or even the sari).

One of the arguments offered by Grewal's (2005) notion of "transnational connectivity" is that in contemporary neoliberal globalization, the dominant power relations of nation, culture, and identity are maintained and fuelled by multiple transnational nodal points. Unlike the West/East or North/South dispensation of earlier colonialism, today we do not see the white female body's multicultural embrace of India exhibiting a linear West/Rest logic. Rather, the cases alluded to in this chapter illustrate complex transnational connectivities where numerous nations, regions, cultures, and identities come together transnationally to secure dominant national logics (in Britain in this case). Cherie's multicultural and globalized nationalism is served by Babs Mahil and Mahil's own Indian/East African history and its colonial relations with Britain. And Ritu Kumar, a national icon in India, whose clothes Diana frequently wore as referenced earlier, bolstered up the multicultural national look of New Britain through the salwar kameez of Diana while partaking in a globalized nationalism of Indian aesthetics (see also Bhachu, 2004). As we

increasingly see privileged white women or celebrities in Indian/Asian garments, we notice a solidarity between rich Asian/Indians/South Asians and
upper-class whites. This is a solidarity that is symptomatic of the complex
transnational connections of contemporary globalization in which, as Gupta
and Ferguson (1997) have noted, "the 'distance' between the rich in Bombay
and those in London may be much shorter than between different classes in
'the same' city" (p. 50).

When white female celebrities wear the sari or the kameez, it is, as noted
earlier, often in settings where they are reaching out to South Asians (usually
privileged) in an attempt to fit in with them to attract their capital (social,
cultural, political, and economic). Or, such white women will often wear
extremely rich, gaudy, heavily gold- or silver-embroidered princesslike garments to fulfill their princesslike Eastern dreams. For example, in 2011, Paris
Hilton arrived in Mumbai to launch her designer handbag. She posed in
Marie Claire's (India) bridal special issue for which she wore a Swarovski-
encrusted sari. Similarly, Victoria Beckham appeared in the cover of a November 2008 issue of *Vogue India*. It was again a bridal special issue. Beckham
appeared dressed in a rich Indian bridal dress. She stated, "I feel like an Indian
princess." Why a British upper-class white woman should be on the cover
of a *bridal* special issue of *Vogue India* is itself confusing, although it does
speak to the power of and fascination with whiteness in India as evidenced
by so many skin-whitening creams, especially for brides (Parameswaran &
Cardoza, 2009). Similarly, Liz Hurley's wedding to Indian business tycoon
Arun Nayar at Umaid Bhavan and Mehrangarh Fort in Rajasthan (India) in
2007 was nothing short of a replay of regal Rajasthan. Magazines splashed
Hurley's princesslike images from that regal wedding. Or, again, Indian fabrics, styles, and embellishments inspired Chanel's Karl Lagerfeld's Pre-Fall
2012 Paris-Bombay show. The entire catwalk design evoked royal Indian
splendor replete with chandeliers, fortlike walls, and royal-style banquet
tables. These regal stylistic embellishments of an earlier era of maharajas and
maharanis (kings and queens) that so fascinate Western designers do not
reflect real India as much as they do contemporary Bollywood chic, which
today is reinventing and marketing royal motifs. High-end Indian designers such as Abu Jani and Sandeep Khosla (among others) have been making
this "princesslike aura" fashionable in the West for white Western women.
In 2012, Jani and Khosla launched their book *India Fantastique* in London.
This book celebrated their 25-year journey with luxury fashion. The book was
launched at Sotheby's by none other than Dame Judi Dench (who herself has
been dressed by these designers and in this instance appeared in a red and
gold embroidered Indian dress) and Bollywood superstar Amitabh Bach-

chan. High-profile Indians and Westerners such as the industrialist Mittal, diasporic South Asian film director Gurinder Chadha, and Robin Woodhead (chair of Sotheby's) attended. Jani and Khosla are stocked in Harrods and Harvey Nicols in London, and their works have also come to Bergdorf and Neiman Marcus in New York.

All this illustrates the complex ways in which today's Western-driven multiculturalism is serviced by the transnational connections of the wealthy in the West and in other parts of the world (such as India in this case).[26] Furthermore, this multiculturalism, in being heavily situated in class and economic privilege, exemplifies how "being" multicultural today requires access to social, economic, and cultural capital. Kamala Visveswaran (2010) has argued that it is important to "examine the ways in which 'culture' often substitutes or stands in for race" and "when culture performs the work of racial difference" (p. 3) (also Gilroy, 2005). The kind of multiculturalism that I have analyzed does precisely this. Here (multi)culturalism overrides race and history, and matters of racial and global inequality are covered over by the aesthetics of (multi)culture.

It must be noted that in only seeing privileged upper-class white Western women in media representations recode themselves as multicultural and cosmopolitan through the embrace of non-Western fashion, we are often led to think that it is somehow working-class whites who are culturally prejudiced and have no interest in a cosmopolitan world. Thus, the racial prejudices of upper-class and even self-proclaimed liberal whites are displaced (implicitly or explicitly) on to working-class whites with whom multiculturalism is simply not associated (Gillies, 2006; Skeggs, 2005; Tyler, 2008). In fashion formations that I have traced here through white women's bodies, the implicit message is often that somehow it is the educated, elite, privileged, urban, metropolitan white people who are open to cultural Others and their styles, but working-class whites are not, as they are "unsophisticated."

One of the issues to also consider in a discussion of whiteness and global multiculturalism is why it is the case that we primarily see representations of the white upper-class female bodies taking on Asian or other non-Western fashion but not upper-class men and white men in particular. Yes, we saw Tony Blair in a Nehru jacket, and yes we saw David Beckham once in a sarong—resembling a lungi, which is a skirt-style cloth wrapped around the waist common with men from South India. And, more recently, we saw Paul Gaultier's Spring/Summer 2013 collection displaying male models in Sikh-styled turbans. But generally we do not see rich white men (unlike white women) retooling their looks through Asian-inspired multicultural garb. Why? I want to suggest that this is because when taking on the garb of an

Other culture deemed less modern than "ours," there is a perceived feminization that occurs (i.e., you are *going down* on the power scale), especially when Asian cultural products are concerned (as Asia is already feminized in Western imaginaries). Thus, white masculinity taking up Asian garments risks a feminization of its image. By contrast, the white female subject position is already hyperfeminized and sexualized in Western cultures. It is easier thus for us to "see" the white female body taking up non-Western fashion for that only expands the scope of operation of its femininity, sexuality, and beauty in a global context.

The discussion offered in this section yields questions regarding cultural ownership. Perhaps one of the most salient questions that the discussion yields is whether a white woman can, should, wear a sari or a salwar kameez? And if and when she does, what are the responsibilities to be confronted? What are the stakes involved? I have never been one to celebrate roots and origins, although I do recognize that at times there is often a political need to do so. But it is important, I will insist, to always be historically aware of our relationship with the objects—in this case garments of another culture—that we may wish to embrace (see also Puwar, 2002). This is true especially when there is a huge historical imbalance in our knowledge about them. In and of itself, a white woman wearing a salwar kameez or a sari is not a problem, but it does become a problem when there is a lack of historical literacy, and an engagement with that literacy as an ethical and political issue—and not just information upload. We are all historically situated subjects and our situatedness in world history is grossly unequal. For a white woman, wearing a sari or salwar kameez produces a historical responsibility that must be faced. It is a responsibility that should guide her—a historical subject—to questions of when, where, how, and if at all, the sari or the salwar kameez should be worn (in a particular context). This is a historical responsibility that requires one to take account of oneself as a historical subject—not historical with a big *H* but a small *h* (the unofficial histories not allowed to rise to the level of History). I am reminded of a statement by postcolonial filmmaker Trinh Minha in a 1992 interview about *Film as Translation*. She states, "In someone else's space I cannot roam about as I may like to. Roaming. . . . is not value free" (1992, p. 117). The sari or the kameez are not value free. The white female national subject must rethink the value-laden history-drenched relation between herself and the sari/salwar kameez before she can go "multiculture" in her fashion choices and self-recoding. It is not a prohibition that is being demanded here, nor a call for permission (i.e., the permission of the other). It is a historical unlearning and relearning that is being asked for—one that must go beyond the sari or salwar kameez. It is a kind of relearning that must encourage or, better still, produce an ethical desire in that white female (multicultural) body to first speak out against the injustices of numerous Satpal Rams that remain violated in Western cultural landscapes. It is an unlearning that must urge that same white female body that wraps itself in the salwar kameez (complete with the scarf) to speak out with Muslim women for their sartorial and religious justice. For the white woman, the wearing of the sari or the salwar kameez has to be a difficult and uncomfortable task. The desire to wear a salwar kameez (or sari) must connect to a desire for historical redress and justice. Nothing less will suffice.

The Black Western Body in Sari and Indian Garments: Transnational Interruption of the Category *Woman of Color*

Although not directly related to the specifics of Cool Britannia multicul-turalism, a few words must be said about a growing representation, still limited, of nonwhite Western women wearing the sari. What do we make of this in terms of Western-driven multiculturalism's pursuit of Asian kool? What do we make of this in terms of a recoding of the black female body? And which black female body? For instance, the 2009 Lakme Fashion Week in Mumbai (Mau Mumbai) saw Naomi Campbell walking the catwalk in a gorgeous black sari with gold border. More recently, in 2012, she organized a super bash for her millionaire Russian beau at the huge Mehengardh Fort in Rajasthan, India (perhaps inspired by socialite Liz Hurley and tycoon Arun Nayar's super wedding in Rajasthan). The fort was decked in detail (from lighting to sitting arrangements) in regal Rajasthani style reminiscent of those bygone princely eras. We saw Campbell in gorgeous Indian saris at this weekend event, which also witnessed Demi Moore and Kate Moss in Indian clothes. We also saw Serena and Vanessa Williams in the 2008 WTA Bangalore Open in gorgeous blue and saffron saris. Furthermore, Oprah's 2012 visit to India saw her in a beautiful sari attending a super bash with high-powered Indian socialites and Bollywood celebrities, all the while mak-ing ignorant comments about India (such as asking whether Indians still eat with their hands), which resulted in a lot of people being enraged. Oprah's lack of any knowledge of the cultural history of India including the origins of eating with the (right) hand in ancient Ayurveda practices and the spiritual, sensual, and hygienic benefits that derive from this practice—as opposed to eating with metal or plastic where your sensual organs such as tongue and fingers touch metal, which is supposed to negatively impact the digestion of the food and health—was minimally embarrassing.[27]

So what do we make of this emerging, although still limited, phenomenon of celebrity black (Western) women and Indo-fascination? I want to suggest that because it is primarily rich high-profile black women who now are seen in Indian fashion styles (like their white counterparts), there is nothing really subversive going on. If anything, it is a continuation of the script of white femininity writ globally now articulating upper-class black female bodies into that script. And these black female bodies are wooed and celebrated in places like India because of their class and economic capital. What must also be noted is how upper-class black female bodies—such as Oprah's or Campbell's—while being sensitive to racial/cultural issues within their nations and in the West at large can end up enacting their nation's dominant attitudes toward other less-privileged nations. So when Oprah makes insensitive comments about eating, this could very well have been an instance of an unreflexive white American woman imagining India through stereotypical tropes of backwardness. Or when Campbell throws an embarrassing bash at a huge fort in Rajasthan, India, where the décor imitates a princely abode, this is, again, no different from white North Americans' or Brits' fascination with India as an ancient land of princes, palaces, and regal luxury—a complete magical mystery tour. Gayatri Spivak had once said, "I cannot comment on the ethico-political agenda of silencing the critical voice of the South by way of a woman of color in the North" (1999, p. 389). Following this statement of Spivak's, I have argued elsewhere that

> the category "woman of color" in which so much of critical race and "multicultural" feminism has invested its energy becomes somewhat meaningless unless we are willing to stretch and situate it across the macro- and micro-cultural, historical, spatial, temporal, and economic relations that connect and disconnect the . . . lives of women and men in different parts of the world. (Shome, 2006, p. 257)

It is this kind of silencing referred to in these quotes that we witness Oprah or Campbell performing. Campbell, for instance, can recreate an entire fortlike environment for her beau's birthday bash, but she is unaware or uncaring of the distance between the environment she creates in the fort and the gendered labor of local women (and men) that has gone into that creation. Or when Oprah asks at an Indian family dining table about people in India *still* eating with hands, she erases the history, pain, labor, and love that have gone into the preparation of her food for that family dinner by the housewives and the female or male helpers. For all such reasons, I am increasingly of the view that it is high time that the category *woman of color* in Western feminist studies be complicated, ruptured, and interrupted through transnational tensions and relations of the Global South. I have rarely found domestic feminists of color, or women of color, in Western nations such as the United Kingdom or the United States (academy and outside) being sensitive to, or interested in, the plight and history of women of the Global South. I have also rarely encountered domestic women or feminists of color (in the academy and outside) relating to women from non-Western worlds in ways that manifest a complex engagement with their culture, communication practices, and identity. Where cultures of the Global South (even when that culture has traveled to a particular Western nation) are concerned, domestic (U.K. or U.S., for instance) women of color can be as unreflexive and discursively violent as privileged white women about "other worlds," including in their interactions with women (and men) of those worlds. Where the Global South (or non-Western worlds in general) is concerned, domestic U.K. or U.S. (or other Western nations) women of color (including often domestic *feminists* of color) often latch on to their nations' scripts of whiteness for viewing other worlds and their peoples at the same time that they extol the virtues of "multicultural feminism" or write about the plight of "women of color" (while often meaning women of color whose situatedness or "origins" are in Western geographies). From the perspective of a woman from the Global South/Non-West, a privileged white woman's view and a domestic Western woman of color's view (of the Global South) are too often the same.[28]

Conclusion

This chapter has raised several linked issues regarding national modernity and gendered appearance—particularly, in contemporary multiculturalism and its links with fashion. At a moment in our contemporary cultural and consumer landscape when fashion constantly crosses borders and a desire for the "exotic" renews itself in the West through new logics and cultural trails of neoliberal globalization, *the terms* under which non-Western fashion crosses borders (and as well creates new borders through that crossing) require constant interrogation. This chapter has suggested that one of the ways in which the privileged white female body functions as a contemporary nationalized "geo-body" (Ware, 2001) is by diffusing multiculturalism's global challenges and rendering invisible its underlying history(ies) of violence and colonialism. Additionally, this chapter has called attention to a point that is not always adequately emphasized in cultural and critical race studies: that today, as privileged spaces and groups in the world remain linked by global capital, the whiteness of privileged white femininity is simultaneously serviced and enabled by the privileged spaces in the so-called non-West as well. A Diana, a

Cherie Blair, a Helen Mirren, or a Judi Dench in an expensive salwar kameez
or sari presents a particular version of a millennium white femininity that
is served by extremely privileged and wealthy businesses of non-Western
fashion (and the underlying capital flows that enable them). Indeed, white
femininity today, as this book suggests, cannot be understood only through
insular and bounded logics of the nation. Geopolitics and global cultural
politics, transnational flows and stasis, historical presences and absences,
all connect and disconnect in unpredictable ways through unpredictable
geopolitical, economic, and cultural routes to constitute contemporary white
cosmopolitan femininity in the West in nations such as the United Kingdom
or the United States.

Finally, this chapter has emphasized the link between fashion and (racialized) national modernity. Discourses of fashion invite us to view the national
body in particular ways in particular contexts and times. To that extent,
fashion is intricately linked to the politics of citizenly belonging. This chapter has highlighted some of the ways in which the politics of whiteness and
national identity articulate each other through the politics of fashion. This
is an important contribution to fashion studies, which, despite producing
wonderful scholarship, remains limited when it comes to matters of whiteness in the context of national identity formation. One of the assertions of
this chapter has been that changing representations of the nation are often
staged and expressed through shifts in (high) fashion, which are for the
most part located in the privileged white (female) body. In contrast, the
nonwhite, non-Western female body, despite all the contemporary rhetoric
about multicultural fashion, continues to be represented through logics of
wildness, barbarism, or exotica in Western fashion discourse. To state this
is not to deny the very limited progress that has occurred in the (Western)
fashion industry on matters of race. Rather, it is to emphasize that change
in fashion and, through it, national temporality is too often associated with
white bodies (given that the notion of change is linked to notions of the
modern).

I end by posing a question that has been an impetus for this chapter and
will continue to inform subsequent chapters: As national modernities are
increasingly written through a globalization and multiculturalism of the
white female body, how is that white female body deployed to suggest the
worldliness of the nation while also revealing the limits of that worldliness?

4. "Global Motherhood"

The Transnational Intimacies of White Femininity

The previous chapter ended with a discussion of the contemporary white female body engaging in a dehistoricized multiculturalism through embracing
Indian fashion styles and garments. In this chapter, I want to continue the
examination of a problematic cosmopolitanism of the white female body in
order to address how it serves as a vehicle through which national modernities in Anglo-dominated nations are frequently written. While much has been
written about how the Diana media phenomenon was situated in complex
transnational media flows and articulations, there is little that has explicitly
addressed how a particular imagination of a "global family" was produced
by this phenomenon through moral visions of white femininity This is an
imagination that exhibited how logics of kinship, familiality, and intimacy
often constitute the grounds upon which contemporary Anglo nations stage
visions of global connectivity through which to rewrite their modern and
caring selves in the 21st century at the same time that they engage in geopolitical and economic violences that make true global harmony impossible.
This is also an imagination in which it is now becoming commonplace and
even fashionable to see white Western women saving, rescuing, or adopting international children through familial frameworks that recenter white
Western (and particularly North Atlantic) heterosexual kinship logics. *Global
motherhood* is the term I use to refer to this logic or imagination through
which white women's bodies today are spilling into the global community
and offering visions and hopes of a multicultural global family.

The issue of white women being positioned as global mothers has certainly had a long history since earlier colonial times. In contemporary times,

Figure 4.1. Two-page spread depicting Diana as mother to the world from the *Daily Mail*'s special supplement of September 6, 1997 (pp. xvii–xix). (Reproduced with permission. Left side [from top to bottom]: Daily Mail/Solo Syndication; AFP and Princess Diana Archive/Getty Images; The Daily Express/Express syndication. Middle page image of Diana in Redcross shirt with baby: Copyright AFP/Getty Images. Middle page image of Diana with baby on lap: Copyright unknown. Right side [top to bottom]: Daily Mail/Solo syndication; Copyright unknown.)

however, this articulation is being shored up in significant ways. Although the Diana phenomenon was certainly one very influential site where we saw this shoring up occur (see figure 4.1), it has become today part of a larger media archive that utilizes the figure of the white mother and ethnic international child to stage visions of a racialized cosmopolitanism. Today, we are bombarded with images of white women adopting international babies, or becoming "good will" charity ambassadors. Whether Angelina Jolie, Madonna, Mia Farrow, Audrey Hepburn, Demi Moore, Susan Sarandon, or others, it has become quite commonplace to see celebrity white women being positioned as transnational caretakers. Princess Diana's representations clearly set a precedent for this, as she (along with Audrey Hepburn) was one of the first women in the late-20th century who was relentlessly positioned as a global mother. Additionally, the last 15 or so years have seen a rise in transnational adoption—especially white Western mothers taking on native children from the Global South as adoptees (Anagnost, 2000; Briggs, 2003,

2006; Cartwright, 2003; Castaneda, 2002; Eng, 2003; Marre & Briggs, 2009; Volkman, 2003, among others).

The Diana phenomenon becomes a useful site through which to explore the construction of global motherhood because this construction played an important role in the New Labor culture of 1990s in recasting the image of Britain through logics of humanitarianism, community, and the international. Kennedy-Pipe and Vickers (2003) note that New Labor's internationalism can best be understood as a moral internationalism. And for Blair—at least in the first years of his office—recasting Britain's image in the world was not going to occur through confrontation or conflict but through moral leadership. Numerous press reports as well as Blair's own biographies and chronicles reveal that right before his election win in 1997, Blair held secret talks with Diana as he was seriously considering her as a global ambassador for Britain. The national brand manager that he was, he recognized early that Diana's global image of compassion and sensitivity was in line with the image of a new compassionate Britain he wanted to project to the world. And Diana herself, as a *Time* magazine article on the 10th anniversary of her death noted, had found that Blair's agenda of building a more inclusive and caring Britain echoed her own vision (Mayer, 2007). Diana's global moralism and the Blair government's desire to secure moral leadership on the global front found strength—at least symbolic strength—in each other.

In this coming together of the project of postcolonial Blairite post-Thatcher Britain and the project of global compassion staged by Diana, what must be emphasized—something that I have also echoed in Chapter 2—is that New Labor's rewriting of Britishness was partly situated in a moral crusade about revamping families and parenting. The Family Law Act of 1996 endorsed by New Labor focused on parenting in order to reduce what Blair consistently termed the "moral deficit" in parenting. The 1998 green paper "Supporting Families" was concerned with providing better services to distribute parenting advice. It also planned a national Family and Parenting Institute. New Labor launched several initiatives on parenting during its years as part of its goal to weed out, as well as raise awareness among, "unfit" parents. For Home Secretary Jack Straw, parenting was to be a legitimate sphere of government intervention. Furedi (2006) describes this as the emergence of "therapeutic governance" (a term originally coined by Pupavac [2001]) during New Labor years in which a holistic approach that meets emotional as well as physical needs of human beings, especially children, was extolled. In such a context, motherhood, as I argued in Chapter 2, became an important vehicle for rewriting the social and for rebuilding the national family. Diana was one of the ultimate symbols of such therapeutic governance domestically and internationally. Thus, media representations foregrounding the United Kingdom's postcolonial internationalism through the image of Diana—who herself had stated numerous times that love is the way to heal the world's pain—acquires significance and illustrates the symbolic centrality of mother-hood and family as cornerstones for rewriting the nation "inside" as well as "outside." But while the writing inside was more explicitly pursued through policies and initiatives, the writing outside was different.[1] It recast Britain's relation with the world through familial logics that ironically recirculated many of the earlier commonwealth logics in which the world was a "family of nations" headed by Britain and bound together by moral goodwill. I clearly do not suggest that there was a direct one-to-one correspondence between the Blairite policies and representations of Diana as a global mother. Clearly, Diana was not just a projection of the New Labor's international agenda. But I *am* suggesting that national makeovers, including in the global arena, need signs and images through which that makeover can be signified and "the people" can reimagine themselves. Diana's global motherhood became one of the signs of such renationalization through a moral embrace of the global that condensed many of the desires and hopes of the New Labor cultural and political ethos. By examining the production of Diana as a global mother, this chapter thus contributes to this limited literature by focusing explicitly on the representational politics through which a white woman comes to suture, name, and frame a global family in contemporary times.

The visual is important in such examinations because of its links with imagination. The imagination of a "global subject"—in this case a global mother—is centrally about ways of seeing (and not seeing) the globe (Eisenstein, 1998). As Spivak (2003) puts it, "no one lives in a global village. The only relationship accessible to the globe so far is that of the gaze" (p. 329). Similarly, no one is a global subject or a global mother—the only relationship informing this fantasy is how we are made to "see" the relationship between particular national modes of white maternity and the "world." In examining the representational politics of white transnational motherhood, questions such as who we see or not see as global mothers, how we see them, what looking relations are centered in such seeing, whose desires are centered in the image, whose histories are invoked and whose rejected, what larger social apparatuses of power are legitimated by particular image politics, what connections are made visible/invisible through particular transnational intimacies are issues to which this chapter speaks.

Other than a limited body of work (Blunt, 1999; Grewal, 1996; Kaplan, 1995, 2001), there is little that has been written specifically on the transnationalization of white femininity in contemporary times—and the ways in which the nation globalizes (and moralizes) its imaginations through the figure of the white woman. The transnationalization of white femininity indeed is not a new phenomenon and was certainly manifest during times of high imperialism (Blunt, 1999; Grewal, 1996) when white women traveled to colonial lands as wives, nurses, missionaries, and teachers. But what the Diana phenomenon, as a contemporary rendition of transnationalized white femininity, manifests are some different logics at work. For one, the logic of linearity that was associated with the white female body during times of territorial colonialism (pre–Second World War days) is disrupted in the image politics of Diana. In pre–Second World War days of British (or other Euro) colonialisms, the trajectory of the white female colonial body in the international sphere was more contained. The colonial male subjects went over to other worlds, parked their flags, took over the land or administration, and then the white female body followed them in the role of missionaries, nurses, teachers, or simply housewives managing colonial domesticity and sexual desires of colonial men (in order to minimize the risk of cross-racial breeding) (Stoler, 1997). There was greater geographical and temporal sequentiality, linearity, and fixity in the colonial movement of white femininity.

But with mediated celebrities such as Princess Diana (or today Angelina Jolie), such a trajectory, fixity, and sequentiality is disrupted. Given the centrality of the media in globalizing Diana's image and producing her as a global figure that was simultaneously located in so many places, it actually seemed to matter little when she was where. The image of Diana, in its spatial and temporal seamlessness, allows a visual stretching of the white female body, and our gaze along with that, across multiple racial and national borders, often at the same time. We see Diana picking up babies in Angola while a few moments later we are exposed to an image of her in Pakistan in the same television program. Similarly, we see Angelina Jolie in Africa, and in the next moment, we see her in Thailand or Vietnam, as the media replays and juxtaposes many images at once. Such an image archive of repetition, at least in the case of Diana, has certainly produced looking relations that have made it normal to see the explosive boundaryless-ness of the white female body today while masking the numerous ways in which that body also functions as a boundary marker (Anthias & Yuval-Davis, 1989; Yuval-Davis, 1997a, 1997b; McClintock, 1995).

A further difference between the transnationalization of the figure of the contemporary white woman such as Diana or Angelina Jolie and earlier transnational travels of white women during times of territorial colonialism is that contemporary renditions of white women as global mothers are often couched in a logic of cosmopolitical morality. In earlier times, white women were not framed or visualized as necessarily occupying the position of "world citizenship" and expressing a cosmopolitical morality. But today, we have a far more complex scenario predicated on a logic of freedom that is symptomatic of our neoliberal times in the West in which, as Gilroy (2005) has argued, imperialism itself is being rearticulated as an "ethical" (p. 62) and moral project. As the introductory essay on the special issue on cosmopolitanism in *Public Culture* (2000) highlighted,

> Where once political discussion focused on the systemic nature of public culture and the distribution of political goods, today there is a revival of the humanist discourse of rights founded on the unique and inviolable presence of "human" personhood. . . . [t]he fetishization of liberal individualism has, in the past years, created a cosmopolitan imaginary signified by icons of singular personhood. What represents the spirit of world citizenship today? In recent years, the answer to this question has not elicited ideas and ideals but philanthropic individuals. . . . (Pollock, Bhabha, Breckenridge, & Chakrabarty, 2000, p. 581)

The displacement of cosmopolitanism onto philanthropic individuals and their activities, while attractive at one level, becomes problematic because its morality is rooted in a politics of transnational pity and love (toward the other) (Boltanski, 1999; Chouliaraki, 2006, 2013; Littler, 2008) instead of transnational justice, which requires the formation of collective resistance and a consideration of historical inequalities. A framework of transnational love and pity deflects attention from larger historical structures and colonial pasts. Jo Littler (2008) drawing on Boltanski (1999) argues that a politics of pity makes it appear as though such global inequalities are primarily about luck and fortune (and hence individual matters).[2] Therefore, we think they are not connected to circumstances of privilege and their histories. Indeed, what makes acceptable images of people like Diana serving as global mothers in other worlds is that the emotions and sentiments such images (of care, love, pity, compassion, etcetera) reify, mask the material violences that produce such states of despair in nations in the Global South.

For instance, since his victory in 1997, Blair had positioned himself as a champion in the fight to reduce international poverty. In several global forums, he pledged to "heal the scar" of African poverty.[3] Yet his aid programs have consistently revealed a different pattern. A 2004 report by Oxfam noted that in the context of the U.N. target of spending 0.7% of the nation's income on aid so as to halve world poverty by 2010, the government had consistently refused to set a timetable for reaching the 0.7% target.[4] Furthermore, while Blair set himself up as a champion for reducing African poverty, the government had consistently espoused an economic model in its technical assistance programs that encouraged privatization and liberalization as keys to poverty reduction—making them a condition for multilateral aid in Africa, despite resistance from local communities. Additionally, the Blair administration was shamefully involved in issuing over two thousand licenses for arms exports to China, Indonesia, Kenya, Uganda, Zambia, Zimbabwe, and several other states not known for embracing human rights. Especially controversial was the "arms to Sierra Leone" affair that involved shipment of arms to Sierra Leone to aid President Tejan's bid to restore his government that was ousted by a military coup. In October 1997, U.N. resolution 1132, which Britain had helped draft, passed a blanket arms embargo to Sierra Leone. Yet a mercenary company Sandline International had supplied arms and AK 47 rifles to Sierra Leone. The company claimed that Whitehall defense intelligence staff were fully informed of the operation and that it had held meetings with British and American officials about their preparation of the countercoup of President Tejan. Later, the *Sunday Times* also published pictures showing Royal Navy engineers in Sierra Leone assisting in servicing the helicopter that had ferried troops and equipment to Sierra Leone.[5] Thus, at the very time that the ethics of the Blair government's policies toward Africa was in question—despite its rhetoric—we were falling in love with images of Princess Diana—as the face of New Britain—in various parts of Africa, tending to children through love and compassion, and arguing for an end to land mines and illegal weapon imports to Africa.

Transnational Intimacies

The subtitle of this chapter, "Transnational Intimacies," calls attention to the transnational connections—always intimate—through which the figure of the global mother is staged in dominant cultural narratives in the West. The term draws on, and extends, notions of intimacy offered by scholars such as Lauren Berlant (see also, Stoler, 2006). Berlant has variously argued (1997, 2000) that intimacy is a highly regulated site through which familial national belongings are staged and notions of publicness and citizenly belonging are legitimated. Berlant uses the term *intimacy* in the broadest sense—to mean not just sex acts but any or all intimate relations of family, kinship, love, caring—to argue that only certain forms of human connections and attachments are recognized and moralized by the nation as legitimate intimate attachments to the social—in this case the global—while many other human attachments that constitute "minor intimacies" (2000, p. 5) are simply not granted any recognition by the state. Extending this point of Berlant's into the realm of the transnational, I explore what forms of attachments are permitted in the production of the global mother. The white lesbian woman, the transgendered individual, the black mother, the mother from the Global South, the brown lesbian woman, and so on are never allowed to function as symbols of global togetherness as morality is never associated with them. They are the nation's immoral faces, its unwanted bodies, its sites of panic. Hence, they cannot function as symbols through which a global public sphere of love and caring can be visualized and moralized. The term *transnational intimacies* also refers to the intimate transnational struggles of maternities and modernities through which white women come to function as humanitarian figures attending to children of the world. Maternities and modernities are intricately linked, as I suggested in Chapter 2. The modern is always gendered, and good mothers, competent mothers, mothers well able to look after their children (and hence the national future) are centrally tied to the imagination of a modern and developed future of the nation (Ram & Jolly, 1998; Stoler, 1997, 2002). Consequently, when we see images of white women caring for children of other nations, or, as is becoming fashionable in today's celebrity culture, simply picking babies for adoption, we need to recognize that implicit in such discourses is a struggle over maternities (and modernities). The white mother can stand in for the global mother, become the body around which global domesticity can be envisioned, only by erasing the nonwhite, non-Western mother in such facile regimes of the cosmopolitan. Transnational maternities of white women are not innocent acts of love and caring; they are sites of articulation through which larger transnational relations of race, sex, gender, nation, and kinship are regulated in the performance of "ethical imperialism" (Gilroy, 2005, p. 62).

I now turn now to the representational logics that inform the visual production of Diana as a transnational mother, although I also broaden my discussion to refer to many other similarly positioned white women in contemporary media culture. My analysis illustrates how the logic of global motherhood, embodied in Diana as well as other celebrity white women, articulates relations of race, colonialism, nation, maternities, notions of kinship, and ethics of love in the imagination of a global family that is, however, mediated by a highly nationalized white female body. There are three particular themes I focus on in the following discussion. First, I address the visual codes through which celebrity white woman such as Diana are moralized as global maternal figures. Second, I examine how the transnational politics of maternal care that the white female body signifies is imbricated in a larger struggle over modernities. Finally, I address how a logic of cosmopolitanism is mobilized through the figure of the native child of the Global South resulting in what I term *infantilized cosmopolitanism* that reinforces a parent-child model in white (Anglo) national femininity's relation to the world.

Rays of Light

The construction of Diana as a moral transnational mother is centrally shored up by visual logics that represent her as an angelic figure emanating compassion, love, and healing. Richard Dyer (1997) has written about the relationship between the aesthetics of photographic technology and the privileging of whiteness. He has noted how in media culture, white women are often bathed through soft white light that represents them as pure, divine, angelic figures. "Idealised white women are bathed in and permeated by light. It streams through them and falls onto them. . . . In short they glow" (p. 127). He further argues that the "angelically glowing white woman is an extreme representation precisely because it is an idealization" (p. 127) in which the white woman becomes the symbol of "white virtuousness and the last word in the claim that what made whites special as a race was their non-physical, spiritual, and indeed ethereal qualities" (p. 127).

It must be noted that not only are white women who come to signify transnational motherhood bathed in a halo of spirituality and religiosity, but they are also always *beautiful*. This point is important to note not only because of the association of beauty with goodness and spirituality, but also because of its association with life. Colebrook (2006), discussing the cultural politics of beauty, notes that beauty serves as an "exemplary image for the furtherance of life" (p. 138). "We regard as beautiful anything that will serve to realize life's potential—anything that is fertile, productive, and conducive to self recognition and self maintenance" (p. 138). It is thus significant that in current Western popular culture, where we are witnessing a plethora of images of white women taking on roles of global mothers, they are all beautiful women. Women coded as ugly do not grace the pages of our magazines as being givers of life in other worlds, for to be ugly or ordinary is to be opposed to enhancement of life, virtue, goodness, and morality. Although this is not totally surprising—given that women who are represented through the logic of global motherhood in popular culture for the most part tend to be celebrities and hence beautiful—the larger issue is that such representations shore up an intersectional economy of representation in which logics of heterosexuality, class, gender, and internationality all come together in securing the construction of the global mother. The ideal mother must not only glow, but must also have the proper body that does not threaten or unsettle frames of familiality that are associated with good motherhood. Women whose bodies are "out of place" and connote immorality—the white trash woman, lesbian woman, nonwhite woman, non-Western woman—do not usually glow, for the glow is always associated with morality and goodness. Life and the ability to give and rescue life in such representations are thus racialized—and simultaneously heterosexualized and classed.

Images of Diana as a global mother reinscribe these visual logics. The images are often saturated in visual codes that moralize her beautiful body and render it as a source of life and light. This is centrally seen in lighting techniques. Consider Figure 4.2, which is an iconic image of Diana with children in Africa that was circulated in numerous magazines. The visual organization of the image invites us to enter it through the framework of light and darkness. We see Diana sitting on a bamboo bench with hungry children who, as the image suggests, have probably just been handed food by Diana as they sit eating next to her. The sunlight falls on Diana and the photograph has been deliberately composed to emphasize Diana through that light. If we look carefully at the composition of the image, we notice that the light flows up to Diana's figure, centralizing her, and the children on her right-hand side are in the light while the kids on her left are in relative shadows. This impartiality of lighting gives us a sense of light gradually beginning to flow into this space, incrementally

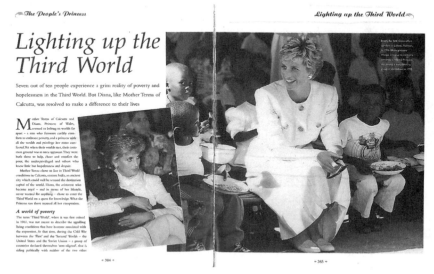

Figure 4.2. Diana with children in Africa. (Left to right: Alpha Press; Rex USA. Text: DeAgostini UK [previously named Orbis Publishing Ltd.]. Reproduced with permission.)

illuminating it. The white female body here is centrally positioned—both narratively in terms of the copy headline—"Lighting up the Third World"—and visually in terms of the photo composition, as the carrier and mediator of this light. Furthermore, most other visual components in the image are also in darkness—the background for instance is in darkness where we only see hazy ill-defined silhouettes of children. The loud copy title "Lighting up the Third World" leaves little to the imagination. It explicitly invites us to look at Diana's body through the trope of light and life and the third world around her through darkness and death.

This play of light through which the white woman's body is often privileged and moralized tends to be a typical visual mode through which white women, occupying positions of global mothers, are framed in relation to the children of the world. Consider this image of Mia Farrow—a goodwill ambassador for the United Nations Children's Fund (UNICEF) (Figure 4.3).The image is from a UNICEF website. Here too the lighting is organized to highlight Farrow. The light illuminates her face, and flows along her arm as she looks down with tenderness at the child on her lap while the face of the child is in relative darkness.

The verbal narrative often functions to shore up the meanings embedded in such visual techniques through which the white female body begins to

Figure 4.3. Mia Farrow, Goodwill ambassador. (Copyright UNICEF. Reproduced with permission.)

occupy a life-giver position. For instance, Diana is often represented through the language of a healer and saint, someone who had some kind of other-worldly power to transform people. Reports describe her in terms such as

> Diana used her power just like a magic wand, waving it in all kinds of places where there was hurt . . . And everywhere she used it, there were changes, almost like a fairy tale.[6]
>
> Or
>
> Diana has this gift to be able to meet people and sit and listen. . . . When she went away, they were absolutely elated, transformed. . . . Some didn't even know what hit them. [7]
>
> Or
>
> Once, at a hospital in Huambo when the photographers had all flown back to their air-conditioned hotel to wire their pictures, I watched Diana, unaware that any journalists were still present, sit and hold the hand of Helena Ussova, a seven-year-old who'd had her intestines blown to pieces. For what seemed an age the pair just sat, no words needed. When Diana finally left, the small girl struggled through her pain to ask me if the beautiful lady was an angel. Could anybody have said no?[8]

This theme, whereby white women are seen as having some innate power to heal and care, is not just unique to the Diana phenomenon but is domi-nant in many other contemporary logics of the cosmopolitan. For instance, in a UNICEF-assembled web photo album devoted to Audrey Hepburn, Hepburn's humanitarian work with children is framed through the caption: "The spirit of Audrey Hepburn."[9] In photos of Hepburn with children from different parts of the world, her face radiates light. She often glows, and her expressions connote a sense of serenity and peace that further shores up her framing through the invocation to her spirit (instead of her corporeality). Similarly, when recent controversies around Madonna's adoption of baby David in Malawi were exploding, one of the most powerful justifications and defenses that Madonna offered for her adoption was that when she saw baby David in the clinic, she was "transfixed" by him, she was drawn to him. The sense one gets is that of a spiritual pull that drew her to this adoption. Additionally, Meg Ryan most recently described her adoption of a baby from China as a "metaphysical kind of labor." She always knew, she said, that she was meant to be a mother to that child.[10] Again, during her adoption of a Korean baby in 2009, actress Katherine Heigl proudly stated that "She [the baby] was actually born the day before me in November, which I thought was really serendipitous and just kind of like a sign."[11]

Such representations are problematic because they elevate white femi-ninity to a status of spiritual transcendence. With the Diana phenomenon, this transcendence was finally sealed through the associations made between her and Mother Teresa. Because the white female position becomes identified with something metaphysical, the white female body transcends history (time) and geographical boundaries (space). And thus, the logic of global motherhood in such narratives offers visions of white femininity that construct an "essence" for whiteness and reproduces a universalist logic in which whiteness becomes associated with spirit and not corporeality. Dyer (1997) has underscored this as being a central logic through which whiteness reproduces itself.

Photos of Diana's humanitarianism frequently highlight the moment in which she is touching someone. Often, it is a shot that has been clicked at the very moment when she is stretching out her hand to touch someone's forehead or extending her arm to cuddle a child or comfort a sick or dying person as in the manner of blessing. For instance, in one image (Figure 4.4), an "untouchable" woman in India, sitting on the road, takes Diana's hand and touches her own forehead with that, as though Diana's touch contains some spiritual healing power. Similarly, in another photo published in a *People* commemorative edition (1997), *The Diana Years* (p. 135), an old disabled woman, on one of Diana's visits to a center for the disabled in Somerset, is

Figure 4.4. Diana's touch depicted as containing some spiritual healing power. (Rex USA. Reproduced with permission.)

sitting and clutching Diana's hand—while Diana is standing tall in the visual frame—as though the woman is receiving Diana's blessing. In numerous other images, the framing of Diana's touching of people—lepers, untouchables, AIDS victims, disabled people, old people—functions similarly where she is touching them in the manner of blessing, healing, or comforting. The touch of Diana has been the focus of numerous media reports about her. And what makes the issue of her touch interesting is that very few white women in history have been the subject of so much discussion in relation to the power of their touch—the power to heal, to give hope, and to give life. In a documentary narrated by Richard Attenborough that was produced as a DVD by the *Daily Mail* (in 2007 on the 10th anniversary of Diana's death) we hear of Diana's touch being compared to that of ancient kings to whom the masses would come seeking healing, hope, and regeneration. And we are reminded that unlike ancient kings, Diana never wore gloves.

John Urry (2000) has argued that social theory has paid far more attention to vision and consequently has neglected the ways in which other senses are imbricated in relations of power. While narratives of touch at one level cannot be separated from the politics of vision, given that how we experience someone's touch and what meanings we attribute to them are tied to how we are socialized to *see* bodies, it is still the case that we pay far less attention to how narratives of touch are given meaning and how those meanings create social and racial hierarchies. For instance, how is the touch of the black man perceived versus the touch of the white woman? Whose touch do we fear, avoid, and whose touch becomes imbued with goodness and healing? Indeed, touch—a sense that we so naturalize and take for granted—has also been important in cultural politics and geopolitics, producing all kinds of disciplinary mechanisms for denying publicness to some bodies. Consider how, in flights, passengers may react if they are sitting next to someone they perceive as a Muslim man. They would probably be vigilant throughout the flight if, by that time, the other passenger has not been deplaned for "looking suspicious." And then consider how at ease we may feel, if the person next to us is a serene innocent-looking young white woman. The social construction of physical touching is a modality for separation as well as connection, and what and who it separates and connects (and how) becomes a matter of cultural politics. Touching and seeing are both implicated in the spectacle of race: for when we see a black man, for instance, and feel fear, what we are fearing is not just what we are seeing but the possibility that who we are seeing (and how) can now come to "harm" us (and hence touch). A limitation in the academic literature on the cultural politics of Diana is this aspect of touching—and particularly, the racialized geopolitical implications of that touching.

The spatial relations framing Diana's touch (and the touch of such do-gooding white women) are situated in, and reify, various inequities. What makes the representational archive of Diana's healing touch political and constitutes it as a racial, heterosexual, able-bodied formation is that the touching is never mutually reciprocal. Diana touches down and the people she touches—disempowered people of color, underprivileged people from the Global South, old people, gay people, physically handicapped people—receive her touch. It is not a lateral touching where the two parties are positioned in terms of their bodies in an equal spatial relation to each other, but one that reinforces a verticality and reproduces an unequal power relation between the subject touching and the subject being touched (the diseased, the untouchables, the lepers, the old people, the cancer patients) who are then rendered into objects. It is this tactile inequality, manifesting "tense and tender ties" (Stoler, 2006, p. 23) of racialized, heterosexualized, nationalized, transnational intimacies that turns the subjects Diana touches into objects that can be touched. No permission is needed here to touch, as the bodies that are touched are already rendered inhuman in our cultural imaginaries, and hence the healing touch of the white woman imbued with spiritual and magical capacity to heal those she touches becomes a touch of *power*. We cannot imagine this any other way. When Diana is allegedly to have said that the biggest disease the world suffers from is a lack of love and that touching heals all barriers of race and culture, such a statement reinforces an unequal tactile cosmopolitanism where the white heterosexual upper-class woman's touch crosses boundaries of race, sexuality, and nation without repercussions but never vice versa. For instance, how freely can a gay man or a lesbian woman even casually, in a gesture of friendliness, touch someone (without wondering how that touch may be received or interpreted)? Or how freely can a black man touch without fearing whether his touch may be perceived as hostile and dangerous? When you are an other, you have to constantly monitor your own body. Touch is situated in a racialized, heteronormative, geopolitical regime of governmentality. The larger issue here has to do with how the borderless compassionate touch of the white woman also reinforces borders of race, sexuality, nation, health, gender, and geopolitics. The white woman's touch of hope, healing, and love renders invisible the very transnational relations of power that even make it possible for her to touch and physically comfort those othered by those very relations.

Other visual assemblages also play a role in attributing goodness and spirituality to the body of Diana as she is made to signify global motherhood. Especially important here is how visual techniques frequently position Diana through the *madonna-child trope*—a trope which also plays out in numerous other representations of white women caring for children of the world. The

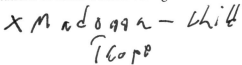

Figure 4.5. Diana cradling a
cancer-ridden child in Pakistan.
(Reuters/John Pryke. Reproduced
with permission.)

madonna-child image, evoking associations of Mary with Jesus, has had a
tremendous visual power in Western religious discourses and has been reproduced in the works of numerous artists from Raphael to Da Vinci to the
ceiling of the Sistine Chapel. Saturated with connotations of salvation, this
highly Christian trope has historically functioned to represent white women
through a logic of morality. Laura Briggs (2003) has powerfully noted that
the prevalence of the madonna-child image in Western culture (especially
in post–cold war U.S. culture). She argues that images such as these have
significantly intersected with and informed (Western) nations' debates about
foreign policy, international aid, political intervention, and family values.

Visual images of Diana functioning as a "mother to the world" (as the
copy framing the very first image at the beginning of this chapter labels her,
and which I address in greater detail later) draw on this trope. Consider for
example, this image of Diana cradling a cancer-ridden child in Pakistan
(Figure 4.5). Her eyes are closed in compassion toward the child (notice
again how the light falls on Diana). The child looks up at Diana with devotion. Diana's hand touches the little hand of the child almost as though she
is giving the child life. This theme of spirituality (where Diana is positioned
as a madonna figure) is also seen in other images of white women. An image

of Angelina Jolie in the British magazine *Hello!* (May 2, 2006, p. 77) is also imbricated in this logic. Angelina is carrying baby Zahara. The image is set against a desert background. Jolie, carrying her adopted child, is looking out into the desert with a peaceful smile gracing her face. The starkness of the image confers an otherworldly and ethereal quality to Jolie. Similarly, in the image of Mia Farrow mentioned earlier, where she is positioned as a goodwill ambassador, the visual composition of the image is imbricated in the madonna-child theme.

Such discursive operations of the madonna-child logic through which white women are often positioned in relation to starving, unhealthy, or deprived children of the Global South are situated in what Bashford (2006) calls "global biopolitics" (p. 67). For instance, in representations of Diana, the children that she visits in other worlds are usually framed as *unhealthy*—they are sick children, children who have been abandoned by their families (read: the nation). Given the normalized assumption that a modern body is a healthy body (for it has the apparatus to attend to its care and development), in such representational logics, the unhealthy body of the child becomes a symbol for the nonmodern future of its nation. The rescue and healing of that unhealthy or neglected body from its nation by white Western subjects such as Diana metaphorizes (and moralizes) a movement from the darkness of nondevelopment to the light of Western modernity. Such representations, in situating white female subjectivity as a site of morality, obscure the role of Western militarism, foreign policy, histories of Anglo colonialism, credit baiting of organizations such as World Bank or International Monetary Fund, and Western-centric population-control policies that often leave such nations in conditions of internal chaos.

Such global biopolitics where health, race, and nation collide manifest a larger phenomenon that has become especially visible in the late 20th and early 21st centuries. This is a phenomenon in which the very battle over modernity and belonging (at one level) is being fought over issues of health. Health has always played a role in imperial projects, in securing borders and prohibiting flows of bodies across racialized boundaries. In such representations health itself becomes temporally framed—that is, third world health is outside of modern time (Bashford, 2006; Briggs, 2003; Cartwright, 2003; Patton, 1992; Treichler, 1999). Additionally, in such representations, health also becomes spatialized in that the places where "unhealthy" third world bodies are found are diseased places (see also Patton, 1992; Treichler, 1999). For instance, Madonna justified her controversial adoption to Oprah, which was cited in many press reports, by stating, "I beg all of those people to go to Africa and see what I saw and walk through those villages. . . . *To see mothers dying, with Kaposi sarcoma lesions all over their bodies. To see open sewers everywhere.* To see what I saw" (emphasis added).[12] Musician and singer Bono supported Madonna's cause when he told Britain's *Sun* newspaper that "Madonna should be applauded for helping to take a child out of the worst poverty imaginable." He is also reported as insisting that "the situation is so desperate in the third world continent that parents are willing to give up their children if there is a chance for them to have a better life." Place (and nation) takes on the connotation of disease and crisis in hygiene in such representations, which ultimately suggests a crisis in the modernity of such nations—a crisis that conceals the fact that larger geopolitical issues related to toxic dumping, clean air, the need for adequate and cheap mobility of health and pharmaceutical products to the Global South, the neoliberal destruction of local economies, the history of colonization are all responsible today for the situation in the Global South that then enables someone like Bono to pity the fact that "parents are willing to give up their children."

In the Diana phenomenon, such spatialization and temporalization of health are significantly at work. For instance, the images of disease-ridden children, sick children, poverty-ridden children, children whose bodies have been maimed by land mines, who Diana visits, are almost always outside of white spaces and geographies. They are in the Global South for the most part. Further, as Briggs (2003) has noted, in such images of children of the Global South, who are awaiting nurturing from Western women, the children are typically shown as being un-homed, that is, they are always outside the home (given that home connotes a sense of stability) and often without parents. This, she notes, is in frequent contrast to how young white children in places like the United States or the United Kingdom are typically represented—in stable environments where they are happy and "homed."

Additionally, in such images the contrast between bodies also performs a visual logic that further renders white maternity as a symbol of the nation's modernity that can and will rescue the children of these nonmodern and diseased nations. For instance, when the robust, toned, tall (i.e., healthy) body of Diana that has been built up with gym equipment, swimming, and other body-attending technologies (read: technologies of the modern and urban) is juxtaposed with starving, small, undernourished, and often seminaked bodies of children in the Global South, such a visual technique highlights the body's (read: the nation) built-up superiority in relation to the damaged (and sickly) bodies of the children of the nations to which she travels.

In fact, a dominant visual technique that is evident in representations of Diana is that the camera angles and lighting are often organized to inspire awe and stature toward her body while the bodies of the native children are visually diminished. Often we look up at her body (or at least her body is at eye level with our gaze) while we look down at the native children surrounding the body of the white woman. Shohat and Stam (1994) make an important point that such tropes of high and low (for instance, when we look up with awe at the body of the white woman and down at the native children) "devolve into symbolic hierarchies that simultaneously embrace class (the 'lower class'), esthetics (high culture), the body (the lower bodily stratum), zoology (lower species) and the mind (the higher and lower faculties)" (p. 140). Camera angles thus become central to how an unequal power hierarchy between the white global mother and the native children of the Global South are secured and maintained.

Transnational Maternities and "Ethics of Care"

Imperialism has always been about a struggle over maternities.[14] Sometimes this struggle has been explicit as during slavery in the United States when the black mother's body was regularly raped by white plantation owners and the child of the rape recirculated as plantation labor. At other times, the struggle has silently informed grand narratives of imperial enlightenment as with cases of white women in British imperialism supporting the empire's cultural mission as teachers, governesses, and missionaries by enculturating upper-class children of the colonized in manners of "civilization." If narratives of imperialism are also grand narratives about modernity, then underlying visions of the modern have always lurked the politics of domesticity, home, and family (Stoler, 1997, 2002). To produce modern subjects is to ensure that the home as the basic unit of the nation is civilized, for home is the site for the production of the nation's future. In Western imperial discourses, where white heterosexual femininity functions as a signifier of "homeliness," the nonwhite non-Western mother by contrast often functions as a failure of civil "homeliness." In contemporary Anglo-centric discourses, for example, the nonwhite mother is often a failed mother. Within the United States, black mothers are "crack mothers"; Latina mothers are seen as overly breeding children while unable to look after them; and Native American mothers are seen as producing babies who suffer from fetal alcohol syndrome.

Imaginations about a global family that circulate in adoption discourses are often underpinned by such a logic of failed nonwhite, non-Western motherhood. For example, a U.S. adoption agency International Adoption Help invokes the trope of maternal abandonment to encourage U.S. families to adopt from Guatemala.[15] It emphasizes that "the easiest way to understand the type of child/children that become available for adoption in Guatemala is to realize" the processes of "abandonment" and "relinquishment" at work. Abandonment, explains the text, is "when a child has been abandoned by his/her biological family or when parental rights have been terminated by the Guatemalan government due to neglect" and "relinquishment" is when a Guatemalan mother relinquishes the child's care to a lawyer because of her inability to give maternal care. The invocation of a crisis in Guatemalan motherhood enables the invitation to white U.S. mothers to step in and rescue those children.

Such a logic of maternal abandonment also informs representations of Diana as a global mother.[16] For example, a popular commemorative book *Diana: An Extraordinary Life* (1998) has a particular chapter (from which an image was displayed earlier) titled "Lighting up the Third World." The chapter offers a detailed description of the conditions of children in Brazil.

> As Diana quickly learned, Brazil, a spectacular country full of beautiful tourist sights had a *horrifying secret*—a mass of starving homeless children, many *abandoned by their mothers and their societies*. . . . When Diana arrived, she saw only the tiniest remnants of these human cast-offs: ten children aged from five months to five years *left in the streets by their mothers who were drug addicts or prostitutes*. . . . (1998, p. 392; emphasis added)

Brazilian mothers here are failed mothers; metaphors of prostitution and drug addiction frame their bodies. Their bodies thus cannot nurture their children—the future of the nation and the world.

A documentary titled *The Diary of a Princess* (1997) that was broadcast on BBC1 (in February 1997) chronicles Diana's humanitarian work with the British Red Cross in Angola. The film invokes the logic of failed non-Western motherhood. The program is replete with images of sick and dying babies and children with broken limbs from land mine explosions. A particular moment in the film captures Diana's arrival at a health clinic where local mothers are waiting with their babies. On Diana's arrival, a young mother hands over her highly overweight baby to Diana. Diana cuddles the baby, laughs, and then says, "He weighs a ton. What is she feeding this young man? He weighs a ton." At this moment, we see the baby's mother, partly eclipsed in the frame by Diana, standing in the background with a shy smile, not understanding the conversation.

While a humorous and affectionate moment, the image of a white mother examining a black baby while that baby's mother is in the background, rendered into silence, is poignant and revealing. The poignancy emerges from the erasure of the African mother by the global motherhood of Diana. The passage of the highly overweight baby from the native mother to Diana is a performative moment through which competing visions of global domesticity are staged in which one (white maternal domesticity) negates the other (nonwhite maternal domesticity). The question "What has she been feeding him?" is addressed to the *local male* officials around Diana and not to the native mother, as she cannot speak English. The male native officials become a point of mediation between the white woman and the native mother. A complex positionality of the third world mother in relation to the white mother becomes visible here. As Diana addresses her query to the local official, this address situates the native men in a position that invites them to "speak for" the native mother.

Spivak (1988) had famously suggested that between patriarchy and imperialism, subject constitution and object formation, the figure of the [third world] woman disappears. In the preceding representation, a complex politics of subalternization reveals itself that symbolically illustrates how the native mother is caught between intersecting structures of her native patriarchy and imperialism. For the native mother, nation and imperialism become interchangeable in this moment. And white motherhood here becomes a staging ground for a subalternization in which the figure of the nonwhite non-Western mother, the white mother, patriarchy, the nation, and the global intersect as well as collide in complex ways. The white mother can only occupy the position of a global mother by erasing the nonwhite maternal body from visions of global domesticity. The white mother's subject position is thus ironically dependent on the necessary failure of the nonwhite native mother. This is the peculiar irony, the ambivalence that disrupts that superiority of the colonial text of white maternity that illustrates (as so many postcolonial theorists have noted) that the colonial-colonized relationship is not so totalistic as it may seem; it is a relationship often of a reverse dependence (of the colonizer on the colonized [or in this case of the white woman on the native woman]).

It is such an irony, where the erasure of one maternity becomes the precondition of the agency of the other, that was addressed in Indian director Ketan Mehta's film *Mangal Pandey* (2005) based on the Sepoy mutiny of 1857 in India. The film has a moment in which the native servant woman is shown as daily functioning as a secret "breast giver"[17] to the memsahib white woman whose empty breasts cannot feed her own newborn baby. The native servant woman—herself a new mother—uses her own breast milk to nourish the white baby. When she returns to her poor dwellings everyday, her empty breast cannot feed her own child for her milk has been depleted. This transracial/transnational maternal transaction remains hidden; no one knows that the white mother's breasts are not generating milk and that her child is being fed by lower-class brown breasts. If a full breast is a cultural metaphor for healthy motherhood, then the native servant woman is a breast giver to the white woman and her child. But when she returns home, she becomes a "failed" mother to her own child and her nation. Her body is being used up daily by the empire and is unable to serve the future of her own nation. This is the performance of national abandonment that the native woman is forced into by the empire; her failure to nourish her own child (and her nation) is what also feeds the health of the empire.

Indeed, when we fast-forward to our times again, where we now see rich white (and increasingly North American) women adopting babies from other worlds, we see this struggle over maternities playing out in the reproduction of white women as bearers of global domesticity. Consider a recent image of Jolie with her babies in the British magazine *Hello* (May 2, 2006). The double-page spread image shows the Jolie-Pitt family relaxing and playing with their adopted children, while waiting the birth of Jolie's birth child, against the vast desert landscape of Namibia. The bold headline copy states: "Brad and Jolie enjoy intimate family moments in Namibia as they await the birth of their child." We see Jolie, her body half reclining and half stretching over toward Zahara (her Ethiopian child). Behind Zahara is her nanny—while her ethnicity is unclear, she is clearly a brown woman (possibly Mexican)—sitting slightly outside the familial circle, looking over at Zahara. The brown nanny here functions as the point of aporia—disrupting the cosmopolitan racialized maternal text through which Jolie is presented as a global mother. She is the one who "cares" for the children picked up during Jolie's cosmopolitan travels. Her figure in this photo reminds us of the always ready presence of the never recognized nonwhite domesticity in zones of transnational white maternal intimacy. Ehrenreich and Hochschild (2002) have discussed the "female underside of globalization, whereby millions [of women] from poor countries in the south migrate to do the 'women's work' of the north" (p. 4) (see also Briggs, 2010). They note how the "lifestyles" of the Global North are "made possible by a global transfer of the services associated with a wife's traditional role . . . from poor countries to rich ones" (p. 4). And in the process, a new logic of imperialism is manifest whereby wealthy countries instead of just seeking to extract hard natural resources now "also seek to extract something. . . . that can very much look like love" (p. 4). And this "love" is extracted not just from the global nannies, but as this chapter illustrates, also from the brown and black children being adopted by white women of wealthy countries. Although Povinelli's (2006) important *Empire of Love* deals with complexities and contexts that are much beyond the scope of this book, it can be said, following some of the insights of that work, that the discourse of global motherhood embodied in the white female body manifests an empire of love—and an empire through love.[18]

The logic of a non-Western native mother's abandonment of her child that simultaneously buttresses the global motherhood of white femininity conceals numerous linkages between political/economic conditions in nations in the Global South and nations such as the United States. For instance, in Western media, we see a lot of coverage of famine and death in Ethiopia. When Jolie adopted from Ethiopia, its failed national structures were highlighted in numerous press reports. But what was often unremarked are the connections between famine in places such as Ethiopia and U.S. international policies regarding food aid. Andrew Natsios, a Georgetown University professor, who led the U.S. Agency for International Development from 2001 to 2006 has disappointedly noted (as stated in a 2008 Bloomberg.com report) that "U.S. farm and shipping lobbyists" often stifle efforts to "simplify aid deliveries leaving Africans to starve when they might have been saved." U.S. policies require the shipment of U.S. produce in international food aid, thus benefiting American farmers. Furthermore, "food must be transported on U.S. flagged vessels benefiting U.S. ship operators" instead of transporting food from a location closer to the starving people that would expedite delivery and save lives. This is in contrast to policies of the European Union and Canada, which will use the closest possible location from which to buy and ship food during famine and international crises. As a senior policy advisor at Oxfam America, Gawain Kripke has noted, U.S. aid programs serve domestic interests more than the world's needy. The humanitarian figure of an U.S. citizen such as Jolie, however, makes such geopolitics invisible, and we as audiences can only feel pity toward (instead of anger about) the children dying in nations such as Ethiopia as we are unable to connect the deaths to larger global politics around food aid.

Transnational struggles over maternities and modernities are also imbricated in a politics of "compulsory heterosexuality."[19] In celebrity culture, white women who signify transnational motherhood are women whose bodies have generally circulated as sites of heteropatriarchal desire nationally and globally in popular culture. And the familial rescue they perform through adoption is usually a rescue into a *heterosexual* kinship structure. This is not surprising given that the political landscapes within which such media representations of global motherhood arise are already coercively heterosexual. In the United States, gay and lesbian adoption is explicitly banned by some states while many other states lack specific laws or court decisions regarding adoption by nonheterosexual couples. Potential gay and lesbian adoptive parents are in the hands of judges and adoption agencies. To date, no foreign nation (that is, foreign to the United States) has allowed open gay and lesbian adoption. To adopt, a gay or lesbian couple would have to remain closeted to adoption agencies domestically and internationally, for such agencies are often unwilling to work with the couple because of the numerous legal, political, and cultural challenges involved. Often only one partner often puts her/his name on adoption papers so that questions do not have to be explicitly answered to agencies about the sexual orientation of the potential adoptive family, which would have to be reported to the allied agencies in the nation where the potential adoptive child resides.

This imbrication of transnational maternal care in heterosexual racialized national forms was recently evident in the presidential campaign of John McCain in which we learned of Cindy McCain's adoption of a baby girl from Bangladesh several years ago. The story of a rescued Bangladeshi baby was utilized as evidence of McCain's character and family values. According to a 2008 *CNN Politics* report, McCain's campaign sent out mailings to South Carolina Republicans before the South Carolina primary that showed a picture of the baby in Cindy's arms with a nun from Mother Teresa's organization next to her.[20] The headline stated: "Rights of the Unborn for 24 Years." According to the report, Cindy used this story to moralize her husband's character: "When a mother comes home with a new child and . . . surprises him with a new baby from Bangladesh—and not only does he open his arms, he loves just like I do. . . . that says something about the character of a man." A Bangladeshi girl we hardly knew about was used to legitimize the character of a right-wing candidate and his family values. At this same time, however, McCain continued his stance against adoption by gay and lesbian families, claiming in an interview with George Stephanopoulos that "I am for the values that two parent families, traditional families represents."[21]

What makes this example particularly fascinating is how a deprived brown baby from the Global South is rescued by a traditional white conservative national family in the West and is rearticulated into a framework of white conservative heterosexual kinship logics. This not only illustrates a domestication of racial difference and transnational otherness, it also illustrates how the cultural politics of transnational maternity is often connected to heteropatriarchal nationalisms of the West, in which the white woman as a global mother performs a rescue function in which the rescued nonwhite non-Western baby is brought into *heterosexual familial scripts*. Colliding intersectional politics of race, gender, sexuality, nation, and transnationality play out in an ethics of care that ultimately buttresses white heteropatriarchal nationalist family values.

Infantilized Cosmopolitanism: The United Colors of Children

Today, a continental collecting of world's impoverished children is becoming a mode through which to represent and visualize a seamless global family in popular culture. In a recent interview, Angelina Jolie, on being asked about her frequent adoption of children from non-Western worlds, made the comment that yes, she was interested in exploring more adoption possibilities, and that she and Brad wanted to travel around the world to find babies from different countries to adopt. As Jolie put it in 2006 (as reported in the *Daily Mail*), "I want to create a rainbow family. That's children of different religions and cultures from different countries. I believe I am meant to find my children in the world and not necessarily have them genetically."[22]

Reports of how she and Brad were first planning to adopt in Russia and then changed their minds and adopted in Ethiopia, or how they were planning to adopt in India and how they would like to name a child adopted from India, *India* "to honor its homeland" shows the pervasiveness of an approach in which worldliness is itself infantilized and framed through an

Figure 4.6. Angelina Jolie's global rainbow (heterosexual) family. Note how the natural lighting has been used here to light up the family in the photo. This was the cover page of *People* on April 4, 2011. (PEOPLE © Time Inc. 2011. All rights reserved. Reproduced with permission.)

additive model in which collecting children becomes a way of assembling different national cultures. For instance, in another report, Jolie is quoted as considering further adoptions through the following statement: "Do you balance the race, so there's another African person in the house for Zahara, after another Asian person in the house for Mad [*sic*]? . . . We think so."[23] Similarly, when Madonna was accused of being racist during her adoption of baby David (seemingly flouting Malani adoption laws), she refuted such racism through a benign internationalism: "I don't worry about it [the charges of racism]. *I don't live in a white world; I live in the world*" (emphasis added).[24] In an interview with Oprah about how her own children were responding to her adoption she again erased racial difference and offered the hope of a color-blind global family when she stated, "they've [her natural children] never once mentioned the difference in his skin colour or questioned his presence in our life."[25]

The larger issue in such celebrations of global families and the recentering of white femininity that occurs in such celebrations has to do with the following question: What does the figure of the child enable in visions of worldliness that figures of adults do not? What logics are secured in such representations of children of the Global South in relation to the white mother? Visual regimes of global motherhood as symbolized by celebrity white women such as Diana or Jolie ultimately constitute symbolic exchanges and transactions between nations. Consequently, how the child figures in these representations becomes a crucial point to analyze, for the representation of the child makes a larger statement about the relationality between nations (and their domesticities) (Castaneda, 2002).

There are several possible responses to the issue of what the representation of the child as a sign around which a facile global family is imagined enables. First, such representation has to do with the psychic comfort generated by the trope of the native child in relation to the white mother.[26] The figure of the child does not represent a threat to our sense of self in the (white) West. It lacks agency. It cannot speak back, it is always "yet to be." As Castaneda (2002) notes, the "child is not only in the making but is also malleable—and so can be made" (p. 3). This is unlike the adult—who is a fully formed human being—whose adultness cannot so easily be stripped of its national and cultural history. In contrast, the child enables an easy dehistoricization.

Second is the issue of what Sara Ahmed (2004) calls "affective economies" (p. 117). Feelings, affects, emotions, Ahmed argues, are not merely psychic or psychological matters. Rather they work to "mediate the relationship" between "the psychic and the social, and between the individual and the collective" (p. 119). They function as sites of "bonding" through which na-

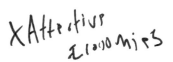

X Affective
    economies

tional and, in this case, transnational attachments are fostered. The child, as opposed to the adult, very easily functions as a love object and thus inspires affection and bonding in ways that the figure of the adult cannot. We can love the child of another nation and love it out of its history (in ways that we cannot for the adult, for to be a child is to be [seemingly] without much of a history). Consequently, feelings of "affection" and "care" that the figure of the child invites are also feelings that can be mobilized and articulated in the imagination of a loving (and dehistoricized) global family.

Such representations of infantilized cosmopolitanism are imbricated in the production of an internationalism (that rests on an additive and affective model) that Lisa Malkki (1994) has discussed as "romantic internationalism" (p. 49). Romantic internationalism, often working through cultural imagery of children of different nations, refers to sentimentalized evocations of a "common humanity" in which difference is domesticated, national inequalities are dehistoricized, and our attachments to the world are romanticized (as in tourism brochures or UNICEF greeting cards that use children of the world to wish us "peace on earth") (see also Banet-Weiser, 1999). Underlying such romantic internationalism, however, is also a sense of hate, a disgust that such facile touchy-feely internationalism conceals. One reason why we in the West can feel pity, compassion, and care for these starving, abandoned children is because we are also simultaneously invited to hate the conditions of their nations (which also influences our political attitudes toward them). We are meant to feel gratitude that we are not them. This underlying gratitude mobilizes our pity and speaks to our sense of superiority. Western national/colonial identities, while professing to forge imagined communities of global belonging through regimes of love and caring, have in reality too often forged imagined communities of belonging through hate and dislike. For without hate, disdain, dislike, narratives of global exceptionalism that are so central to the interiority of the Western national psyche are not fully possible. Consider how easily we make statements such as "I *hate* the poverty in the third world"; "I *hate* seeing diseased African children on television"; "I *hate* those barbaric terrorists"; "I *hate* the way women are oppressed in the Middle East"; "I *hate* seeing poor children in the third world"; and so on. In expressing such statements, one knows (and is grateful) that one is not like "them." And it is this knowing that enables one to position oneself through a narrative of love and caring for that other (whose social and national conditions one hates). Thus, underlying all the love—for instance for the adopted child, the abandoned child, or the sick poverty-stricken child—that the global white mother feels is always the troubling haunting of that original hate of that nation from which the adopted child may have been rescued, the abandoned child found a home, or the sick child given medical treatment. As Ahmed (2004) writes, "It is the emotional reading of hate that works to bind the imagined white subject and the nation together" (p. 118). And the irony is this: Our hatred of the original national conditions of the child always interrupts our capacity to seriously love it on an equal cultural level, for to love the child with dignity and equality (instead of patronizing love) is to love its nation and culture with dignity. Thus, while romantic internationalism mobilizes our love (in the West) as conditions of attachment to so-called third world nations, it also simultaneously mobilizes our underlying disgust for these nations.

Sara Ahmed's (2004) work on the cultural politics of emotions including love calls attention to the importance of recognizing love as site of cultural politics. What occurs in the name of love? What relations of power are forged and reproduced? Noting how the politics of love can function to secure a multicultural imagination in which loving the (host) nation (for example, by an adopted child, an immigrant, or an exile) as an ideal becomes a precondition of being recognized by the nation, Ahmed asks, "What happens when love is extended to others who are recognized as 'being different'" (p. 153)? And where others who are different are also expected to return the love of the nation that seemingly embraces them? While Ahmed's work is focused less on transnational connections, her provocative arguments are relevant in understanding how transnational connections of the nation, symbolized by the figure of the white woman, are often organized around love and the expected "return" of that love by the adopted native child (and hence the child's "original" nation). In discourses of adoption, for instance, the white mother who adopts the native non-Western child gives love in adoption but also receives the promise of the return of that love from the child that is adopted. But in this return of love, the child inevitably has to distance itself from (and perhaps even hate) its original maternal body (of the former nation that has abandoned it) for the dominant love is now (or is expected to be) toward the adopted mother (and therefore toward the mother's nation and culture). This is an affective politics of white femininity that reproduces a dangerous cosmopolitanism in which a nation (such as the United Kingdom or the United States) with a violent colonial history, recirculates its white postcolonial body through the redistribution of love as the logic of attachment to its national body. The white female body becomes a site of negotiation for two regimes of affects—racial love and racial hatred. It visibly performs the first and conceals the latter.

Third, the native adopted child, as a sign of its nation, also allows a *naturalization* of that nation. Consequently, the native adopted child is often used to promote an essentialist rhetoric that equates nations of the Global South with logics of naturalness. For example, a persistent visual trope through which abandoned children that Diana rescues or loves is that of the naked, seminaked, or the half-clothed child where the lack of clothing functions as a metaphor for a lack of care and civilization. Representations of seminaked bodies or even fully naked bodies reduce those bodies to a "natural" state (Malkki, 1994; Shohat & Stam, 1994). This naturalness consequently also situates those bodies (and the corresponding nation) in the realm of the primitive, outside of modern time.

This plays out for instance in a powerful episode in the documentary referred earlier—*Diary of a Princess* (1997)—that is based on Diana's travels in Angola. There is a segment "Road to Kikoko" that captures Diana's Red Cross jeep arriving at a health clinic. We are given visual shots of native African people dancing, swaying their half-clothed bodies and rear ends to the beat of drums. Such a representation reproduces age-old stereotypes about African bodies; the wild drumbeat essentializes and sexualizes those bodies through the trope of the primitive and the natural. And it is against the sound of the wild drumbeats that the *modern* jeep carrying Diana, the white woman, rolls into a village to visit a health clinic.

The narrative of the film is presented to us in a travelogue format, meta-phorically captured by the term *Diary*—a term that itself is gendered in that diary writing in colonial narratives has always been associated with upper-class white women of leisure. The colonial diary was also a site for recording and observing the exotic. The decision to use a travel narrative format is significant. Day 1 is titled "Road to Kikoko." Similarly, Day 2 and the other days are also entitled through such road metaphors. Travel narratives have historically been a mode for producing knowledge about others (Pratt, 1992). Yet, travel narratives of white people from Anglo-dominant nations are usually less about others and more about the audience back at "home"—the Anglo nation—who is invited to respond in particular ways to the knowledge about the natives being produced in the narrative. As the narrator (in this case, Diana as a cosmopolitan white woman) becomes the "eye" of her imperial nation for whom the narrative is being ultimately pro-duced, she renationalizes herself through the travelogue.

An interesting difference between colonial travel narratives—which were written travelogues—and contemporary media travel narratives, as is this documentary, is the issue of authority and credibility. In colonial literary travel narratives, the written form of the narrative could potentially be seen as a "lie"—we have access only to whatever the writer textually records. But today, mediated narratives provide what seems like "evidence"—in the form of moving pictures and scenes. Thus, they confer more authority on the subject recording the images—in this case Diana, as we view Africa through her eyes. Instead of the white male gaze of earlier colonial times, we now have the white female gaze recording and mediating other worlds in a spirit of global humanitarianism.

The Red Cross jeep in which Diana travels through the lands is visually prominent in the documentary. Every now and then, we see this tough-looking white jeep with its Red Cross sign tearing through dusty roads often playfully chased by half-clothed African children. As we witness this visual travel narrative, we cannot help but notice the symbolicity of the Red Cross. The Red Cross organization historically has been deeply entrenched in British colonialist enterprises and their militarisms. It emerged in the early part of the 20th century to medically assist war-torn soldiers during times of war. The Red Cross, in its humanitarianism, was ultimately a part of the imperial war machine. Thus, the Red Cross jeep in this era of postcolonial British humanitarianism is ironic. The jeep firmly establishes Diana as a British national subject who, while crossing global borders of despairs, does so with imperial instruments of the nation.

Representations of children in visual regimes of global motherhood often situate the child through particular stereotypical national markers where the condition of the child is equated with an essentialized cultural vision of that particular nation. For instance, the children that Diana visits in different parts of the world are represented through traditional dresses of their nations such that their bodies function as markers of national/regional difference against which the (universal) white female body of Diana can engage in the global display of children. In Figure 4.7, we seen an exotically dressed Indian child in a traditional cultural costume, which marks the region of India she is from, on Diana's lap. The child (and it is often female children who are depicted in their cultural clothing) carries the sign of her nation and region in her clothing. Regular everyday clothing of a simple skirt and blouse/shirt, or a dress, would not have enabled such a national signification.

Angelina Jolie also embraces this kind of an exotic touristic logic in her adoption of children when she notes to *People* magazine her fascination with adopting from different parts of the world: "There is something about making a choice, waking up and travelling somewhere and finding your family. . . . Sooner or later, I'll end up everywhere."[27] Jolie once stated in a CNN interview in 2006, "I loved Ethiopia, Brad loved Ethiopia . . . And so it just felt like a natural place to adopt."[28] In such comments, the native child becomes positioned as a route for the white woman to enter a particular culture and geography even while the child, in such representations, becomes "rooted" in that culture as it is often made to embody the stereotypical markers of its

Figure 4.7. Tour of India in 1992. (Rex USA. Reproduced with permission.)

national difference. One of the ultimate manifestations of such a logic of cultural and geographical rootedness that seems to underlie Jolie's global adoptive desires is the way in which she has recently transformed her body into a world map. On her left arm the geographical coordinates—the latitudes and longitudes—of the birth places of her different children have been tattooed (Figure 4.8). And media images constantly zoom in on this in their shots of Jolie. In this example, the white female upper-class heterosexual body of Jolie is literally recrafting itself as a global maternal body through the mapping of global coordinates of her children's birthplaces onto her body. And thus the white woman equals nation equation is now extended to become white woman equals the world itself. The white female upper-class body becomes the site through and upon which the contours of a harmonious global family are etched (or tattooed in Jolie's case). Further, the utilization of geographical coordinates to signify a global family reifies a colonial logic of place making. During European imperialism, geographical coordinates were first identified by explorers who wished to conquer particular lands and places. A desire for conquest of indigenous worlds usually preceded the task of producing geo-

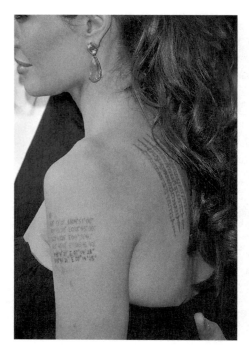

Figure 4.8. Angelina Jolie. Her arm displaying the tattoo with the geographical coordinates of her family. (Rex USA. Reproduced with permission.)

graphical coordinates necessary to plan an imperial expedition. Additionally, as many postcolonial geographers have suggested, the Cartesian perspective that informs the production of such geographical coordinates is based on a logic of universality where the coordinates become transcendental markers and even makers of place and time. In etching such geographical coordinates on her body, Jolie (whether aware or not) explicitly reifies a European colonial logic of conquest and invokes a fixed and transcendental notion of place and time in which the viewer—the colonial explorer or map maker (in this case Jolie)—remains somehow above place and time. It is from her (or his) vantage point that the world is being viewed. And such invocation of universality seems to occur at the very same time that Jolie proudly seems to assert the cosmopolitanism of her family.

Another egregious instance of infantilized cosmopolitanism, enacted through transnational white femininity, is Madonna's recently established charity Raising Malawi formed after her controversial adoption of baby David from Malawi. The charity is dedicated to improving lives of children in Malawi. The top section of the web page of the Raising Malawi charity features Madonna with African children. As in other images of white women, Madonna glows. The name Raising Malawi equates the nation of Malawi with a child, who now has to be "raised" by a parent (i.e., Madonna and by extension white femininity of the Global North). Child and this nation of the Global South here become absolute equivalents of each other producing an epistemic violence (Spivak, 1988) in which we are able to think of Malawi only as an abandoned child.

International adoption web sites catering to white women in the West too exhibit such infantilized and touristic logics. For example, the "Sponsor a Child" section of Children's International that is clearly targeted at white heterosexual families in the United States states, "At Children International, in our efforts to fight poverty, we unite sponsors with children around the world—bringing different nations and cultures together. So take a peek by clicking below and learn about the children and their countries, their traditions and their lives." When potential sponsors click on the image of a child from a country, they are directed to a section that provides a stereotypical cultural description of the traditions of that particular country (and less background of the child itself) from food and cultural festivals to language and social styles. One almost feels that one could be shopping for a tourist place to visit. In choosing to adopt a child, one chooses to affiliate oneself with a particular nation that may take one's fantasy. The child becomes a carrier of its national difference and it is this difference that is sold and marketed to international sponsors. Yahoo, for instance, even contains a directory of group lists devoted to potential adoption parents in the West. These lists bear names such as "Ichild" (for children from India), or "AdoptAfrica" (for adopting from Africa), or "Single-attach China" (for children from China).

A tension reveals itself here again that ruptures the seamless fantasy of a global family. On the one hand, the global mother promises a cosmopolitan humanism; on the other, this promise is ruptured by the symbolic (and not historical) embrace of the international child. As the child symbolizes an exoticized version of the nation that the global mother wishes to bring into her familial space, the child can never be too real, for to engage the child's reality fully is to confront its national history and its linkage with Western colonial relations.

An interesting point about such facile cosmopolitanism of children, shored up by celebrity white women, is how its representations contrast with that of domestic transracial adoption in Western nations such as the United States. In media culture, as well as larger everyday adoption narratives, international adoption or international humanitarian acts toward international children by white women receive far more recognition. And these adoptive acts are frequently exoticized. In contrast, there is far less desire to adopt domestic nonwhite children within the nation. And there is also limited representation of white women with domestic children of color in the nation. This was certainly the case with the Diana media archive. In my research, I found that many of the images of Diana with impoverished hungry children were children of the non-Western world or marginalized East European sites. Ortiz and Briggs (2003), explaining this as a feature that also plays out in adoption narratives, suggest that in discourses of transnational adoption there is a far greater sentimentalization, love, and pleasure attached to embracing a child from an other nation than from within the nation. One reason has to do with the fact that the discourse of underprivileged children within the nation is racialized in that children are seen to come from characterologically flawed and toxic families—where mothers may have been crack mothers raising children in environments infused by drugs and guns. These children are thus often seen as being psychologically damaged or flawed in terms of their character development.

In contrast, Ortiz and Briggs (2003) note, international children are usually not seen as characterologically flawed. While seen as poor, starving, abandoned by their poverty-stricken families, or physically unhealthy due to lack of proper health infrastructure, they are usually seen as innocent, docile, and simply in need of rescue by the modern family structures of Western nations. Underclass children (usually children of color) within the United Kingdom or United States, on the other hand, are seen as products of antisocial families that have rejected the citizenly values of their nations. Rita Soren, executive director for the Dave Thomas Foundation, confirmed this view when she noted to Fox News in the context of the United States (but it is relevant to other nations such as United Kingdom or other European nations) that more Americans go abroad to adopt instead of taking on domestic kids because "there is an idea that because these kids [domestic kids] come from unfortunate circumstances, that they are juvenile delinquents."[29] There is indeed a disproportionate celebration of international adoption in contrast to transracial adoptions within the nation. One famous celebrity case of interracial adoption within the nation is that of Sandra Bullock. In an April 2010 *People* cover image, we see Sandra Bullock with her adopted son. The baby is African American. And yet an exotic-looking beaded necklace that is associated with African handicraft is deliberately strung around the baby's neck in order to exoticize it, perhaps producing a fantasy of an African baby. Just with a beaded necklace, an African American baby becomes geographically moved to, and fixed by, the continent of Africa, in ways that ironically betray the baby (and by extension the African American community). The adopted baby is not seen as American. Rather, through the beaded necklace, we are invited to associate it with its supposed origins—Africa. This also revives a slave narrative and projects it onto the adopted African American child. This problematic image reinforces white women's fascination with the specter of a black African child—bringing light to the "dark continent." Indeed, one problem of the rhetoric of international adoption is the way in which it resurrects a discourse of racial and national origins, based upon which the Western mother then chooses her adoptive child.

What must additionally be noted is how this discourse of transnational/transracial adoption often functions as an instrument for the rehabilitation of damaged lives of such privileged white women who adopt. Negra (2010) writes that such family ties (in adoption) not only confer "significant forms of identity capital," they also "recuperate" and "stabilize" any "identity crisis" that the white woman may be undergoing. Such multicultural or transnational adoptions thus also enable the solidification of "narratives of motherhood as recovery" (p. 60). The children become routes and passages for the white female upper-class self to remoralize and revitalize itself.[30] Bullock's new black baby has been presented in the media as giving her a new life of joy that enabled her to move beyond the betrayal of her working-class—white trash—husband Jesse James who reportedly was never comfortable in Bullock's privileged world. An interesting fact is that often the visual coverage of Jesse James calls attention to his heavily tattooed arm—just so that we, the audience, know he is white trash. In Bullock's case, we see a significant collision of class and race through which her white womanhood is salvaged. Adopting a black baby enables her to move away from the white trash Jesse James.

We also saw a similar pattern with Angelina Jolie.[31] Wild girl, bad girl, always on the high, sexually reckless, and emotionally disturbed are themes through which Jolie existed for us before her adoptive motherhood phase. But once she started collecting children from Africa and Asia, these children became routes through which she became (positioned) as the super mother of the 21st century. Indeed, it is worth noting that the place on her left arm on which Jolie now bears the geographical coordinates of the birthplaces of her children previously carried the name Billy Bob—her ex-husband—who like Jolie also had a wild and "bad boy" image. The Billy Bob tattoo has now been erased to make room for the coordinates of her global family. Thus, black and brown babies constitute the grounds upon which the maternal agency of privileged white women are resecured and their lives rehabilitated. They also constitute the terrain upon which privileged white women carve new possibilities for their selves and futures.

Conclusion

On September 1, 1997, the *Daily Mail* ran a special 80-page supplement devoted to Diana's memory (see Figure 4.1). The double-page spread centerfold consisted of numerous images of Diana with children from all over the world. The bold and loud caption declared, "now she could be a mother to the world." This centerfold was preceded by several double-page spreads replete with iconic images of Diana through which her emergence as a national subject—from days of her courtship, marriage, pregnancy (which is interestingly framed as "nation expects") and modern motherhood—was charted. And then followed the centerfold, with the headline "now she could be a mother to the world." The strange temporality invoked in the word *now* has intrigued me for sometime. Why *now* she could be a mother to the world? Why not just "she could be a mother to the world"? What is the *now* stabilizing or fixing? Clearly, the word *now* serves an important rhetorical function. When we read this in relation to the trajectory of Diana's development as a national subject that the newspaper supplement charts, it seems to assert some important claims about white motherhood in relation to the global that are worth unpacking as a conclusive comment to this chapter.

The temporality of the *now* seems to suggest that the white mother's intimate attachment to a global domesticity can be permitted *after* she has served as a maternal figure for/in her own nation. Diana can now be a global mother because her body has first been attached to the nation's familial future—through her motherly love of William and Harry. What is to be especially remarked upon is that the kind of transnational motherhood that the likes of Princess Diana and privileged white women who cross borders today perform is in stark contrast to the realities of forced regimes of transnational motherhood that also mark the late 20th and early 21st centuries. Impoverished migrant mothers from the Global South are often forced to leave their nations to earn money and take on caretaker positions for families in the Global North. For such global mothers, there is no seamless harmony between the nation and the global. There is no "*now* she can be a mother to the world." Rather, their imbrication in transnational maternity interrupts their ability to be desirable national mothers to their nation. Such mothers are not celebrated in media regimes. They are frequently coded as having "abandoned" their children and by extension their nation. They are "bad mothers." Yet they signify the unacknowledged realities of transnational maternities in our times.

This chapter has highlighted how representations of global motherhood function to renationalize white femininity (and by extension the nation) through seemingly postimperial cosmopolitan humanitarian logics. It has also illustrated how transnational intimacies written, celebrated, and absorbed through the logic of white global motherhood render invisible the realities of many other forms of transnational motherhood that are located in the brutal excesses of flexible neoliberal capitalism and its violent ethics of care. Finally, the discussion offered in this chapter invites us to ask how whiteness—in particular the white heterosexual family form—today is being bolstered by, and remaking itself through, particular kinds of transnational flows of children who occupy positions of extreme global otherness.

5. White Femininity and Transnational Masculinit(ies)

Desire and the "Muslim Man"

Did they really kill her because the establishment would not have a Muslim stepfather to the future king of England? Was MI-6 involved in her killing? Was she really pregnant with his baby, a Muslim baby? Was Mohammed Al Fayed really getting back at the establishment through the Diana-Dodi romance for having been denied citizenship? Did she really have another secret Muslim lover? These are the kinds of questions I have encountered when discussing this project with people. This slice of Diana's life has probably been the one that has most titillated people. The scenario evoked by the questions certainly carries the juicy flavors of a Hollywood thriller or a Harlequin desert romance—complete with the playboy sheikh and his patriarchal father, the blonde princess and the Arab lover, Mediterranean cruises and car chases, forbidden loves and conspiracy theories, and then the mythic finale: the meeting of the cross-faith star-crossed lovers in heaven that could not occur on earth.[1]

The scenario is neither Hollywood nor Harlequin. It reflects a charged narrative through which the last days of one of the most visualized women of the 20th century was given meaning. Of all the various aspects of white womanhood that the Diana phenomenon brings to the fore, the one that has most intrigued me is this element where white femininity becomes a transnationalized battleground between Muslim masculinity and Anglo-national patriarchy. This aspect of white femininity that the Diana phenomenon illustrates reveals how, in the battle over national modernities, Muslim masculinity is often evaluated and represented through the lens of white femininity in globally dominant fields of representations. It is almost as if Muslim masculinities do not have any independence on their own; any time Muslim men are evoked, the white woman always lurks somewhere—visibly or not so visibly. It is this aspect that I wish to focus on here—*how framings of Muslim men in Western popular culture are mediated through the figure of the white woman; how such framings keep alive particular logics of a "Muslim man" that (Western) nations need in order to assert their own national selves; and how such representations tell us as much about "Muslim masculinity" as they do about Anglo patriarchy.* The history of geopolitics, since the Crusades, has taught us that Anglo Christian patriarchy has always defined itself (without marking itself as such) by constructing Muslim men in particular ways. Central to that construction have been particular imaginations of white women in relation to the Muslim male other that then easily enables the West to construct the Muslim male as a national enemy—potential or established. In our times—the late 20th and early 21st centuries—representations of Muslim men with whom Diana allegedly had affairs provide us with some of the richest contemporary images of Muslim men in a nationalized media phenomenon that was organized around the dead/alive body of a white upper-class heterosexually identified British woman. I say richest because these representations exist within a frame of celebrity glamour that the Diana phenomenon evokes—thus seducing us far more easily into their narrative structure than do representations of Muslim men as terrorists—which tend to have more of an exceptional quality to them.

Although much has been written about representations of Muslim women in contemporary Western media—evidenced by the plethora of work on veiling—little has been discussed about representations of Muslim masculinities—beyond the framework of the "terrorist." Through what meanings are Muslim masculinities framed in Western media? What geopolitical purposes do those framings serve? In one of the few critical studies that exist of Muslim men, Katherine Ewing (2008) states that

> with all the attention directed at the Muslim woman as victim, no one has stopped to investigate how the Muslim man has been depicted. . . . These representations. . . . play a major role in the political processes in many European countries shaping public policy, citizenship legislation, and the course of elections. (p. 2)

While Hollywood screens have consistently used the logic of the terrorist to frame Muslim masculinity—as Jack Shaheen's (2001) work has demonstrated—not much has been done to examine some of the other ways in which a racially, religious, and geopolitically charged assemblage called the "Muslim man" or Arab (since these categories collapse in our reductive orientalist fantasies) acquire meaning and become reduced to a monolith. Although scholars such as Edward Said, Ella Shohat, and Jack Shaheen, among others, have offered insights into the construction of the Muslim/Arab man in Western culture, overall the body of work focused solely on representations of Muslim masculinity is still limited. While this book is not exclusively about Muslim masculinity, in devoting an entire chapter to this topic, this project invites a greater investigation of this subject. Indeed, it is important to understand how the extreme logics through which the construct of the *Muslim "terrorist"* is represented are the same as ones that also inform non-terrorist and seemingly benign representations of Muslim men. It is just a matter of being positioned differently on the spectrum. Further, examining representations of Muslim men in relation to white femininity enables us to perform the critical task of provincializing European men. As Ewing notes, probing representations of Muslim men "parochializes images of the modern Western man, challenging their foundation in a universalized understanding of modernity by questioning the contrasts . . ." (2008, p. 28).[2]

Images, we know, create visual fields upon which larger cultural politics and geopolitics play out. Images are simultaneously visual fields that are outcomes of geopolitics. Minoo Moallem writes that "storing, organizing and transmitting meaning by means of writing and images . . . is as fundamental as the production and storage of wealth" (1999, p. 320). The relentless image making of the Muslim male in various popular and political cultural sites in globally dominant regimes of representations is also about the production and storage of "wealth"—a kind of cultural, religious, and racial capital (in which white femininity figures significantly) that can be drawn upon as evidence of how "*they* are" whenever things become geopolitically sensitive in Western nations' relations with the Muslim world. This chapter argues that a significant way in which Western national imaginaries engage Muslim masculinity is through the figure of the white woman. In this engagement, Muslim masculinity acquires its meanings through how white womanhood is perceived in relation to it. White femininity, as a multilayered and multimodal transnational script, is intimately entangled with geopolitically dominant scripts of Muslim masculinity. The primary focus of this chapter is on how the Fayeds (and Hasnat Khan, Diana's "real love") were represented by the media and how those representations invoked age-old stereotypes of Muslim men.

In the geopolitically charged representational minefields of the late 20th and early 21st centuries, to invoke the Muslim man—even benignly—is to invoke geopolitics and nationalism. For instance, after Diana's death, the press in the Middle East saw the death as a murder. A film called the *The Last Supper* by Egyptian director Khairi Beshera (whose work is well known in European festivals) that was based on the Diana-Dodi subject was in the works (although I have not found any reports confirming whether it was finally produced). According to Associated Press writer Nasrawi, the director's reason for wanting to make the film was stated as follows: "the notion that she [Diana] was killed because she was about to convert to Islam to wed Egyptian Dodi Fayed . . . is too popular [in Eygpt] to ignore" (Nasrawi, 1997). Other Muslim media personnel such as Anis Mansour of the Egyptian daily *Al Ahram* stated that British intelligence killed Diana "just like the CIA killed Marilyn Monroe."[3] This is because she chose a Muslim man "with the possibility of having a child called Mohammad . . . to be the brother of Britain's crown prince. . . ."[4] The Iranian press broke its usual silence when its women's magazine *Zan'e Ruz* (*Today's Woman*) claimed the same.[5] Many Middle East newspapers such as the Egyptian government newspaper *Al Akhbar* celebrated the notion that an Egyptian (Dodi) had won the "gold medal" (Diana) in the "Olympic game of love."[6]

Colonel Gaddafi of Libya took all these steps further. He linked Diana's and Dodi's deaths to the Lockerbie case. When two Libyans were accused of blowing up a Pan Am flight in 1988 over Lockerbie, Scotland, Gaddafi had been reluctant to hand over the suspects to the British and Americans. Gaddafi is supposed to have argued that such a handover could occur only after the allegation of the Diana-Dodi murder by the British establishment was investigated.[7] Although things did not pan out the way Gadaffi wanted, the geopolitical currents giving meaning to Diana's and Dodi's deaths far exceeded a pretty, sunny Mediterranean romance. It illustrated that when a white upper-class British woman comes close to a Muslim man, larger global politics over "civilization" can become activated. On September 1, 1997 (the day after Diana's and Dodi's deaths), Gadaffi boldly stated in a Libyan television address that

> Britain does not have a constitution. . . . yet is given as an example of a civilized country. . . . The crime committed yesterday [Di's and Dodi's deaths] is but an example. It was one of the most repulsive racist acts; an anti-Islamic and anti-Arab act; an act against Islam. . . . They [the British] no longer have any right to talk about terrorism or human rights.[8]

I have offered some details of the reactions of the Muslim world because they were rarely made visible to us in the global (yet British) love fest that followed Diana's death. We were not allowed to see how a battle over national patriarchies and modernity was playing out over the dead, yet symbolically alive, body of a white British woman. This was also borne out on the British side, as the rest of the chapter illustrates through an analysis of the racist media framings of the Fayeds. But more explicitly, reports tell us that Tony Blair had directly advised Diana to stay away from the Fayeds and that Prince

William at that time in 1997 was horrified and "did not think that Mr Al Fayed was good for his mother."[9]

In light of all this, it is difficult to read the Diana and Dodi romance as evidence of cosmopolitanism of a New Britain as cultural studies scholar Mica Nava (2007) suggests. Although after Diana's death, tributes were left for both Diana and Dodi—suggesting that some people at an individual level were willing to embrace a more cosmopolitan future (as Nava suggests)—it is important to note that when we analyze media narratives about Diana and Dodi in the *context* of the anti-Muslim climate of Britain in the 1990s (which I detail shortly), it is difficult to see a serious cosmopolitanism at work in the Di and Dodi phenomenon. In fact, in 1990s Britain, there was a heightening of anti-Muslim attitudes. The thing is that any individualized coming together of a white woman and a Muslim man is not necessarily cosmopolitanism. Rather, *how* the relationship is framed, within *what social/national context, and with what consequences, is a more important matter.* It is the positionality, politics, and the power relations of the interracial interreligious mixing and not just the *fact* of mixing of white Christian and Muslim national cultures that makes something cosmopolitan or not. Cosmopolitanism is not colorful global identity politics. Ultimately, it has to do with a mindset and national ethos that can embrace a serious and even uncomfortable worldliness through which the other is radically allowed to penetrate, disturb, unsettle, and even rework the cultural fabrics of the people.

In 1999, Alison Jackson, English photographer, produced fantasy photographs (Figure 5.1) showing Diana and Dodi with a mixed-race child. I have reproduced one such image. This caused strong reactions.

In her book *Visceral Cosmopolitanism*, Mica Nava (2007) uses this photo of Jackson's to suggest that

Figure 5.1. Fantasy image of Diana, Dodi, and a mixed-race baby produced by photographer Alison Jackson. (Copyright Alison Jackson. Reproduced with permission.)

maybe a child of Diana and Dodi, mixed race half sibling to the future king would have done the trick. It would certainly have confirmed Britain's new sense of self . . . The modern rainbow nation . . . would have been not just a multicultural nation . . . but a postcolonial one where the descendants of the colonizers can no longer be distinguished from the descendants of the colonized. . . . (p. 127)

Mica Nava's reading of the Diana and Dodi romance, in my view, misses the point about cosmopolitanism. Like arguments about "postracialism" floating around in the United States since Obama's entry into the White House, such a reading seems to minimize the structural inequalities that persisted in 1990s Britain and even today. What I have been struck by in my research is how the Diana–Dodi Fayed relationship (and less so the Hasnat Khan relationship—Diana's apparent real love) was framed through some of the same old barbaric narratives through which Muslim leaders, dictators, and Middle Eastern sheikhs have been historically framed in Western popular culture. There is no doubt that in recent years white female national and global icons, in turning to Muslim men or converting to Islam, have shaken certain boundaries of their national belonging (for example, Jemima Khan [British heiress and ex-wife of Pakistani politician Imran Khan], Yvonne Ridley [journalist], Kristiane Backer [MTV anchor], Myriam Cerrah [a model], and Sarah Joseph [founder and editor of Emel, a British magazine celebrating Muslim life] among others).[10] Diana's action as an *individual* white woman was certainly brave and subversive within her context. But it also allowed a particular *renationalization* that fit the rhetoric of the New Labor, in that it (falsely) suggested the arrival of a multicultural postcolonial Britain that easily became attached to New Labor's shallow vision of a postimperial New Britain. Furthermore, it is easier to claim a cosmopolitan vision when the actors are dead. There is comfort in the fact that we do not have to confront their physicality. Once we have moved them to the celestial sphere, we can construct any and all stories of cosmopolitanism from them (and we did so after Diana's and Dodi's deaths). Indeed, one wonders whether New Labor's multicultural rhetoric of the late 1990s would so easily have articulated Diana's cultural crossings had she really married one of her Muslim lovers and, in the process, demolished the very Protestant Anglo basis of Britishness.

National Sentiments Toward Muslims in Britain in the 1990s

Before proceeding with my analysis of the Muslim men–white women dialectic, I want to provide the reader with a sense of the British national context of the 1990s with regard to Muslims. This will help us contextualize the representations of Diana's relationship with Muslim men so that we can better understand how impossible the times were for seriously engaging with Muslims in a dignified way. It will also enable us to challenge a perception that grew in some scholarly and journalistic quarters after Diana's death—that her relationships with Muslim men illustrated a growing cosmopolitanism in Britain that converged with the postimperial rhetoric being spun by the incoming New Labor administration.

Islamophobia without Apologies

Despite the collapse of the monoculturalism of Thatcherism and the gradual emergence of a self-proclaimed cosmopolitanism of New Labor in the mid-1990s, the decade of the 1990s was anything but hospitable for Muslims in the United Kingdom. There were many reasons for this. The year 1989 had given rise to the Rushdie affair. Khomeini, the Iranian religious leader at that time, issued a fatwa on Rushdie, a British Muslim citizen, for publishing *The Satanic Verses* (1988). As a result, the general outrage on the part of many Muslims toward what they considered blasphemy secured a view in the United Kingdom, and the rest of the Western world, that Islam was about the lack of free speech, fundamentalism, and irrationality. The Rushdie affair expressed a fundamental fear and loathing that the British society already had toward Muslims. Whereas Rushdie's free speech and artistic license were considered absolute by the Western press, the same Western media vilified demonstrations by the Muslim community. As a report by the Islamic Human Rights Commission (2002) stated: "Whilst Rushdie's right to free speech was deemed absolute, Muslims' right to hold not just 'extreme views' but political values has been continuously undermined. . . ."[11] Since the Rushdie affair, media demonization of Muslims was reflected also in national reactions to the Oklahoma City bombing in 1995. We have to remember that until one learned later that the bombing had been carried out by a white man, Timothy McVeigh, the initial nationwide reaction in the United States clearly assumed the hand of a Muslim terrorist. At that time, Bernard Levin of the *Times* wrote the following:

> We do not know who primed and put the Oklahoma bomb in its place; we do know that they were in the fullest meaning of the word fanatics. . . . Do you realise that in perhaps, half a century, not more and perhaps a good deal less, there will be wars in which fanatical Muslims will be winning? As for Oklahoma it will be called Khartoum-on-the-Mississippi, and woe betide anyone who calls it anything else.[12]

For our purpose, it is important to note a particular moment in this anti-Muslim British ethos of the 1990s. In October 1997 (a month after the spectacle of Diana's funeral), the Runnymede Trust's "Report of the Commission on British Muslims and Islamophobia" was launched.[13] The report concluded that Muslims in the United Kingdom faced deep prejudice in all quarters of society. As the first major study of "Islamophobia" in the United Kingdom (the term has become commonplace after this study), the report asserted that a new legal framework of "religious violence," along with the existing racial violence framework, was needed to protect Muslims. The feeling was that racial violence framework does not cover religious discrimination. At the launch of this highly anticipated report, the New Labor Home Secretary Jack Straw, while agreeing that the matter was "difficult and sensitive," asserted that legislation creating *anti-religious* discrimination was not the answer. When asked about the continuous media criminalizing of Muslims and what it would take to urge the media to be responsible in its treatment of Muslims, Straw could only weakly suggest greater self-regulation by media and trusting the media's good intentions. Straw, a New Labor honcho, wanted to avoid the matter, although he did not deny that it was a difficult issue.

Right after the Runnymede report was launched, journalist Polly Toynbee wrote an article in the *Independent* headlined "In defence of Islamophobia: Religion and the State," which became famous. Toynbee opened the article declaring proudly, "I am an Islamophobe" and that "I judge Islam not by its words—the teachings of Koran interpreted by those Thought-for-the Day moderate Islamic theologians. I judge Islam by the religion's deeds in the societies where it dominates. Does that make me a racist?" (Toynbee, 1997, p. 23). Criticizing the Runnymede report—and in particular its claim that Islam is prejudicially perceived in British society as "barbaric, irrational, primitive, and sexist"—Toynbee argued that that if people held such a view of Islam, then it is understandable given that it is "a religion that describes women as of inferior status, placing them one step behind in the divine order of things. That is not equally worthy of respect" (p. 23). Toynbee made no effort to offer actual religious evidence from Islamic scriptures and texts to support the claims.

Another significant incident of the 1990s was the terror attack at Luxor, Egypt, in 1997 at the 3,400-year-old Temple of Hatshepsu that killed 58 foreigners and resulted in further intensification of anti-Muslim hatred in the United Kingdom. An Islamic "militant" group was seen as being behind this attack. With the Luxor massacre, the press squarely used national *security* as a theme with which to vilify Islam (Richardson, 2004). Richardson, in his marvelous analysis of the British press's treatment of Islam, quotes from a *Daily Telegraph* editorial of November 1997. The editorial stated, "there are too many people resident [*sic*] in this country who use British liberty to take liberties." And that these people, are "Middle Eastern and Far East Asian students" who come to the United Kingdom because of "indiscriminate recruitment" (cited in Richardson, 2004, p. 132).

While space does not permit a more detailed discussion of the anti-Muslim ethos in the United Kingdom in the 1990s, the preceding discussion provides a context within which to situate the media narratives about the Fayeds so that we can see how they draw upon the anti-Muslim sentiments of the times, thus betraying a rhetoric of cosmopolitanism.

The White Woman and the Muslim Man: At the Limits of the Nation

In what follows, I discuss how sexuality, sexual relations, and mental perversity function as optics through which the Muslim male is depicted in relation to white women in the Diana phenomenon and popular culture at large. It is quite surprising that despite the work that exists on Diana, there has been little scholarship on media's representations of the Fayeds as "typical Muslim" men who are outside of reason and civilization. The representations of the Fayeds in the Diana phenomenon are important to analyze because Diana was one of the first celebrity white woman of our times who came intimately close to Muslim/Arab men, and out of her own choice. How is the Muslim man in such instances represented? This is not only a popular culture question but also geopolitical one. I address how representations of the Fayeds recycle age-old themes through which Western imaginaries have depicted Muslim men. The trope of the playboy sheikh, the theme of perverse Muslim male sexuality, and the madness of Muslim men are three motifs that will be discussed here to illustrate how white femininity becomes a standpoint against which these motifs are given life.

Western popular culture has a long history of looking at Muslim men (and by extension Islamic cultures) through the lens of white women. Early films such as *Sheikh* (1921), *The Arab* (1915), *Captured by Bedouins* (1912), *The Thief of Baghdad* (1924) and more contemporary films such as *Sex and the City 2* (STC2) (2010), *Sahara* (1983), *Not Without My Daughter* (1991), *The Siege,* (1998), *The Mummy* (1999), *Patriot Games* (1992), *True Lies (1994),* *Sheltering the Sky* (1990), as well as the 2009 representations of the Muslim U.S. army psychiatrist, Nidal Hassan, who gunned down individuals on the Fort Hood, Texas, military campus, are only a few examples.[14] Jessica Taylor (2007) argues that although romance novels in North America rarely have nonwhite heroes or heroines, the one time this logic breaks is when the genre of "sheikh romance" is produced, where typically a white woman falls in love with, or is seduced by, a dark exotic Arab or Muslim Sheikh. Taylor notes that at least every month one novel in this genre is produced. So the white woman–Arab or Muslim man dynamic has been very alive in Western popular culture. Yet, it has hardly been theorized in a developed way as transnational politics.

The last couple of decades have witnessed quite a few celebrity cases of white Western women romancing or marrying Muslim men or converting to Islam. Princess Diana's case was one of the most visible in that her romances became caught in a larger cultural politics over national identity and multicultural belonging in Britain. But there have been others as well, as indicated earlier: Jemima Khan and her marriage to handsome ex-Pakistani cricketer turned politician Imran Khan, and Queen Noor of Jordan. Queen Noor is of mixed descent—Swedish and Syrian—but she grew up an "all American girl" who ultimately fell in love with the dashing King of Jordan. More recently, Lauren Booth, Cherie Blair's sister, converted to Islam. Then there is also Kristiane Backer, the anchor of MTV Europe who grew up in Germany and later lived in London. Under the influence of her former friend Pakistani cricketer Imran Khan (as discussed in her book *From MTV to Mecca*, 2012), she found herself drawn to Islam. From North America, the two famous cases are Nicole Queen—a fashion photographer—from Texas and Ingrid Mattson from Canada. Mattson was the first convert to lead the Islamic Society of North America. There is also the intriguing example of the British white woman Yvonne Ridley who was captured by the Taliban in 2001. They then released her but asked her to read the Koran. She apparently did, and in the process found tremendous value in Islam and converted. Some Western reporters labeled her conversion as exhibiting the psychological Stockholm syndrome, where one becomes dependent on or attached to one's captor. The possibility that she may truly have found something of value in the Koran seems too difficult for them to accept. Recent journalistic reports and research surveys in the United Kingdom have also noted an emerging trend of white British women converting to Islam.[15]

I do not suggest that the situation of every white woman turning to Islam or embracing Muslim men is the same. Nor am I interested in the individual motives that lead white women to associate with Islam and/or become intimate with Muslim men. What is more interesting to me is how Muslim men or Islamic cultures are represented vis-à-vis white women and what representational roles white women play in narrativizing Muslim cultures for our Western national imaginations. Additionally, as Nilufer Gole (2011) has argued, the matter of Islam is very much a European matter. "We must therefore focus on this zone of contact and confrontation in order to study the relationship between Islam and Europe" (p. 31). Although Gole rightly marks Europe, her point can be extended to many North Atlantic nations today for *how* we—in the West (and beyond)—frame zones of contact with Muslims is one of the most urgent matters of our times. Celebrity images and popular cultural interactions are as important as any to analyze in the geopolitical relationship between Islam and the West, given the seductive power of popular and celebrity culture.

The works of Edward Said, Ella Shohat, Reina Lewis, Rana Kabbani, Leila Abu Lughod, and Meyda Yegenoglu, among others, have demonstrated how Orientalist discourses have often been organized around sexuality and desire—which then function to racialize, temporalize, and spatialize (as belonging to dark sinister geographies) Muslim cultures. Ella Shohat (2011) has especially argued that in representations of white women with Arabs (and also men of other national origins), there is often a displacement of white male heterosexual desires onto the Muslim male. The argument here has a psychoanalytic leaning: Those suppressed desires that the Western white man cannot enact under the lid of "civilization" become projected and displaced onto the Arab/Muslim male. The Arab man, or we can say the Muslim man— as these two distinct categories are usually conflated—becomes the "id" in relation to the "Western masculinist superego" (p. 57). Thus, the rape fantasy, the sexual fantasy, the narrative of capture of the white woman, the narrative of the sexually perverted Muslim male, and so on, which have been frozen on Hollywood screens, tell us as much about Western popular culture's views of white Muslim/Arab men as they do about white patriarchal (forbidden) desires themselves. In the Diana phenomenon, this played out particularly in representations of the Fayeds—the family so disliked by the establishment and constantly denied citizenship (as was Al Fayed Sr.).

During the Diana inquest, we learned that Diana's birth mother, Frances Shand Kydd, had humiliated the princess by calling her a whore who slept with Muslim men (English & Harris, 2008). This was revealed by her butler Paul Burrell. Newspapers went berserk publishing this information: "Diana's mother called her a whore for sleeping with Muslim men" screamed the *Daily Mail* on its online site.[16] Many other papers pretty much headlined the same way. I begin with this because if in 2008, the press could still manage to titillate its readers by being able to scream Diana's status as "a fallen" woman who was corporeally and symbolically penetrated by Muslim men, then it does suggest that after *all* the multicultural hype about New Britain in the 1990s, the image of a degraded sexual Muslim man (i.e., Dodi) is what people could still latch on to.

Something that I have noted in scanning numerous images of Diana is that she rarely looks sinister, remote, or dangerous. She may look defiant, depressed, or sad, but she always looks beautiful, radiating warmth and care even when looking unhappy. One image, which is relevant to our topic here, is the exception. In 2000, Granada published what became an international best seller written by Kate Snell titled *Diana: Her Last Love* (2000). The book is primarily about Diana's relationship with the then little-known Muslim Pakistani doctor Hasnat Khan, although it also deals with the Dodi Fayed romance. The cover visual of the book is significant. The image is actually from one of Diana's trips with the Fayeds to St. Tropez. Her animal-print swimsuit, wet hair pulled back, dark glasses staring at us from a distance, arms crossed over her chest (suggesting perhaps "do not come near me") make her look sinister and remote even though glamorous. The animal-print suit evokes danger and wildness (e.g., degradation). Diana seems to be look-ing at us from forbidden territories—reified also by the visual of the barred window at the back. In contrast to white women glowing in images discussed in previous chapters, in this image she is darkened. This image caught my attention because despite Snell's story of Diana's "real love" for the gentle and noble Pakistani doctor Hasnat Khan, the cover image somehow seems to produce a different narrative—one of a woman embodying danger. And while the title is about her "last love," the cover visual is from a scene with her holidays with the Fayeds in the Mediterranean.

Although white womanhood can become "fallen" and "degraded" via as-sociations with Muslim men, the reverse is hardly true in Western imagina-tions: A white man marrying a Muslim woman does not make the Muslim woman a fallen woman—rather she climbs *up* in social perception. Her proximity to the white man makes her safe (she is away from those barbaric men) and somewhat understandable to the Western imaginary for she has moved toward rationality and freedom. This illustrates another logic of white masculinity in relation to other masculinities: The white (heterosexual) man never moves from his position of modernity. He is fixed by it; he is it. On the contrary, the white woman, depending on her proximity to particular masculinities, can occupy a range of positions from virtuosity to degradation. This is why, as I indicated in Chapter 1, white femininity, in a given moment, can occupy a range of contradictory positions. And those positions are often outcomes of how far the white woman is seen to have moved away from white heteropatriarchal nationalized masculinity toward other masculinities.

If the white woman becomes a fallen woman by associating with the Muslim man, then the Muslim man has to be examined. What is it about how we understand him that invites us to see a white woman as a whore when she comes close to him? The "it" is his sexuality. One of the important contributions of Edward Said's *Orientalism* (1978) is his discussion of how the sexuality of Muslims is something that has obsessed Europeans and informed the works of many novelists and artists. In this obsession which, Said suggests, reveals much about the intense regulation, disciplining, and institutionalization of sex in Europe from the 18th century (that Foucault had also critiqued—without however referring to Muslims), the Muslim man was frequently seen as crazed, deviant, and a threat. And all these deviances that prevented him from being seen as a full civilized human being, despite wealth and riches, were frequently explained by his sexuality, just as his sexuality would be frequently explained by the pathologies of his mind and character.

Jasbir Puar, in her excellent work (2007) on the Abu Ghraib scandal, has discussed how particular historical constructions of the Muslim body as sexually pathological is what enables that body to be so easily violated by Western practices of torture. The body can be easily turned into an object of torture. As the place of forbidden and pathological sex, the "Orient is the site of carefully suppressed animalistic, perverse, homo- and hypersexual instincts. This paradox is at the heart of Orientalist notions of sexuality that are reanimated through *the transnational production of the Muslim terrorist as torture object*" (p. 87; emphasis added). Indeed, even though in racializing others, sexuality has always been an issue (consider, for example, the myth of black male hypersexuality or the desexualization of East Asian men), no other group perhaps has had their sexuality be so literally and violently linked to global politics as the Muslim male. Black men, for instance, were owned by the white masters. Hence, once they arrived from slave migrations, they were contained and chained within national/racial boundaries. But Muslims were hardly directly owned that way by Westerners. In fact, especially in the latter part of the 20th century, as rich Middle Eastern Muslims began to buy property and wealth in the postcolonial economies of the West, Muslim masculinity became more and more of a threat. While Western economies today remain financially dependent on the Middle East in many ways, the West however cannot culturally accept the Muslim man as a social equal, for that acceptance would mean having to write a different future for the world.[17] One way in which this anxiety about the Muslim male—and his ability to penetrate Western economies today—is expressed is through the pathologization of his sexuality where that sexuality ironically also becomes an object of perverse fascination (by the West)—and consequently an abstraction. I say abstraction, because in Western representations, Muslim sexuality becomes so dehistoricized and decontextualized that it seems to lack any variation and historical specificity. Muslim male sexuality ironically becomes reduced to an object that is constituted in and through Western representations. In fact, it would not be inaccurate to say that Muslim male sexuality, as we in the West are given to understand it, does not exist a priori; it acquires meaning only through (Western) representations.

Playboy Sheikh

In representations of the Fayeds, age-old themes of sexual Orientalism of Muslim masculinity are visible. For instance, a prevalent theme is the rich sheikh playboy.[18] Dodi Fayed is depicted as a rich playboy who has romanced a bevy of white female celebrities but lacks commitment or responsibility for a serious relationship. This is the theme we encounter repeatedly in press reports. We learn, as described in a famous *Vanity Fair* December 1997 exposé of Dodi by Sally Bedell Smith, titled "Dodi's Life in the Fast Lane," that Dodi was a "man/child": not very grown up.[19] He was boyish, gentle, had all kinds of toys, and was fully dependent on his father financially and for his personal life. Dodi sought famous white women, we learn, to give himself importance. We are also told that he lacked "any real professional distinction" and "defined himself by women—the more famous and beautiful the better." His attitude was the bigger (in fame) these women were, the better they "reflected on him." Princess Diana was his final trophy because "as an adult he had to prove to himself and make himself bigger than he was." In this same account, we are also told, through an interview with the nightclub owner of a prestigious London club that "Dodi's manner was that of friendly puppy, always eager to please."

This image of Dodi very easily reproduces Western stereotypes of rich sons of Arab sheikhs. They chase and buy white female celebrities for their own self-esteem, splurge money, buy properties in Beverly Hills or Malibu, engage in shady business deals (Dodi is known for having a string of debts), and are emotionally damaged people, terrified of their sheikh daddy. Being seen with white celebrity women is what gives them their sense of self. Although many Muslim celebrity men have been represented through such logics, two are especially worth noting. Imran Khan, the one-time dashing Pakistani cricketer who married British socialite Jemima Khan but has now become a Pakistani politician, occupied this playboy framing in media during his days in London in the 1970s and 1980s. He was seen as having a fast London nightlife scene and was frequently reported being seen with a string of famous white women (although there was no sheikh daddy in Imran's case). In fact, even today, when Western journalists interview Imran or cover his profile, his earlier playboy image is often evoked. To what extent does this happen when serious profiles of notable white male leaders such as a JFK or a Bill Clinton are presented? Another example is the playboy sheikh Mohammed Al Fassi who died in 2003. When he died, the *Telegraph* reminded us that he was "notorious for his wild behavior and extravagant lifestyle."[20] He too had a string of unpaid debts, a bevy of white women, and two wives who were Westerners—one an Italian and another an aspiring American actress.

Such playboy sheikh narratives have significant commercial value. They sell magazines and newspapers—and they become themes in romance novels. Just out of curiosity, I went to Amazon books and typed "playboy sheikh" to see what contemporary book titles would come up. These are examples of romance novel titles that were on top of the list: *The Playboy Sheikh's Virgin Stable Girl, Surrender to the Playboy Sheikh, Surrender to the Sheikh, Woman in a Sheikh's World*, and *Breaking the Sheikh's Rules.* One notices the theme of entrapment and seduction of white women in the titles. One also notices the point that Ella Shohat made (referenced earlier) about the displacement of forbidden white patriarchal heterosexual desires for the white woman onto Arab men. Such romance novels clearly are written for a Western audience. The white woman heroine is imagined through the lens of the (white) male gaze even if the author might be a woman. These novels are not written for Muslim men. Thus, we find a double displacement in that Muslim/Arab men become the heroes and onto them are projected white patriarchal heterosexual forbidden desires for the white woman. This illustrates again how representations of Muslim men in popular culture tell us perhaps more about white heteropatriarchal desires than about the reality of Muslim men.

Perverse Sexuality

Perhaps the most grotesque and barbaric description of the Fayeds that emerged in many media narratives is about Al Fayed's alleged sexual perversity. In numerous sites, the picture that emerges of Al Fayed is of a person with pathological sexuality. We learn, for instance, that Fayed ran the store Harrods like a harem. Details are provided especially in two significant sources—a controversial 1995 (September) *Vanity Fair* exposé by Maureen Orth called "Holy War at Harrods," and *Fayed: The Unauthorized Biography* by Tom Bower (2001 [first published in 1998 right after Diana's death]). It is significant that Fayed had sued *Vanity Fair* for what he considered to be a biased and offensive article (although later he is supposed to have dropped

the suit). We learn in the *Vanity Fair* report that Fayed would walk the Harrods store regularly looking for young attractive women to work in his office.
Such women would be given splendid gifts and he would say, "come to papa"
or "give papa a hug" (p. 82). And "those who rebuffed him would often be
subjected to crude humiliating comments about their appearance or dress"
(p. 82). The report also paints vivid pictures of how Mohammed Fayed would
chase his secretaries around the office and "sometimes try to stuff money
down women's blouses" or that "he would brandish a two foot plastic penis
at male visitors and ask, 'How's your cock?'" (p. 82). We further learn that his
office was heavily scented and that the "Room of Luxury" and the Egyptian
Hall that he installed in Harrods had his own face carved on the sphinxes
around the molding (p. 72).

What is interesting is that similar details are also provided in Bower's 1998
biography of Mohammed Al Fayed. In Bower's unauthorized biography, the
back cover quotes the *Sunday Times* stating that "there is enough sex and
intrigue here for a sequel to *The Arabian Nights*" and the *Spectator* commenting that the book was a "brilliant account of one man's appalling life
. . . Tom Bower has triumphantly told the truth about an awful life." Lynn
Barber of the *Daily Telegraph* is also quoted in the blurb for the book. The
blurb states that it is a "'fuggin good read'" mimicking Al Fayed's broken,
accented English and his alleged frequent use of "fuggin." Such racist framing
is also apparent in references to *The Arabian Nights,* which were similarly
invoked by the *Vanity Fair* (1995) report that stated that "Fayed's life story is
right out of Aladdin or Ali Baba" (p. 79). In reading about the Fayeds in such
sources, I had to remind myself that (1) I was reading about the *Fayeds* and
not any Middle Eastern dictator such as Saddam since the representational
frameworks are so similar and (2) that I was reading about real people and
not some movie script about a Muslim villain or sheikh obsessed with sex
and entrapping (white) women.

The first problem with such representations is the reductionism at work.
Lusting after white women seems to be one of the predominant occupations
of upper-class and aristocratic Muslim men, as is splurging wealth in the
West. There seems to be nothing else to their character—no sophistication,
no complexity, and no brain. Al Fayed comes across as a buffoon while Dodi,
although shown as less aggressive than his father, is infantilized. Further, the
reduction of their personalities to sexual lustfulness situates them as outside
of reason and enlightenment and reduces them to the body.

The second problem is that such narratives normalize existing and past
geopolitical frameworks in which Muslim men are criminally associated with
white women in particular and women in general. For instance, in Holland,

there is now a phenomenon of the Lover Boys. Lover Boys are pimps often posing as "boyfriends" to young Dutch women. They then enslave these girls and throw them into sex trafficking. The Lover Boys are primarily seen as Islamic men in public narratives. While to be sure such men are involved, to see Muslim men today in Netherlands (as is becoming the case) only through this association reduces them to violence and criminal sex.

The third problem is that such representations deny that white Western men are also sexually lustful and violent; they erase the fact that during various military occupations in non-Western worlds, white men in diplomatic positions, as soldiers (Enloe, 1990, 2000), or as colonial masters have engaged in all kinds of sexual wrongdoings with native and local women. Yet, they do not acquire the tag of sexual lustfulness or perversity. Indeed, when it comes to sexually playing with, or violating women of the Global South (or nonwhite women in general), we do not seem to care much as the bodies of these women have little worth. This is unlike the white woman (signifier of the purity of Western nations and the world). This is the age-old colonial double standard through which the struggles of Western and non-Western patriarchies have played out in global politics. Additionally, as Sarah Projansky (2001), drawing on Shohat notes, such representations of interracial sexual misconduct also "displace questions of sexualized violence from a U.S. context" (p. 49) or we could say, generally, white Western national contexts. It is almost as though white women are in danger of being sexually violated or imposed upon by men of color—and in this case Muslim men—but are seemingly safe around white national men. Yet, empirical evidence suggests otherwise.

Such representations of the Fayeds, when situated in the context of so many other similar Western logics of Muslim masculinity illustrate a complex convergence of sexual politics, race, religion, nation, and geopolitics in a battle over modernity. Judith Butler (2009) has suggested that questions such as "who has arrived in modernity and who has not" (p. 102) are centrally linked to sexual politics where Europe becomes the site of sexual freedom in relation to sexualities of all other cultures. Indeed, one of the ways in which the narratives of sexual freedom and exceptionalism through which North Atlantic modernities have expressed themselves in popular culture is through a dialectical play of Muslim masculinity and white femininity where the positionality of white womanhood serves to reveal the (seeming) pathological minds of Muslim men. To see this further, let us briefly turn to some recent examples from our times. We will then see how the Diana phenomenon, instead of narrating cosmopolitan possibilities, actually only recycles age-old patterns of framing white women and Muslim men relationships in Western public culture.

In 2009, at the Fort Hood military campus in Texas, we had the infamous case of the military psychiatrist Nidal Hassan who opened fire. Until then, we did not know much about him. In the midst of all the questions—Why did he do it? Was he connected to terrorists? Did he lose his mind?—a racialized sexual twist crept into the story. We learned that he frequently visited a strip club close to the Fort Hood campus to unwind after a hard day's work. Reports tell us how he often sat close to the dancing pole, was always quiet, and did not make any trouble. Some of the white women strippers interviewed in newspaper reports stated that he was polite but tipped well for every dance (something that seemed to be a code for his forbidden desire for white women's sexuality). The *Telegraph* (2009, November 11) stated that

> Hasan was a regular customer at a club close to the Texas military base and on one occasion spent six hours there watching women pole dancing.

> His behaviour in the run-up to the shooting spree is similar to that of some of the September 11 hijackers who also sampled Western decadence before committing their atrocity.[21]

Why this piece of information should even have become big news (since corporate white men and politicians constantly visit such places after work— think Eliot Spitzer) is what seized my attention. This information became a game changer of sorts as we were now invited to view Hassan's lapse of reason through the added prism of (his) sexuality and its link to white women strippers. His visiting a strip club is supposed to tell us something about his perverse mind; yet when high-profile white men engage in all sorts of illicit sexual affairs (think John F. Kennedy, Bill Clinton, John Edwards, and so on) we rarely see those as expressions of a weird pathological mind. In fact, often the rhetoric that emerges is that "great men often do such things." This reinforces the point that the minds of white heterosexual national men are not necessarily seen as reflections of, or reduced to, their bodies (hence the universal rationality of white heteronormative masculinity). We see the Cartesian mind/body dualism at work—a dualism that is only attached to white men but rarely any other men (and especially not Muslim men).

Another recent example is *Sex and the City 2* (2010)—one of the most Orientalist and racist films of recent times.[22] A significant moment in the film—that captures the intermix of sexuality, nation, white femininity, and Muslim masculinity (and culture)—is when at a *souk* (marketplace), Samantha's bag pops open spilling out condom packs. We see Arab men crowding around her and her fallen condoms, as they crazily yell at her in their language. In an obscene gesture of rebelliousness that mimics sexual intercourse, Samantha waves the condom packs in front of the men's faces screaming: "Yes, I have sex!" This is a white woman stating that I own my sexuality, unlike your women whose sexuality you control. (The condom functions as sign of reproductive freedom reflecting the sexual exceptionalism of the United States.) Seen through Samantha's lens, the Arab men scolding her for using condoms seems pretty barbaric, as though the notion of female reproductive freedom is sacrilege. This moment preserves a white (hetero)patriarchal nationalism of the United States that is linked to freedom and is naturalized by a white woman–crazy Arab dynamic. It is also worth noting that in the film, the Muslim women covered in veils who usher these American women into a secret room where there are many other Muslim women, are all fashion-conscious (Manhattan) designer-wearing women (under their veils). Their haute couture (i.e., consumerism)—that they reveal to these fashion-obsessed white American women—seems to function as a fulcrum upon which possibilities of a global multicultural and transfaith sisterhood, which can bypass the crazy Muslim/Arab men, is hinted at in the film. An implicit narrative of white women, if not directly rescuing, then at least recognizing, the needs of their otherwise (seemingly) oppressed Muslim female (potential) friends who desire the West (as designated by their clothes under their *Abaya* [the fully covered black cloak]) also seems to be at work in this narrative.

In 2003, paintings and murals were found in Saddam Hussein's trove by American soldiers. Jonathan Jones of the *Guardian* (2003, April 14), commenting on the paintings stated that they "betray a mind obsessed with sex and violence."[23] Naming a painting (see Figure 5.2) "the iconography of psychotic porn," the report points attention to the white "naked blonde maidens menaced by dragons and trolls. . . ." Figure 5.2 is the original Associated Press photo by photographer John Moore that shows a U.S. solider looking at the painting. When this Associated Press photo was reproduced in the *Guardian* article, the photo was compressed a little. And unless one looks very closely in the *Guardian* image, it seems as though the solider is looking at a real live fearful scenario (and not a painting as the frame of the painting is not very visible) of a naked blonde being dragged by dragons.

The *Guardian* report tells us that such erotic art pieces represent the "hysterical aesthetic, the hyperpornography of power and violence." The report asserts that these erotic art pieces are "proof of the dictator's execrable sensibility" and that "they are from the universal cultural gutter—pure dreck." What is visually significant is the American soldier looking at the painting.

Figure 5.2. U.S. solider looks at a fantasy painting in one of Saddam Hussein's Baghdad residences. (AP Photo/John Moore. Reproduced with permission.)

In the visual structure of the photo, one can read Shohat's (2011) point (cited earlier): the displacement of the white masculine heterosexual desires/gaze onto the Muslim man (Saddam, in this case, who we do not see but imagine him gazing at this painting). The *Guardian* reporter stated: "Looking at these paintings is like seeing the owner [i.e., Saddam]) naked." But looking at this piece, could we not also say that it like looking at the viewer—the white American solider gazing at the painting—naked (that is, his desires bared)? Saddam is absent here, and we, as audience, can only see the white solider (read: the masculinist U.S. nation) viewing the paintings. A complex and intimate entanglement of Muslim male desires and white male desires is ironically betrayed in this moment. Such perverse sexualization of the Muslim man—or "dictator"—was also seen in the case of Osama Bin Laden. After Osama's death, it was revealed that he (apparently) had a "fairly extensive" collection of pornography in his hideout in Abbottabad that the Navy Seals discovered.[24]

What is interesting about such (seeming) "hyperpornography of power"— as the *Guardian* reporter claims these paintings of Saddam express—is that no one would object (nor has objected) when since medieval times we have seen representations of white European women in "erotic" poses painted for the white male gaze. John Berger's (1972) classic work has done much to point to this. Such art today still hangs in some of the most prestigious galleries and museums in the world, but there seems to be nothing "psychotic" about it. Yet, when found in the palaces, halls, and homes of a Muslim dictator, such art becomes lowly expressions of the cultural gutter. Pierre Bourdieu would probably have a lot to say about how the meaning of taste and judgment operate in this geopolitics of culture. For us, what is to be marked is how the Islamic context already renders these paintings as low art that signifies the mind of that Islamic culture. In contrast, paintings of white women with naked breasts and erotic poses in a place like the Louvre can only signify the high art of Western civilization and the refinement of the European mind.

Madness and Civilization

Edward Said's work has shown how the Westerner has always been obsessed with the "Muslim mind." Indeed, rarely have Muslim kings or presidents—especially ones who have dared to show independence from the West—come to our screens as sane people with whom dialogue is possible. In the Diana phenomenon, press reports as well as popular books released after Diana's death call attention to weird obsessions and paranoia that both Al Fayed Sr. and Dodi harbored. While neither of them was a political leader, they nonetheless—especially Mohammed Al Fayed because of his wealth—held a significant, even if disliked, position in British society.

In Tom Bower's biography on Al Fayed, we learn that Dodi would subject his women (who are white women since we do not learn of any other) "to his strange fantasies" (2001, p. 253) (we are given no details of such fantasies but can assume in the context of the book's narrative that these are sexual fantasies). He had even "intimidated one [woman] with the Berretta revolver he kept near his bed . . ." (p. 253). He often abandoned these women once he was done with them. Similarly, in Smith's (1997) *Vanity Fair* exposé on Dodi, we learn that Kelly Fisher, to whom Dodi was engaged while courting Diana, had affirmed that "Dodi kept an 'astonishing array of weapons.'" Another account in the same article tells us that "he once threatened her [Traci Lind] with a nine mm Beretta" and that they fought like "children" "trading pushes and slaps." Although in many reports Dodi is also described as gentle, his gentleness is portrayed as not being very normal—for example, Dodi is supposed to have loved toys and possessed a vast array of soft toys. His is a gentleness of childlike powerlessness, hence his weird behavior with women (we are meant to infer).

On the contrary, Mohammed Al Fayed comes to us as crazy, evil, and sick, resurrecting the stereotype of the evil Arab from fantasy literature. The theme of crazy Mohammed that frames several discussions of him became particularly prominent after Diana's death. Orth's (1995) *Vanity Fair* exposé offered the most famous rendition of this theme. Although it was published before Diana and Dodi met, it became an important reference point about Fayed in public narratives especially after Diana's death. It is a piece in which there is no positive discussion of Mohammed Al Fayed. We learn of Al Fayed's paranoia about security. His buildings were apparently connected to the Dorchester Hotel through secret passageways. He is supposed to have had an elaborate alarm and bugging system. He had phobia about germs, and he expected the plates he ate out of to be boiled and disinfected with a lime piece. His obsessive fears about germs and contamination apparently even extended to running HIV tests for would-be employees, carrying wet wipes that he would use after every handshake, preventing his children from attending Harrods's Christmas party lest they catch germs, and wearing a gas mask while traveling in a helicopter from his country house to London to avoid inhaling city fumes (pp. 80–81).

Such details about Fayed's phobias repeat what has been said in the Western media about so many Muslim leaders and dictators. For instance, numerous media reports have told us that Gaddafi had a phobia about flying and heights, that he would demand to stay on the ground floor, and he never flew long distances (and always took a break). According to an ABC report (October 20, 2011) we learn that Gaddafi traveled with his "bulletproof tent": "this 'Bedouin' brought a bit of desert with him, camping out in the world's capitals. . . . To complete the *Arabian Nights* theme, Gaddafi would often tether a camel or two outside."[25] Similarly, Saddam Hussein has also been represented in Western reports as being obsessed with cleanliness. This was also revealed in the film *Uncle Saddam* (2000) made by French filmmaker Joel Soler.[26] People wanting to meet him apparently had to wash and cleanse themselves in front of men who were in charge of his security. An ABC *Good Morning America* report quotes Al Janabi, who was apparently personal secretary to one of Saddam's sons at one time. "They take you to a shower," says Al Janabi, who fled Iraq two years ago. "You have to take a shower in front of the people who are responsible for his safety."[27]

A theme of homoeroticism is also hinted at, and subtextually criticized, in these reports as an expression of a perverse sexual mindset. We saw this in the *Vanity Fair* (1995) report of Mohammed Al Fayed where we learned of him waving a two-foot-long penis at his male visitors. Same-sex male contact (or its possibility) is degraded, and that degradation is projected onto the Muslim male body. We see one of the ultimate expressions of this in our times in the instance of an alleged CIA secret plot to fake and create a gay sex video of Saddam Hussein having sex with a teenage boy. The video, we learn, "would look like it was taken by a hidden camera. Very grainy like it was a secret videotaping of a sex session," stated an unnamed CIA agent according to a 2010 report in the *Guardian*.[28] According to reports, the video would have used fake actors and the purpose was to destabilize Saddam's regime. Although the plot was apparently halted, the *Washington Post* (cited in the same report) had revealed that Osama had been similarly targeted. And a similar film (falsely) showing Osama around a campfire with his cronies discussing their conquests of young boys had been thought of.[29] It does not seem as though such films were made at all; apparently, "top CIA brass repeatedly rejected the ideas."[30] But reports from these credible news sources do certainly suggest that these plots may have been conceived of by the CIA.

What is interesting is that gay sex is implicitly criminalized in the conceptualizations of these would-have-been films. And that criminalization is projected onto the Muslim male body. This once again exhibits a complex interweaving of sexuality, masculinit(ies), nation, and geopolitics. But as important is that the category of gay—which is very much a category of Western sexual epistemology (as Joseph Massad's [2002, 2008] work has so brilliantly discussed)—is displaced onto Muslim cultures and men here. Massad (2002), among others, has cogently argued that male same-sex contact, desires, or relationships in the Muslim world cannot be understood through Western notions of desire and their underlying categories (gay, heterosexual, and so on). Additionally, he explains, in most Muslim countries, there is no law against same-sex male contact. Yet, organizations like the Gay International impose and create notions of homosexuality (which is a Western sexual category) in the Muslim world where no such categories existed. Or, they suppress or disregard same-sex desires in the Muslim world when those desires cannot be recuperated into Western epistemological categories of sexual contact or identities.[31]

Such framings of phobia, paranoia, and sexuality of Muslim men since the Crusades have geopolitically functioned to produce Muslim men as pathologized villains of the West ready to take over Western civilization through their insanity. Indeed, popular culture and geopolitical culture fuse where the narrative of Muslim madness is concerned. The Diana phenomenon represents one more high-profile instance of a framing of Muslim madness in the late 20th century. For instance, the *Vanity Fair* article (September 1995) is titled "*Holy War* at Harrods" (emphasis added). This language—evoking jihad—suggests a takeover of Christian Englishness (symbolized by Harrods—a highly nationalized British space) by Muslim fanatics. (Harrods is one of the oldest shopping stores and institutions in Britain and a classic sign of white upper-class Englishness. When Harrods was bought by Fayed, the royalty distanced itself from the store.) Even before the reader has entered the narrative of the article, the title "Holy War" has already positioned the audience in an oppositional relation to the Fayeds as well as to Muslim cultures.

The "Good Muslim": The Structure of Invisibility

An interesting dichotomy set up in the Diana phenomenon—that also attests to a growing discursive pattern since 9-11—is that of the "good Muslim/bad Muslim" (Mamdani, 2002, 2005).[32] The *bad Muslim* is whom the West likes to hate, he (always a man) threatens "our character," "our civilization," and "our morality." The *good Muslim,* when in the West, likes to remain invisible. He does not call attention to himself and, for the most part, is proper and noble. He is not in your face. The good Muslim legitimizes the existence of the bad Muslim (Mamdani, 2002, 2005). Allen (2010) argues that in European (and we can say U.S., as well) settings, the term *Muslim* can never be neutral: it is already politically saturated. To invoke the term *Muslim* is already to ask (explicitly or implicitly) whether he is "good," "moderate," "radical," "fanatical," and so on. The underlying assumption is that there is something problematic about being Muslim. Hence, when someone is a good Muslim—one whom we like—we make it a point to assert that "goodness." This is unlike any other religious faith: We never say good Christians and bad Christians, just Christians, or we never say good Hindu or bad Hindu (although we do say "traditional" Hindu and "modern" Hindu, which have different social connotations). The thing is that one can only be a bad or a good "person" (Allen, 2010) but not a good or bad *religious* person. With Islam, however, good and bad have become discursive instruments through which we in the West pit different parts of the faith against each other.

I have often wondered what it is that enabled the narrative of Hasnat Khan, the Pakistani Muslim doctor, with whom Diana was supposed to have been in love, emerge from the media without a scratch. Why is that in an anti-Muslim climate in the 1990s, his dating Diana did not cause much reaction? Or even later when we found out more about their relationship? In contrast, the Al Fayeds became a subject of media obsession where they (especially Senior Fayed) were seen as being out to entrap the most prized national possession: the blonde princess and the mother of the future king of Britain. One of the only images of Khan that circulated around that time of Diana's death in 1997 was of him invisible, hidden under dark glasses, and barely noticeable among a host of other attendees, in Westminster Abbey at Diana's funeral ceremony. (See Figure 5.3.)

Figure 5.3. Hasnat Khan in dark glasses at Diana's funeral. (Copyright Alpha Press. Reproduced with permission.)

In the image, Khan is unremarkable; he looks as though he does not want to be seen. It is only when papers later identified him in the crowd that most of us even learned of his existence. I find this photo symbolic. Hasnat literally attempts to erase himself from the mediated national gaze—working hard to distance himself from any association with the white national princess. In fact, when we see this image through a longer shot of the abbey in other photos, we see how nondescript he seems among hundreds of important personnel in seats next to him. While Hasnat seems visually unnoticeable around the time of Diana's death, the Fayeds built a Diana and Dodi memorial in Harrods (that still exists today) and had condolence books at Harrods that many lined up to sign. And the famous image of Dodi half-naked in a swimsuit with Diana in a boat circulated around the world at this time. We see Dodi's glistening sun-kissed body exhibiting a dark mat of chest hair while beaming at Diana. They both look happy. (See Figure 5.4.)

Another image of Hasnat Khan that circulated heavily is of him carrying a small medical equipment bag, walking in the street (presumably near Royal Brompton Hospital). In this image—one of the few that exists of Khan—Khan is associated with a noble profession—that of saving lives (in contrast to the destruction of lives that the West associates with Muslim men). We

Figure 5.4. Diana and Dodi vacationing in the summer of 1997. (Copyright Alpha Press. Reproduced with permission.)

also learned later that he had come to England specifically to work with and train under Sir Magdi Yacoub, the renowned heart surgeon.

This contrast of visibility and invisibility through which the Fayeds and Khan have visually circulated in the media invokes—intentionally or not—the logic of the good Muslim versus the bad Muslim. The good Muslim is an "absence"—he does not demand the attention of the nation. We may know he exists, but we do not have to recognize him or, if we recognize him, see him as a Muslim person. At the time of Diana's death, there was a significant visual absence of Khan's body in the mediated realm beyond the few images discussed. One function of visual images is to constitute subjects and publics in particular ways. How we see, what we see, and in what contexts we see images not only confer meaning to the visual text, they also confer meaning for whom those texts are distributed and circulated. And those meanings, as Stuart Hall's work has taught us, arise in relation to a host of other related visual texts—past and present. This is the notion of visual intertextuality that cultural studies scholars are familiar with. Images and narratives of the Fayeds are caught in a historical structure of hypervisibility of Muslim men that has served to criminalize and pathologize them. In contrast, when we see Khan walking down the street with medical equipment, we are for the most part unable to visually draw upon any established historical visual structure of saving lives that we can associate with Muslim men. (In contrast, we have learned to associate them with brutal killings of others.) In fact, we hardly see Khan and Diana together in images (after her death), partly because they were not available—he is supposed to have hated media attention and would go out with Diana when she was in disguise (again the logic of invisibility). His almost unseen presence in the visual field called Diana (read: the white gendered nation) functions through an invisibility that tells us that he knows where his place is—*behind* the public screens, and not confronting the white male gaze of the nation. He understands that his body is there to serve the nation (as in being a doctor), not to threaten it.

What I am suggesting is that the politics of visual representation itself plays a role here in producing the Fayeds as bad Muslims in contrast to Khan. The images that exist of the Fayeds invoke an already existing visual regime about Muslim men where they are always a problem. Consequently, that hypervisibility renders them ironically more invisible for we cannot really "see" them for who they might be as individual human beings. In contrast, Khan does not signify anything about Muslim men that is already familiar to us (after all, it was Diana who went after him—thus reversing the captive narrative). And it was he who finally broke off the relationship, allegedly for reasons of cultural difference and her high profile. Thus Khan is an ambivalence. And little wonder that there is not much storytelling about him in the media because he does not fit an established visual regime about Muslim men. His overall visual absence (although now there is an increasing visual presence—but it is still limited) is ironically also what gives so much meaning to the Fayeds as bad Muslims out to devour the religious white core of the nation.

Conclusion

The main argument of this chapter has been that white femininity constitutes one of the main assemblages through which Muslim men are given problematic meanings in globally dominant regimes of representation. I have further suggested that meanings that circulate about Muslim masculinity (playboy sheikh, perverse sexuality, madness, and violence) tell us not only about Muslim men, but also about the forbidden desires of white (national) men. I have also posited that Muslim (male) sexuality, as we are given to understand it, is constituted through and in Western representations where white femininity figures centrally. Muslim sexuality (as we are given to understand it) does not exist prior to the Western representations but is, in fact, the product of Western fantasies. To understand Western constructions of the Muslim man, thus, requires probing into a complex structure of displacements of (suppressed) desires of white patriarchal nationalism that inform global geopolitics, yet remain hidden under the lid of "civilization."

This chapter has asserted that there is a particular structure of hypervisibility that exists about Muslim men in Western media discourses that make it difficult for those in the West to imagine Muslim men outside of this narrative structure. However, unlike many earlier representations, in the Diana phenomenon we begin to also see the emergence of a visual logic of the good Muslim—where the good Muslim is either hidden and/or associated with a profession that is considered noble for the nation. For example, after 9-11, we have been witnessing, as Evelyn Alsultany (2012) argues, this logic of the good Muslim man who is proximal to the nation's institutions (such as security [for example, Mohammed Elibiary or Arif Alikhan in U.S. Homeland Security] or media [for example, Ali Velshi, Fareed Zakaria, both associated with CNN]). To this extent, it would perhaps not be inaccurate to suggest that the Diana phenomenon, as an instance that both attempts to embrace multiculturalism and renationalize the (British) nation, portends many later Western nationalist instances (9-11 being the most prominent) of managing the nation's multicultural face where Muslims are concerned (where some of them are brought into folds of national "goodness"). This allows the continuous vilification of other Muslims (the bad Muslims) through age-old Orientalist logics.

The Diana phenomenon, as one of the most visible phenomena of our times that depicts a relation between white national femininity and Muslim

masculinity, poses some interesting issues. Unlike some of the earlier historical or Hollywood narratives of white women being trapped or violated
by evil Muslim men, Diana is not represented through that overt logic of
violation, given that she herself wanted relationships with Muslim men. And
along with some other white female celebrities that I mentioned earlier, the
Diana phenomenon opens up the possibility for white women at least being with Muslim men. ("For if Princess Di found them attractive, why can't
we?") Thus, sociologically it is not too far off to think that we may see more
instances in the future of individual white women being proximal to Muslim cultures and men. The issue for us then is to probe the structure of the
representations through which transracial, transfaith, and more specifically
white woman–Muslim man romance is framed in popular culture. Do those
representational structures really move us toward the possibility of imagining
a serious and equitable relationship between a white (national) woman and
a Muslim/Arab man? What are the terms that circumscribe a transnational,
transracial romance between a white woman and a Middle Eastern man or
Muslim man in popular culture? As I have argued, the structure and pa-
rameters of representation of the transfaith, transracial romance that we call
Diana—while allowing the white woman some agency (that is, she herself
seems to have desired these men with whom she had relationships)—ultimately suggests the impossibility of permanence in such cross-faith relationships. In the Diana phenomenon, the Muslim man dies (Dodi); his family
is pathological, perverse, and violent (Fayeds); or he is so traditional that
he cannot accommodate the cultural difference and the hypervisibility of
white femininity and thus breaks off the relationship (Hasnat Khan). These
are not encouraging narratives that suggest the possibility of permanence.
And while these are facts (in that they did happen), the point is that when we
look at the mediation of the Diana phenomenon—as an instance of a rather
subversive transnational romance—it only suggests temporary excitement,
not permanence. It suggests that despite superficial Westernization, Muslim
men are still the same as we have always known them to be—perverse sex
maniacs, mentally damaged, or too grounded in their conservative cultures
(i.e., not modern). Finally the Diana phenomenon reveals that white (national) womanhood will always be betrayed by Muslim masculinity (via
death or breakup) and brought back to where it belongs—white national
heteropatriarchy. This is sealed in that iconic image of Diana's coffin, draped
by the Royal Standard, being followed by three generations of royal British
men. The "whore" transformed back into an "English rose" while the whole
world was watching.

6. Cosmopolitan Healing
The Spiritual Fix of White Femininity

This chapter is concerned with a particular kind of borderlessness of white femininity that marks our times, of which Princess Diana, especially later Diana, became one of the original symbols. This borderlessness is organized around a discourse of spirituality, well-being, and healing, and frequently incorporates the ethos of non-Anglo and Asian-inflected therapeutic practices of inner wellness, planetary connectivity, and "finding yourself." We see this in numerous contemporary new age discourses that are represented through, and embraced by, upper-/middle-class white women who seek inner healing and wellness to fashion seemingly liberatory modes of selfhood. Astrology, tarot card reading, séances, psychic healing, reflexology, acupuncture, detox ayurveda diets, energy crystals, herbal medicines, colonic irrigation, homeopathy, meditation, yoga, spiritual retreat packages, reiki, tai chi, massage therapies, tarot cards, lifestyle spas, chantings, and other wellness practices celebrated in Western mass culture today have emerged as technologies for recrafting (usually the female) self through a turn toward the interior (Carrette & King, 2005; Heelas, 1996; Heelas & Woodhead; 2005; Franklin, Lury, & Stacey, 2000).

The United Kingdom, especially metropolitan London, from the mid- to late 1990s reflected such a shift toward a logic of interiority in which connecting to one's inner world became a means of connecting to, and making sense of, the external world. For instance, this was a time when what has been called the "therapeutic turn" (Ecclestone & Hayes, 2008; Furedi, 2004) in public culture emerged as a visible mode for the production of a reflexive self both at a cultural and political level as New Labor prioritized emotional literacy in its Health Care Agenda from its very first term in office. *Reflexivity* (and the reflexive self) is a term associated with Tony Giddens ("reflexive modernization") who was the architect of New Labor's "third way" politics. He stated in his influential text *Modernity and Self Identity* that "living every moment reflectively is a matter of heightened awareness of thoughts, feelings, and bodily sensations. Awareness creates potential change . . ." (1991, p. 71). In this 1991 book, the elements of Gidden's thinking that were to have such a profound influence on New Labor's policies were already visible. In 2001 (January 20), the *Observer* ran an article with the subtitle: "New Labour's Best Minds Want to Help You Find Your Inner Child." The article opened with the lines: "How are you feeling today? In touch with your inner emotions to run the economy, the health service and the criminal justice system? Good. Then let us begin."[1] The article stated that the goal of trying to connect to your "inner child" was to "wipe away generations of stiff upper lips, bulldog spirit, clenched jaws, explosive tempers. . . . and sons who call their dad 'sir.'" Thus, as sociologist Frank Furedi (2005) notes, the 1990s and onward in the United Kingdom became an age of "life style gurus . . . makeover experts, healers, facilitators, mentors and guides." In fact, these tendencies were symptomatic of a larger trend in which many nations in the West since the 1990s have focused on "wellness" and happiness as measures of national productivity instead of only the traditional economic determinants of the gross national product. The New Economics Foundation, an independent think tank based in the United Kingdom, even lobbied for substituting the gross domestic product with measures of "national accounts of well-being" calling for governments in Europe to directly measure "people's subjective well-being" as a new way of evaluating society's progress.[2]

Ecclestone and Hayes (2008), who have written a lot on the therapeutic turn in education in the United Kingdom, argue that this movement toward the interior symbolically began with the death of Diana—for instance, with people's baring of their emotions at the time of Diana's death. Indeed, there is no denying that the story of Princess Diana is central to viewing a shifting national sensibility toward inner life. For instance, any brief storyline of Diana's life published anywhere roughly follows a logic that gives primacy to exploring one's inner world as a way to self-empowerment. The story of Diana is almost always presented as the story of a princess of suffering, who finds a way to deal with her pain by turning to her inner life force (through astrology, acupuncture, psychotherapy, non-Western holistic treatments, non-Western religions, psychics, and more). This revitalizes her and produces a higher and more liberated self that enables a transcendental and even spiritual connection to the world and its people. When Diana died, she certainly became "saint Diana" (Richards et al., 1999). Numerous tributes left for her by ordinary people framed her as such. On the day of Diana's funeral, a columnist in the *Independent* cemented the popular responses to Diana by announcing the birth of a "new religion" in the United Kingdom.[3]

> People have a new religion. Most did not gather outside the Abbey and Kensington Palace to find God. *They came together for a more internal exercise, to explore their all-important inner selves and feelings, an event prompted by the death of a woman who excelled in expressing her own emotions.* (emphasis added)
>   This religion is the creed of the confessional society and has been developed by a priesthood of analysts, therapists, counsellors, agony aunts and psychobabblers. . . . *Its first commandment is to get in touch with your inner self. [. . .]* (emphasis added)

In scanning numerous media materials on Diana, I have observed that her life story, equated with the story of the birth of New Britain, is often depicted via different bodily postures. If we lay out the various iconic images from each phase of her life side by side, we would see a body rising up—emerging from under the weight of billowy clothes (in the early to mid-1980s)—and manifesting a more free, straight body that stands tall—to the days after her death when her body began to be remembered through nature symbols (for instance, in images of Diana buried in the gardens of Althrop or flowing as a water fountain in Hyde Park, or signifying, through Elton John, "an English rose" in England's rolling hills—as in Elton John's song). What we have is a narrative of transcendence of corporeality, which is equated with natural freedom. An iconic image (see Figure 6.1) that often represents the last days of Diana's life is of her perched on the diving board of the *Jonikal* (Dodi's yacht in the Mediterranean where she was cruising before her death) wearing a swimsuit. It is a long-distance shot. Her body looks small from the distance as it hangs from the edge of the diving board visually merging with the azure sea and the open blue sky. The picture evokes the wondrous stillness of nature, and Diana seems to have become one with it. The image, frequently used to define a new phase in Diana's life, evokes a sense of limitless freedom—metaphorized through the expansive ocean—that she seems to have achieved. The seagull above seems to signify peace and tranquility.

Diana's representations are important to analyze because they anticipate the growing inner wellness trend (mind-body connection) that informs the contemporary ethos of trans-Atlantic cultures (see, for example, McGee, 2005; Miller, 2008)—an ethos that tends to be represented by middle- and upper-middle-class white women. Additionally, the images of inner freedom that link Diana to nature tend to recycle earlier colonial logics of representing white women where, in the pursuit of inner wellness, white women fuse with

Figure 6.1. Diana on holiday in Portofino. This image has been reproduced in several places including in *Vanity Fair* in July 2007. (Copyright Corbis. Reproduced with permission.)

the spirit of nature. And as with the goal of this book, the question for us is what does all this reveal about white femininity and the nation given that such representations of interiority, inner healing, and natural connectivity are lodged in white (upper-/middle-class) femininity? A survey of numerous wellness web sites, brochures, and magazines from spiritual wellness and holistic spa programs reveals that, more often than not, the images in the photo galleries are of white women because this is the clientele that tends to be targeted and can afford such services. It is not that men do not participate in these (although clearly far less than women do). I think men tend not to be represented as much in such wellness practices because these are often seen as feminized practices reflecting a feminized space of nature (and in Western cultures, anything alternatively spiritual and holistic tends to be feminized). In fact, new-age kind of (Western) men who *do* participate in these kinds of wellness centers or spa retreats are often somehow demasculinized or even comically portrayed. We see this in films such as the *Next Best Thing* (2000) where Madonna plays a yoga instructor and the male lead character (played by Rupert Everett) is gay. Or, in *Darjeeling Limited* (2007) where three (white men) brothers plan a therapeutic trip to India in order to bond, but the film is a comedy and the spiritual "East" of India is comically represented, inviting laughs from the audience.

What is especially ironic is that this turn toward the interior, increasingly made popular by celebrities, is occurring at the very time that women's bodies, including white women's bodies, are being hypersexualized and commodified in Western popular culture in ways never seen before (and coded through a neoliberal rhetoric of "freedom" as scholars writing on postfeminism have argued).[4] What is also remarkable is that this turn to the interior, the (cosmo) spiritual, the embrace of alternate holistic practices, and the implied veneration toward nature that such practices call for, has been occurring at the same time (since the mid-1990s) that white masculinist nationalist discourses in nations such as the United States and the United Kingdom have been militarizing the world (evidenced by overwhelming defense spending and the increasing rhetoric of securitization and surveillance). All this pushes us even further to ask what a turn toward interiority, symbolized by white women, might be managing; or why it is that a rhetoric of gendered interiority can be on the rise at the same time as a rhetoric of militarization; or why it is that instead of producing a resistant and oppositional public (as one would think), this turn toward the inner self exists side by side with, and even feeds, a hypercommercial cultural landscape; or why white women are turning to non-Western holistic therapies to feel empowered but do not seem to find resources for empowerment in their own national spaces; or how this rhetoric of interiority is marketed in popular culture such that white women can embrace and dehistoricize non-Western healing practices but do not feel the need to speak out for the very cultures and their struggles—for instance environmental struggles—from where they (mis)appropriate cultural practices of inner healing and empowerment. For instance, Diana was able to say after visiting Africa that love is the answer, and that a lack of love is the world's biggest disease. If only it were that simple—then every white woman's "love" for other cultures would have by now leveled the geopolitical field.

If the global mother in Chapter 4 promised transnational connections through a borderless maternity and infantilized cosmopolitanism, then the late-20th-century/early-21st-century "post-political" (Mouffe, 2005, p. 64), spiritually healed (or healing) white female subject of modernity promises a transcendental cosmopolitanism by connecting to, and radiating, a global soul. This is no more just a subject of "I feel your pain." In its turn toward the interior, it has become a subject of "I feel your energy" and (in some cases like Diana or Shirley MacLaine or Angelina Jolie) "can heal your pain." Once again, a politics of global justice becomes replaced by an affective project in which white women become transmitters of global wellness. Such a turn toward interiority provides evidence (again) of how the politics of citizenship in the late 20th century and continuing into the 21st has shifted from publicness to the private so that an expression of an "appropriate" publicness itself relies on the regulation, management, and nurturing of one's inner landscape. As some scholars have argued (Wood & Newman, 2005) wellness has replaced welfare today.

Before moving specifically to Diana, New Britain, and the emergence of a "reflexive self" in British culture, I want to offer some examples of celebrity white women embodying such logics of interiority so as to mark a larger millennial trend within which to situate Diana's turn to interiority. I also want to mark a larger equation in which a particular relation among white femininity, inner wellness, transcendence, and citizenly belonging is being forged in contemporary culture since the mid-to-late 1990s. Celebrities and stars make these trends both visible and desirable. This is because we worship celebrities; we construct them as transcendental beings (Dyer, 1986; Nayar, 2009; Rojek, 2001; Turner, 2004). As Rojek notes, "celebrities take themselves and their fans higher. They are the ambassadors of the celestial sphere" (2001, p. 781).[5] So when white female stars embody this turn toward interiority and even transcendence, they already operate within a cultural matrix that codes stardom as a site of idealized whiteness. And, in the process, they make desirable a particular subject position of interiority that can deflect attention from neoliberal inequalities of the social.

Today, we have icons such as Deepak Chopra, whose clientele is predominantly upper-class white women, appearing regularly on talk shows and running a wellness center in Los Angeles. Madonna, the wild material girl, has turned into a spiritual girl since the late 1990s and is deeply engaged in healing practices from Kaballah as well as mind-body fitness regimes such as yoga drawn from Hinduism. A fascination with Hinduism is also on the rise. The Hindu "Om" tattoo has been branded on some celebrity bodies such as Ashley Tisdale, Miley Cyrus, and Vanessa Hudgens just as converting to Hinduism, as with the likes of Julia Roberts, is becoming an "in thing" (Figure 6.2). *Elle* magazine (September 2010) notes that Roberts, after her film *Eat Pray Love*, has become a "practicing Hindu," and her entire family goes to temple together. She has already named her production company Red Om Films, and her children have been given Hindu names. Reports also note that Roberts is planning to adopt from India.[6] This again calls attention to the interconnection between white femininity, global saintliness, transnational maternity, and national identity that was addressed in Chapter 4.

Figure 6.2. Julia Roberts meets with Swami Dharmadev at Hari Mandir Ashram in Pataudi, India, in September 2009. Notice again how the lighting illuminates her (especially her left side). (Rex USA. Reproduced with permission.)

Figure 6.3. Goldie Hawn
in Varanasi India in
November 2009 meditating
on a boat. (Copyright Rex
USA. Reproduced with
permission.)

A few years back, when Olivia Newton John was plagued with breast
cancer, she is reported to have engaged in alternate therapies and Buddhist
chanting to clear her energy field. In 2009, Goldie Hawn performed the
Ganga Aarti (holy cleansing prayer on the divine River of Hinduism—the
Ganges in North India whose water source is the Himalayas) dressed in white
and sporting a vermillion tilak (very much a Hindu religious sign) on her
forehead (Figure 6.3).

Recent reports have claimed that Brad Pitt and Angelina Jolie have a Hindu
guru who has given them mantras to chant and asked them to practice *Sidha*
yoga together for harmony.[7]

As a result of such celebratory narratives that teach us that mastering our
inner experience through cultural crossovers is a way to self-empowerment
(McGee, 2005), there is now also a rise of wellness (or holistic or spiritual)
tourism. Retreat packages and wellness web sites have exploded seeking
clients pursuing natural and non-Western healing to reenergize themselves.
For instance, the famous Integrated Medical Centre in London organizes
regular health tours to the western state of Rajasthan and the mountains of
the Himalayas, in India. Fashion industry icons such as Donna Karan—alleged to be an ardent spiritual healing fan—have successfully cashed in on
this spiritual "market" with a fashion line for yoga activities. Karan now has
an Urban Zen fashion and home store in Los Angeles. The exclusive Manhattan yoga and sports clothing store Lululemon has also cashed in on this.
Lululemon recently marketed a small tote bag for its clients with the word
Brahmacharya on it. The word is broken into three colorful rows of letters
against a vibrant background. *Brahmacharya* in Hinduism refers to someone
who has renounced material and earthly life to seek spiritual transcendence.

Brahmacharya is also someone who practices celibacy in this higher goal of spiritual transcendence. Lululemon, however, co-opts this very complex notion of Hinduism to appeal to its clients—upper-class Manhattan women (and men) practicing yoga to revitalize their bodies and energies.

Time magazine in April 2001, ran a special issue *Power of Yoga,* which was presented through the image of model Christy Turlington, an apparent yoga fanatic. The issue opened with the lines: "Stars do it. Sports do it. Judges in the high court do it. Let's do it: that yoga thing. A path to enlightenment that winds back 5000 years in its native India, yoga has suddenly become so hot, so cool, so very this minute. It's the exercise cum meditation for the new millennium. One that doesn't so much pump you as bliss you out."[8] Yoga, as anyone who has any knowledge of it knows, is not a "thing" and its goal is not to "bliss you out" as much as to help you attain spiritual self-awareness. Celebrities such as Gwyneth Paltrow and Madonna have been photographed with their yoga mats in ashtanga classes, and Christy Turlington has lined up with the German company Puma to start a line of clothing for yoga and other mind-body activities. Yoga, like many other practices of healing today, has also ended up as a modality through which privileged affluent white women express their seeming self-worth, self-care, and connectivity to life, while all around us racial, geopolitical, military, environmental, and economic violence increasingly function to destroy life or the ability to sustain life (especially economically) for the ordinary and the poor—and particularly in the Global South.

Franklin, Lury, and Stacey (2000) argue that such millennial trends reflect a new cultural formation that constitutes subjects as "part of a global order" and "signals the *emergence of Life* rather than God as the site of worship" (p. 124; original emphasis). For them, this seeking of life constitutes an example of what they term the "global within" (p. 97)—where the body is no longer just a physical matter but "reconceptualized" as a site for the "flows of life, systems of energy" (p. 125). Although spirituality, including the embrace of non-Western spirituality—and its alternative rationales of well-being—continue to have an everyday normalized social *rationality* in many Asian countries, the striking feature of this logic of the global within in contemporary Western nations is the way in which *it begins to replace the state as a source of life support and empowerment for the people.* This is in contrast to some of the very cultures from which alternative practices of therapy, healing, and spirituality are lifted, reworked, and dehistoricized in the West, where such mind-body practices have historically functioned to build *collectivities of resistance* as during colonialism. They were not about individualized modes of self-empowerment or a retreat from social justice and struggles where you remain "blissed out."

I thus argue in this final chapter that this late-20th and early-21st century discourse of spiritual capital secures a new interlinked national and global morality in which the inner self, or more precisely the inner spirit or inner energy, becomes a site of governmentality. Scholars such as Nikolas Rose have discussed the late-20th century "governing [of] the soul" (Rose, 1989) in which life itself becomes a project of governmentality. However, as Angela McRobbie (2009) and Lisa Blackman (2004) have suggested, the work of Rose and others (such as Beck and Giddens) have not paid adequate attention to how such logics are complicated by issues of gender, race, class, and other social formations. For instance, does the inner self of white women, acquiring spiritual capital, represent the same life value as that of a woman from the Global South? Whose inner wellness and inner transcendence "counts" as soul force? What gestures and acts are made available to us as constituting inner capital, and what acts of historical erasure have to be performed for such an articulation of interiority to be offered as a solution for self-empowerment especially by women (but normalized through the position of white women) in North Atlantic national polities today? While scholars have paid attention to the growth of self-help discourse—to which this chapter also refers—there has been far less attention paid to the logics of global healing as a component of contemporary self-help logics of white female freedom.[9] This kind of an extracorporeal packaging of "life power" reflects a new cosmopolitanism that invokes a planetary spiritual connection to cross social and material borders. And in the process, it renders invisible numerous geopolitical inequities, for if our mode of connecting to the world itself is through life energy, then the materialities of borders do not have to matter. We are all the same; we are all part of a larger network of life flows and energies.

To appreciate more fully the representational politics of the media's framing of later Diana through a logic of wellness and interiority, we need to first address the New Labor initiatives related to wellness and emotional literacy in the 1990s. These were initiatives that reflected a shifting national sensibility toward interiority, even as this sensibility existed in consonance with (instead of contradiction to) the very corporeal logics of New Britain in which reworking the body, as discussed in Chapter 3, became an important site of symbolic capital for a nation trying to brand itself as "cool" and "active." In fact, one of the arguments of this book is that the relationship between white femininity and national identity is at once hypercorporeal and immaterial. It is a relationship that reflects what Radhika Mohanram (2007) calls "a tense interplay between the body as im-material, a concept, and the body as material, fleshy" (p. 177). Such interplay between the white female body as material and immaterial, as spirit and object for the nation's viewing pleasure reflects how Anglo-dominant national discourses often regulate the white female body through a simultaneous logic of embodiment and disembodiment. Not much, however, has been written about the disembodied intangible expressions of white femininity in national discourses. We know far more about white femininity's constructed corporeality in national discourses than about its constructed interiority/spirituality through which the nation also writes its national and global desires. Although this book charts these dual tendencies of embodiment and disembodiment, this particular chapter pays more attention to how logics of disembodied whiteness or "dematerialized" (Mohanram, 2007, p. 177) whiteness are secured through white femininity. As Mohanram (2007) notes, "if the dematerialized body is ironically also the idealized body and deemed hierarchically superior, there is still an urgent political need to comprehend why it is so" (2007, p. 177).

Lifestyle, Wellness, and the Soul of Britain

The mid-1990s saw important shifts in British society. Some of these shifts had to do with health and lifestyle regulation and a turn toward interiority and a new age spirituality (as opposed to formalized religion) as ways of navigating through life. One of the most insightful books of the times, *The Tyranny of Health* (2001), was written by Michael Fitzpatrick, a general practitioner from Hackney, London. Fitzpatrick argues that under New Labor's refashioning of health, the focus was not just on health (as in treatment of diseases) but also on healthy lifestyle and well-being, which became linked to a morality in which lifestyle choices—domains previously outside the medical sphere—became integral target areas for government's intervention into health care. National Health Service (NHS) doctors were compelled to be not just doctors but also moral guardians of patients, enhancing wellness in their lifestyles.

> Once health is linked to virtue, then the regulation of lifestyle in the name of health becomes a mechanism for deterring vice and for disciplining society as a whole. The new government health policies no longer focus on health in the familiar sense of treating illness and disease but rather encourage a redefinition of health in terms of the ways in which we live our lives. (Fitzpatrick, 2001, p. 8)

Exercise and fitness, healthy eating, nutritional diet, participation in wellness programs, emotional literacy (Ecclestone & Hayes, 2009), and more were areas reflecting intervention by the state, which worked with local communities through programs such as Health Action Zones and Healthy Living Centres. An important argument that Fitzpatrick makes is that this turning of health into a moral order must be linked to a society that has abandoned any large-scale project of social support and in which "the horizons of the individual have been reduced to their own body" (p. 7) and, one can add, their inner world itself. Whatever may go wrong (including injustices toward your body), you must now draw upon your inner resources to survive. Thus, you must cultivate those resources and revitalize your inner energy. Issues of social exclusion and marginalization constituted evidence of damaged inner worlds. Ecclestone (2007) notes that

> New Labour has created widespread agreement in all areas of public policy that social exclusion is inextricably linked to destructive influences that damage self esteem and emotional well being. Although other aspects of poverty and social exclusion are seen as important, emotional "dysfunction" and corresponding interest in happiness and emotional wellbeing. . . . have become central political concerns. (p. 457)

This was also a time when practices such as homeopathy found official support by the NHS for the first time under the Blair administration. Around the year 2000, it was reported that there were 362,000 general practitioners in the United Kingdom, but 398,000 practitioners of complementary medicine. Forty percent of general practitioners enabled access to alternative practitioners. In 1998, herbal medicine sales were around £50 million.[10]

In 2000, the BBC ran a number of television programs significantly titled *Soul of Britain*. The goal was to assess the spiritual condition of the nation at the turn of the century. The data for the program was based on a national survey commissioned by the BBC working with other groups (Hay, 2002). A particular episode that explored the rise of alternative spiritualities was presented by Michael Buerk (July 2000). It referred to a survey (as posted on the web site of Facing the Challenge) that revealed that 32% of people surveyed had tried aromatherapy, 16% astrology, 17% fortune telling, and 44% believed in a god outside of formal religion. The program enlisted a number of beliefs of New Agers, including linking alternative spiritualities with a "green agenda"—the idea that everything is connected and interdependent. In a 2001 article in the *Guardian*, Paul Heelas, a noted sociology professor, argued that people have begun to treat the body as a "thermometer"—a bad back may suggest emotional problems or absence of spirituality (Ward, 2001). It is not surprising then that within a few years, in 2003, *Cosmopolitan* magazine—usually so focused on the body—appointed a spirituality editor who stated that the magazine "already cover[s] the mind and the body but we needed the spirit as well."[11] Nina Ahmed, the acting editor of the magazine (in 2004) stated that it "want[ed] women to be the best they can in every respect of their lives" and that it did not want readers to "feel alone on their spiritual journey."[12] In fact, popular culture became an important realm in which we witnessed such new logics of national subject formations occurring. In 1995, the famous celebrity psychologist Susie Orbach, who had reportedly also treated Diana, directly linked people's inner worlds of emotions to *"our capacity for citizenship"* (emphasis added).[13]

In what follows, I analyze two themes regarding the logic of interiority through which Diana, as the face of New Britain, was discussed in media culture especially in the 1990s and after her death. This discussion of Diana, and her turn toward the interior, do not represent definitive conclusions about the logic of interiority operating in national culture in the late 1990s. This is because the so-called spiritual and alternative healing tendencies of Diana in the last years of her life were just beginning to emerge and receive attention from the media. Whether these practices would have continued had she lived on, one does not know. But they are important to focus on in terms of what they portend about the more visible rise of wellness practices in Britain (and the United States as well) since her death. Along with other white national women such as Cherie Blair or Sarah Ferguson (or even Jerry Hall, ex-wife of Mick Jagger) who engaged holistic multicultural therapies, these representations of Diana thus indicate the emergence of a new mode of selfhood through which one can read the rewriting of "the people" of Britain—particularly in metropolitan sites at the turn of the century.

A particular theme informing the representation of Diana's interiority in media assemblages that especially interests me is multicultural healing. The following section analyzes this representation in order to address the way in which interiority was being constructed through the logic of multicultural-ism. Relatedly, this analysis also enables us to explore *what* is being materi-alized and naturalized in the representations of white nationalized women such as Diana acquiring spiritual capital and harnessing life force through the embrace of non-Western healing logics. Although I focus on Diana, I also ad-dress other national celebrity white women of the times such as Cherie Blair and Sarah Ferguson to indicate a larger millennial synergy between white nationalized women and non-Western healing cultures in Britain and how the latter was reworked and dehistoricized through the former. As with other topics in this book, my larger interest here is to understand how multicultural, non-Western intimacies and domesticities are absorbed into white Western nationalism through the guise of cosmopolitanism. In what follows, I first provide some specific examples of the embrace of multicultural healing and spiritual practices by white women such as Diana. Then I explore the theo-retical implications of all this for comprehending the relation among white femininity, nation, the nonwhite non-Western woman, and a transnational cultural traffic in the "spiritual."

Cosmo Healing

New Energies, New Selves, and New Souls

A persistent theme through which Princess Diana's embrace of non-Western healing therapies is represented is that of a birth of a "new self"—and usually a more free and natural self than her earlier self. The broken-down damaged psyche of Diana, following her alleged struggles with the royal establishment, has been represented in countless media narratives as being replaced by an emerging new self in her later life that was partly produced by alternative non-Western healing practices. For instance, we learn that Diana was a regular client of North London Chinese acupuncturist Dr. Lily Hua Yu who treated her for tension and stress in the last years of her life and assisted her in overcoming eating disorders. Acupuncture is an ancient Chinese medical treatment. It works on the principle of unblocking the energy flows in the body through the use of pins and needles. A *Daily Mail* one-page coverage of Diana's acupuncture in 1998 (February 24) (Figure 6.4) stated, "Diana was very receptive to alternative therapies. The needles made her feel refreshed and active." The report quotes the staff at the acupuncture center saying,

Figure 6.4. Full page coverage of Diana's acupuncture in the *Daily Mail* on February 24, 1998. (Diana's ear and Diana: Getty Images; Coin and Pin image: Daily Mail/ Solo Syndication; Text: Daily Mail/ Solo Syndication; Acupunturist Lily Hua: Unknown Copyright; Right side Jean Cummins: Copyright unknown. Reproduced with permission.)

"the needles had been key to Diana's new found vitality." The article carries a close-up image of one of Diana's ears pierced with pins at different points; the energy flow functions are explained to us through markers in the picture so that we can understand how energy is unblocked. The article highlights the acupuncturist's own statement about Diana's recovery by placing the statement in an insert box: "*We restored her inner balance*" (my emphasis).

Similarly, we learn that feng shui, the Chinese art of rearranging furniture to enhance energy flow in the home, and tai chi, the Chinese art of restoring energy flows in the body, were utilized by Diana to restore harmony in her life. Andrew Morton, in the popular book, *Diana, Her True Story* (1998 [1992]) writes that

> she also had a personal instructor who trained her in the subtle skills of tai chi chuan, a slow-moving meditation popular in the far East. These movements are graceful and flowing . . . enabling an individual to harmonize mind, body, and spirit. . . . This gentle physical meditation was *matched by inner peace she found through meditation and prayer* often with Oonagh Toofolo, whose Catholic faith had been tempered by her work in India and the Far East. (p. 235; emphasis added)

In addition, media reports frequently focus on how related practices such as colonic irrigation, detox diet, and aromatherapy were used by Diana to clean up her energy and produce new life flows within herself. The sense one gets from reading these reports is that these practices functioned to free Diana and release her natural energy. For instance, a June 1993 report by the *Globe* provides details about colonic irrigation that Diana regularly underwent.

Colonic irrigation actually has its origins in ancient Egypt, and references to it are also found on tablets of Babylon.[14] It was reportedly also used in ancient India. While it is increasingly fashionable in the West, its origins and the rationale for inner cleansing are very much rooted in non-Western views about mind-body balance with nature. The *Globe* report described Diana as follows: "She has her bowels washed out with 12 gallons of water 3 times a week. Now she's *free from tiredness, anorexia, headaches, allergies, depression, candida*" (emphasis added). We learn in the report that the water "washed out years of collected fecal matter, mucous, and built up poisons" and that the process is concluded by a "special acidophilus tea," which restores "good bacteria" to the system. The article reports Diana stating that the treatment "makes me feel brand new and pure." If we read this metaphorically, one could be reading about the new self/body of New Labor washing out years of toxins from the (national) body's system in an attempt to free Britain.

This theme of cleaning out the inner self—especially inner energy—and producing a new energy system within is also discussed in relation to Diana's detox diet. Much has been made about Diana's detox guru Nish Joshi. In the year of the 10th anniversary of Diana's death, the *Guardian* ran a report on this celebrity health guru in which we learn that "it was she [Diana] who urged him to look to the East, to the ayurvedic medicine on which his Indian family had relied for generations, for solutions to common Western ailments: 'Go back to your roots,' she said."[15] Nish Joshi is quoted as stating that he helped Diana through bulimia with his detox treatment and that "you saw how she flourished, how she started to glow."[16] Similarly, from Andrew Morton's book, we learn about Diana's aromatherapy and about a therapist from whom Diana used to acquire healing oils and who, over 20 years, had practiced the art of making such oils that enabled the "serenity of the mind" (1998, p. 234).

The overall theme in all these descriptions is how Diana's broken-down soul is given new life through multicultural healing techniques. In fact, media reports often visually call attention to a revitalized Diana whose insides have been cleansed out through alternative healing techniques and who is now "new." In the wake of Diana's death, the *Daily Mail* produced a 12-part glossy magazine supplement, *Diana: The Untold Story* (1998) authored by journalist

Figure 6.5. *Diana, The Untold Story,* a series of special supplements, published by the *Daily Mail* in 1998. This is the cover image of Part 9 of the supplement. Notice also how the light plays on Diana, once again, to make her glow. (Photo: Frank Spooner Pictures. Text: Daily Mail/Solo Syndication.)

Richard Kay. Each part is devoted to an aspect of her life. The cover page of Part 9 frames itself directly through the title "New Age Diana" (Figure 6.5).

In the opening pages of this supplement, we learn that she often wore "white crystal, symbolizing a clear mind, stability and harmony" (p. 148). The rest of the magazine supplement gives us various details of Diana's engagement with alternative therapies. The cover visual is especially striking. Diana, in a swimsuit, sits on a bamboo-framed lounger on a wooden deck; behind her is a thick green tropical kind of foliage evoking an Asian landscape (whether in reality that was the case or not). It is bright and sunny (so we are to think that this is not England). The bamboo-framed loungers, wooden deck, a thick tropical kind of foliage in the background, all work visually to produce an Asian ambience. Diana's sun-glassed face looks up to the sunlight. A towel and sandals are casually strewn around. Diana's body is glowing and the sunlight soaking her body further highlights this. Her body seems to radiate a kind of energy that is emphasized with the loud caption on the cover page: "New Age Diana." This is not just a "new" Diana. This is a "new age" Diana. The association of New Age with its connections to nature is visually significant in this image. Similarly, there is another iconic image of Diana frolicking in the ocean in a two-piece swimsuit. Her toned glowing body radiates a natural energy that seems to burst from within. And the copy, framing the image, tells us that after undergoing many alternative treatments, Diana's new vitality—evidenced by her body—was evident.

Diana, however, was not the only high profile national white woman during New Labor's time who invoked multicultural practices of inner purification. Cherie Blair and Sarah Ferguson were also known for their embrace of alternative healing energies. Blair was particularly known for her focus on non-Western therapies and has shown a decided interest in energy cleansing through the use of Asian therapies such as acupuncture. She has been photographed wearing an acupuncture needle at a Labor Party conference (in 2001) to balance energy. She has also been seen wearing a "bio-electric shield" pendant with magic crystals to ward off harmful energy emanating from cell phones and computers. After the Blairs came into Downing Street, a feng shui expert had been brought to Downing Street to balance energy flows—the act working as a metaphor for cleaning out the energy of earlier Britain from the prime minister's official residence. In fact, the Blair government (and many think on the advice of Cherie) had recruited a feng shui expert for advice on how to improve inner city council estates. It was told by the expert that "red and orange" flowers would reduce crime and introducing a "water feature" would reduce poverty.[17] Cherie has also been a client of Bharti Vyas, the Indian new age ayurvedic guru, whose motto was "beauty on the outside begins from the inside." Furthermore, NHS's support of homeopathy during the Blair administration is also considered by many to have occurred due to Cherie's influence.

Perhaps the most remarkable practice of producing a new self that has been cleansed from inside was of the Blairs participating in an ancient Mayan "rebirthing" ritual in Mexico in summer of 2001. The Sunday Telegraph (2001) (Sydney) elaborates on this ritual. "Clad in swimming costumes, they were guided through a ritual—including bowing to the four winds as Mayan prayers were read out—invited to imagine animas in the steam from the bath and to smear watermelon, papaya and mud over each other's bodies."[18] They were invited "to scream out aloud to signify the pain of rebirth" and Tony Blair made a wish for "world peace."

Sarah Ferguson, like Cherie and Diana, is famous for her faith in non-Western therapies. She regularly imbibed homeopathy and underwent spiritual tours for healing. In fact, in her most recent book *Finding Sarah: A Duchess' Journey to Find Herself* (2012), that is about her self-renewal, Sarah provides detailed discussions of her healing in Kamalaya—the Thai wellness center. She discusses her diets, her spiritual mentoring by Rajesh Raman, the Hindu chanting of Om, and much more. Sarah is also known for having been a follower of the highly controversial now-dead Hindu guru Sai Baba. She had once traveled 120 miles north of Bangalore to visit him in 1997. She is also known for her trips to the homeopathic healer Dr. Isac Mathai's Soukya Hoslitic Center in Bangalore. In fact, in her book, Sarah makes a typical white Orientalist statement, possible only by upper-class whites as they breeze in and out of high-end ashrams and holistic treatment centers: "One of the most spiritual places on earth is India. I love the country and its people and culture for personal reasons. India has given me decades of discovery, learning and friendships. India is in my heart" (2012, p. 149). (As an aside I must say that having been born in India and having lived the first part of my life there, I would not disagree there is a depth of spirituality among people that does exist at the level of everyday. But, and here is the main thing, it exists seamlessly in tandem with an urban, and increasingly globalized, cultural space. More important, it is a kind of spirituality that you are also able to observe among the vast sections of population who live in unimaginable poverty alongside gross wealth and urban splendor, which then makes you wonder what faith in God can produce such a desire for survival among people in such poverty. But this kind of spiritual reflection is not something that you can access by breezing in and out of ashrams and health centers. It is not something you can capture simply by meditating and detoxing your body. It emerges out of your engagement with the real struggles of the disempowered.)

In 2010, when Prince Charles and Camilla Parker visited Delhi for Commonwealth Games, Camilla also went to the famous Soukya Holistic Health Centre in Bangalore where she experienced *Shirodhara*—the pouring of warm medicated oil from a mud pot on the forehead. The South Indian leading newspaper, the *Deccan Herald* (2010, September 30) noted that "the Duchess is also being taught 'Suryanamaskar' a salutation to the Sun God."[19] In fact, Hollywood celebrities such as Jennifer Aniston and Victoria Beckham are known to regularly practice *surya namaskar* to develop their bodies. According to the *Deccan Herald* report, Camilla ate "satvic" food comprising homegrown vegetables, "a far cry from her typical English supper" and that before sunset she would sit "cross legged on a 'chatai' (choir mat)" and practice meditation with a teacher. Although Camilla's example comes from a later time, I include it to illustrate how the turn to interiority symbolized by turn-of-the-century national subjects such as Diana, Cherie, or even Sarah, becomes more pronounced within a few years of the late 1990s. Which is why Diana's representations, as I stated earlier, are important to focus on because they function as a precursor to understanding the internal sensibilities of a changing "new" Britain.

A few comments are necessary to address why someone like Cherie Blair was frequently ridiculed by the media (especially the conservative media) for her new age therapy practices while Diana did not face that kind of criticism. There is no doubt that Cherie, as the prime minister's wife, played an important role in raising the visibility of new age practices. At the same time, however, images of Cherie in a political context in which she might have been wearing a crystal or bioelectric shield are frequently distorted and she is sometimes made to look very odd in the photos. Often her eyes seem to be protruding in the images, suggesting perhaps an unstable personality. Terms such as "Cherie's cranks"[20] or "bonkers"[21] have been used to describe her new age affinities. So what did Cherie do wrong that some of the media often chastised her new age sensibilities but not Diana's (who was only celebrated for her seeming transcendence)? As I suggested in Chapter 3, class and cultural capital are central to national identity. Like Sarah, who was a fashion disaster and was seen as lacking class, Cherie too is punished for lacking class. In a long article on Cherie Blair in 2008, *Vanity Fair* quoted *Sunday Times* columnist Carole Malone on Cherie's new age leanings: "No matter how many style gurus she employs, no matter how many designer outfits she buys, no matter how many therapists. . . . Cherie will always be that awkward, envious, frumpy lass from Liverpool who by dint of a decent brain and a lorry-load of ambition catapulted herself into the heart of High Society." Similarly, a

Telegraph article in 2002 explained that Cherie was far more vulnerable to "professional manipulators" (like new age therapists and so on) because she was a "child of a broken home in working-class Liverpool" and "she had to apply herself with single minded fervor to get what she wanted" while other girls were experimenting with fashion and clothes. Because Cherie is seen as lacking class, her body is often presented as undisciplined and ungovernable. Media reports have emphasized her lack of fashion sense, and her tendency to say the wrong things at the wrong time. We are meant to understand that Cherie sometimes comes across as a working-class "disaster" who does not fit "naturally" into the kind of society in which she travels. Thus, Cherie's (upper-class) new age leanings are often trivialized by the (seeming) crassness of her working-class body that she cannot transcend. In contrast, Diana's new age orientation, as I have suggested, is seen as somehow transcending her body and moving her to a saintlike plane of existence. Through these examples, we see, again, how white womanhood of the kind idealized by the nation, is elevated, pure, and spiritlike—an attribute denied to white working-class women and their unseemly bodies and style.

The Implications of Transnational/Multicultural Reworking of White Female Interiorities

The transnational dynamics between white (upper-/middle-class) national femininity (and its interiority) and nonwhite non-Western domesticity illustrated in the preceding examples highlight the ways in which a cosmopolitan (gendered) whiteness has been nationalizing itself since the mid-1990s. In particular, they call attention once again to how the intimacies (in this case interiority as a site of intimacy) of the white Western woman are being reconstructed and renationalized through domesticities (visible or invisible) of the Global South. The renewal of white national female subjects through the embrace of non-Western and in particular Asian holistic therapies is part of the same contemporary racial assemblage that extends to salons in the United States and the United Kingdom where Asian women pedicure, manicure, groom (for example through herbal facials), massage, and detox white women's bodies (Kang, 2010) in order to revitalize them as appropriate national subjects who can emotionally stand the stresses and pressures of their lives. It is part of the same global racial assemblage that makes transnational surrogacy popular and in which lower-class, poverty-stricken Asian women (particularly Indian women) bear the children of white women of the North and in the process renew white women's interiorities, filling them with hope and love, while the energies, emotions, and procreative potential of the surrogate woman of the Global South are incrementally depleted. Indeed, it is also part of the same assemblage in which domestic labor from the Global South takes care of upper-class white women's families and children (i.e., national families) as illustrated in Chapter 4.

Part of what this book has been arguing is that new expressions and subject positions of white nationalized femininity are too often serviced by the material and immaterial labor of non-Western domesticity and, in the case of this chapter, non-Western spirituality and holistic practices. In a recent *Daily Mail* report by British celebrity writer and columnist Anna Pasternak who visited the famous Chiva Som spa in Thailand, we are told through the loud copy title that Thai spas "excavate the 'sediments of sadness' from your soul."[22] We are further told that "they will detox you, rebalance you, banish fat and wrinkles, tone you up and even, in my case, excavate 'sediments of sadness' from your soul"(emphasis added). "They" here presumably refers to the healers (primarily female workers) in the spa. Read another way, the statement sounds like "they" will revive you, bring your broken self back to life, so that you can go on. And that is all you need to know about the "they." The image of Anna standing against a natural water background at the Thai spa clearly positions this narrative for identification by white upper-class women (and not men).

As stated earlier, we do not learn much about the nonwhite non-Western female, and sometimes male, workers renewing the white woman's body in such Asian spas. Who are they? Where do they come from? How much are they being paid for their services in the spas that have employed them? What about their health? Their souls? Are they able to use these holistic practices (which cost time and money today) on their own selves to renew their tired hands and tired lives? Indeed, one rarely sees white upper-class women, now so dependent on ayurveda treatments for their souls and bodies, speaking out, or even having adequate knowledge, about biocolonialism and biopiracy, which cut through all these holistic non-Western formations of New Age. Perhaps every wellness center catering to upper-class whites—whether in a Western geography or in the non-West—should include such information in their brochures (as in cigarette packs or fair trade coffee information) so that we know that underneath the expensive beauty chairs and detox tables is a transnational gendered politics of violence and appropriation at work. And that underlying the revitalized "souls of white folks" languish souls of non-Western nonwhite lower-class folks, especially women. White women's soul treatments are not just about renewing the white (national) soul. They must be seen as implicated in biocolonialism and the commercialization of non-Western indigenous medical practices. I will return to this point shortly.

Such de/materialized practices of caring for, renewing, or even excavating white women's interiority enforce "the treatment of white women's bodies [and one may add souls] as special" (Kang, 2010, p. 9). And they simultaneously discipline the bodies that perform such labor as they put those bodies in a relation of deference and service to white women. Furthermore, such disembodied cleansing of the (white) national female soul through incorporation of non-Western healing techniques reinforces a dehistoricized and hybridized cut-and-paste approach of white cosmopolitanism: picking what you want, whenever you want, from whatever religion and culture, in order to reinvent the individual white self in ways that do not produce any global criticality. So when Diana revives her energy after acupuncture, or Cherie Blair attempts to clean the energy of 10 Downing Street with feng shui, or rebirth herself in Mexico, the "multicultural," as a source of healing, simply functions as value (Fortier, 2008)—a value that renews the life force of whiteness. Instead of situating non-Western holistic therapies in a context of larger non-Western critical philosophies about life and how such therapies in colonial times often played a role in postcolonial justice (Alexander, 2006), these treatments now are simply techniques of hybridity to be plucked at will to reenergize the white nation through a new life force of whiteness. bell hooks (2001) writes about such practices by whites: "I am often struck by the dangerous naricissism fostered by spiritual rhetoric that pays so much attention on *individual* self improvement. . . . *spirituality becomes no different from an exercise program*" (p. 76; emphasis added).

Native American writers and feminists have similarly discussed (in the U.S. context) (see, for example, Crowley, 2011; Smith, 2005) white women's appropriation of Native American crafts and practices through which liberal white women seek a global multiracial sisterhood in order to escape the historical burden of whiteness. Or through embracing Native American practices, they attempt to disassociate themselves from white patriarchy, as though that is possible. Yet white women continue to remain quiet or even ignore the structural injustices toward Native Americans by the white patriarchal system in the United States even as they frequently claim that such experiences with non-Western/non-Anglo spirituality change them "forever." Sherene Razack (2002) notes that in such schemas, "indigenous cultures are fantasized . . . as repositories of health and wholeness" (p. 242) for whites, especially white women.[23] This reproduces a discourse of exoticization and naturalization of non-Western cultures (Lau, 2000).[24] So when Diana is reported as telling her African Indian dietician Nish Joshi, "go back to your roots" (to India), we see the desire for authentic nativist treatments offered by an *authentic* native. Or when the Blairs pray to the four winds and rub fruit over each other's bodies in the Mexican Rivera in a seminaked state, we see the same romanticized primitivism at work.

What I find especially alarming in this recent turn toward (white) interiority, made fashionable by global goddesses such as Diana in the 1990s, is that it essentializes both white and nonwhite/non-Western cultures/nations. One of the seductions of contemporary globalization is that we think globalization produces "flexible subjects." Indeed contemporary academic literature has also reinforced this. What has been examined less is how global logics simultaneously fix and essentialize nations and cultures. The equation between cosmopolitanism and fluidity (of identities) needs to be rethought in a far more contextual fashion, especially where race is concerned. For instance, in the examples offered in this chapter, we encounter a dangerous rhetoric that suggests that white women (and whiteness) have an "inner essence" that can be accessed, cleansed, purified, and even reconnected to nature. On the flip side, we see non-Western nations such as India, Thailand, and so on still defined by the exotic, the nonmodern, and the traditional in such rhetoric. They symbolize "nature" that is then distilled selectively (hybrid- × cosmo- ized) into the matrix of whiteness to offer liberal white national subjects a spilituality new subject position—of cosmospirituality—in the late 20th and early 21st centuries through which they can now declare their love for, and interconnection with, the whole of humanity, as did Diana.[25] Recent films such as *Eat Pray Love,* focusing again on the spiritual healing of white femininity, also showcase these desires. In fact, since the 1990s, a lot about what may called the life project of whiteness is being outsourced to, and being revitalized by, the Global South. As I write this, I am reminded of the recent film *The Best Exotic Marigold Hotel* (2012) that encourages the "outsourcing" of white British retirement to India (and note the connection between retirement and a movement toward one's inner self).

All this once again reveals that when the "national" and the "global" come together in seemingly harmonious ways to shore up national subjectivities (in the West), often the underlying economic, colonial, and geopolitical violences are hidden in such narratives of coming together. And such images of harmony, more often than not, are visualized through the figure of the white (national) woman and, in the case of this chapter, her very interiority. As I have argued in this book, white femininity—given its associations with beauty, morality, purity, love, spirituality, nature, motherhood, family, and so on—easily makes desirable numerous subject positions of (seemingly) harmonious transnational intimacies.

Yet, such transnational narratives of healing often remain walled by borders of class, as I also noted in my discussion of crossover fashion in Chapter 3. Ghassan Hage's (2000) important discussion of white cosmopolitanism and the nation must be invoked here. Hage argues that contemporary white cosmopolitanism practices reveal that only certain whites are (seemingly) competent and sophisticated enough to absorb cultural otherness into their lives. "The very language" of white cosmopolitanism "presupposes a 'cultured' and sublimated approach to otherness devoid of a too materialist functionality which the upper classes use to distinguish themselves and exclude less 'cultured' people" (p. 204). The classiness invoked by cosmo-multiculturalism suggests the need for the possession of "cosmopolitan capital" (p. 205), which is symbolically and materially denied to working class "white trash." White women, in contemporary celebrity and popular culture, who represent new planetary cosmosubjectivities are all upper-class women with cultural capital.

Indeed, a perusal of web sites marketing numerous non-Western healing practices in Western cities such as London or New York clearly illustrate which kind of white souls—upper-/upper-middle-class white women—are worth being renewed, excavated, and revitalized. Not the white trash woman who cannot financially access these places or lacks the spiritual capital to transcend her corporeality and not the nonwhite domestic woman who is coded as incapable of having an inner morality and purity (that can be renewed). And certainly not the non-Western nonwhite working-class woman of the Global South for even though she may be the historical practitioner of the very integrated holistic treatments offered to white souls, her role is to service the upper-class white female soul and the body. She cannot signify the modern but can serve the modern body and soul of white, upper-class (and usually heterosexual) femininity. I say heterosexual because in the media often the representations of the benefits reaped from such treatments focus on acquiring a beautiful (white) body type that invites heteropatriarchal desire toward that body. In a larger project on new age spirituality, Lau (2000) notes how practices like yoga and other alternative therapies are often framed in Western cultural spaces through the ideal of the Western body type—so if you engage in these therapies, the underlying message is that you will achieve a certain body type (which actually conforms to a well-groomed glowing upper-class white female body type). Yet nothing is said of the cultural norms of the bodies for and by whom these therapies were originally developed.

Scholars writing on postfeminism (Banet-Weiser, 2007; Blackman, 2004; Douglas, 2010; Gill, 2007; McRobbie, 2009; Negra, 2009; Projansky, 2007; Tasker & Negra, 2007) have noted how postfeminist logics produce new visions of "female individualization" (McRobbie, 1998) in which the management of one's lifestyle (and not oppressive social structures) is often touted as central to female empowerment. As Tasker and Negra (2007) note, "one of postfeminism's key functions is to negotiate the failure of contemporary institutions and the prospect of social death. Postfeminism frequently imagines femininity as a state of vitality in opposition to the symbolically deathly social and economic fields of contemporary western cultures" (p. 9). Clearly, the logics of white femininity that this chapter explores offer a particular subject position of female empowerment through a turn to the interior that is consistent with the observations offered by scholars of postfeminism. In presenting a shallow dehistoricized cosmopolitical/multicultural spirituality/holism that can renew the energy of a (white) national culture, such discourses of "spiritual fix" rewrite whiteness, nation, and femininity through very traditional individualized logics of structural transcendence. The problem is that these subject positions of white femininity offered by discourses of interiority overlook all other bodies of femininity (and even masculinity) that are not white upper class. Consequently, such rhetorics end up blaming those marginalized groups who simply cannot "lift" themselves up and excavate, as Anna Pasternak mentioned earlier, "the sediments of sadness" from their souls.

A few words must also be said here about biodiversity, biopiracy, biocolonialism, and the white woman (Shiva, 1999). Detox diets, colonic irrigation with its roots in the ancient Egyptian practice of enema, ayurveda, aromatherapy, homeopathy, herbal massages, and facials that high-profile white celebrity women have made popular in the West, however, are dependent on a constant supply of rich natural indigenous resources. They are also rooted in traditional indigenous pre(Euro)colonial knowledge systems of non-Western cultures (where many of these practices have an everyday currency). Until recently, these holistic healing practices have not had much commercial value. Making profits off them was never the object. Having been raised with homeopathy and ayurveda myself in India along with pharmaceutical medicines (which is called allopathy), I know from personal experience that these practices were often based on a culture of sharing (where, for instance, in family and neighborly communities, folks would have these therapies in their houses and often shared them, if necessary, with family members). Or they were sold at minimal costs at a homeopathic medicine center. My grandfather's friend—I used to call him "Doctor grandfather" as a child—had his own beautiful wooden carved box inside which were several thin homeopathy/ayurveda bottles of medicine, along with a small book (containing the knowledge behind these medicines). As a child, I often visited him with my

grandfather, especially if any family member needed medicine for some everyday ailment. Such local knowledge about homeopathy/ayurveda treatment
was usually passed down from one generation to another in families. It was
common sense (although not anymore). Yet, as environmental activist, Vandana Shiva's works have shown, Western nations—now increasingly alarmed
by pesticides and chemicals in their food, cosmetic, and beauty products, or
by the adverse reactions to strong medicines by the body—have attempted to
patent, license, or in some cases pirate the natural earthly resources on which
such holistic products are dependent. This produces a situation where indigenous cultures are denied ownership of their own earth, natural resources,
and knowledge systems as big Western corporations (often in alliance with
local companies interested in sharing profits) attempt to stake a claim to
these resources. Not only is this a plunder of the earth, land, nature, and
indigeneity itself, it is also a violation of local knowledge systems that over
centuries have produced alternative and more healthy relations to the body.
Yet, until recently, such knowledge was denigrated as nonmodern, irrational,
and primitive by European medical systems.[26] Vandana Shiva (1999) writes,
"capital now has to look for new colonies to invade and exploit . . . These new
colonies are, in my view, the interior spaces of bodies of women, plants, and
animals. Resistance to biopiracy is a resistance to the ultimate colonization
of life itself—of the future . . . of non western traditions of relation to and
knowing nature" (p. 5). The women that Shiva is talking of are non-Western
local women of the Global South involved with the earth and nature, and
not white Anglo women, nor even urban metropolitan women in the Global
South. The practice of alternative (i.e., alternative to us in the West) healing
systems in homes was often within the domestic orb of women. Clearly, we do
not want to romanticize such alternative knowledge systems or cultures or see
them frozen in the past. Ayurveda and homeopathy are very alive knowledge
systems and constantly create new discoveries. The issue is not that these
natural holistic practices from the Global South or indigenous cultures (as
in Native American cultures) cannot be used for the overall betterment of
people of the world, including in the North. The problem, however, is that
if we were to claim a logic of "global commons" for these products, as is the
tendency, we first have to recognize that "commons" is a concept that serves
the powerful. It is not so free and transparent where everyone can enjoy the
commons; it is a product of a network of power relations and geopolitics
(Coombe, 1998; Coombe & Herman, 2004; Goldman, 1998; Shiva, 1999).
Since the 1980s, there has been a huge controversy over the desire to patent
Neem (which is a plant that has tremendous health benefits and is used in
ayurveda and homeopathy). A U.S. patent was obtained by W. R. Grace on

a pesticide from seeds of the Neem tree. The patent was challenged by India and although the U.S. office dismissed the challenge, the European office finally revoked the patent. Constant struggles such as these occur against biocolonialism and patenting of indigenous medical practices. Most recently, in response to this aggressive biocolonialism and biopiracy, the Indian government has created a database of traditional Indian knowledge—Traditional Knowledge Digital Library—to prevent misappropriation and false ownership attempts. Additionally, non-Western/Asian healing practices are geared toward treating the individual (body and psyche) as a whole. Thus, doctors will often want to know about the personality of the individual. Unlike Western medicine, standardization does not occur, for it is not just the symptoms that are being treated but the individual as a whole person. The Cartesian mind-body dichotomy simply does not work here. To bring this kind of a healing culture into the context of a body-oriented culture (such as in the North Atlantic West) will immediately result in a misrecognition of the underlying philosophies about the human condition upon which different non-Western medical and healing practices are based (although increasingly forgotten). For instance, today, there is a widespread reaction by Hindus not just in North American but even worldwide to the commodification and misrepresentation of yoga in the United States. With the rise of U.S.-based practices such as nude yoga or naked yoga, yoga's link to Hindu philosophy about life, the body, and so on is damaged and transformed into something quite different and even degrading. Nude yoga becomes easy to sell to clients. Thus, the Take Back Yoga Movement has now arisen as a reaction by Hindus to this kind of sexualization. And many Hindus committed to yoga are highlighting the need to understand yoga as a philosophy and not just an exercise for the body.

Conclusion

Although the narrativization of Diana's (cosmo)spirituality and interest in holistic therapies is far less defined in the media than are other aspects of her identity—and that is because these signify the very late days of her life and hence the material available is limited—the narrativization does provide us with significant resources through which to understand the connections between (white) interiority, cosmopolitanism, nationalism, and gender—connections that as I have shown offer a framework through which to study several millennial white national women of the late 20th and early 21st centuries. What I have attempted to illustrate is how the renewal of white female interiorities through various holistic and spiritual practices borrowed from the non-West are not innocent transcendental phenomena—they are fully imbricated in national politics. There are many other aspects of Diana's "spirituality" that also circulated in mediated public spheres that I have not dealt with in this chapter: for example, the numerous discussions of Diana being channeled by psychics and mediums after her death, or the associations made with Mother Teresa, or the associations between Diana and nature after her death (as in symbolisms of nature in her burial ground in Althrop, or the Diana water fountain in Hyde Park, or the numerous visual shots during her funeral ceremony when she was represented through landscape images evoking a natural [white] English spirit).

To prevent this from becoming an endless chapter, I deliberately chose to focus more on the multicultural/transnational crossover aspects of her cleansing of the inner self in order to connect this to a neoliberal self-help national logic. But this is not to say that other spiritual aspects of the Diana phenomenon are not important or that they are not situated in the reinvention of white nationhood. If more space had been available, these would have become detailed subjects of investigation. However, for some of these topics much has already been written—for example, the association with Mother Teresa. Further, discourses about channeling Diana that are on the rise even as late as today provide important subjects that might better fit a different investigation about society's increasing fascination with the "ghostly," with "hauntings" (Gordon, 1997), and the connections to renewed white nationalisms. At the end, this chapter has simply tried to show how, in signifying the liberal/global soul of the 21st-century Anglo nation(s), white national femininity (of a certain privileged kind) constantly but invisibly relies on the gendered intimacies of the Global South to stage its soul force and renew itself as site for the representation and distribution of national life force. This enables it to mask the external, material violences of national (and racialized) neoliberalisms.

Afterword

The main goal of the book has been to highlight how white femininity, as an assemblage of power, is utilized in the production of a national modernity, in a given time and context. I have underscored that white femininity is a formation that continually shapes new contours or rearticulates old ones of the nation. One significant contribution of this book—I hope—has been to illustrate how transnational relations and contexts (even when they are not apparent) are always embedded in the processes through which white femininity and the nation articulate each other. To that extent, not only has this project rejected the (seeming) binary of the nation/global but has in fact attempted to show how the (white) female body functions as a site through which the (seeming) binary relation between the nation and global becomes unsettled. This project has also asserted that white femininity—especially white, heterosexual, middle-/upper-class, able-bodied—is a dependent formation. Its existence and assertions are dependent on the negations and cancellations of nonwhite, non-Western femininities from the Global South, working class femininities (which may be white but are often coded in as "not quite white"), and nonheterosexual femininities. To think of white femininity as a structure, an assemblage, or a formation is to consider how its operations are intimately and intricately linked to these other kinds of (often unseen) femininities. And, as I have suggested in this book, it is also to consider how white femininity is linked to nonwhite/non-Western masculinities. The project has further illustrated how in contemporary times, in many Western nations (such as the United Kingdom or the United States), the constant enactment and representations of "love" and "care" by the (privileged) white

female body—that are targeted however toward specific subjects/objects—
enables a renationalization of the nation through the production of new life
scripts of living and being.

This book has particularly focused on specific late-20th and early-21st
century national logics (especially in North Atlantic Western nations)—such
as the veneration of active motherhood, the turn to interiority for self-help,
or engagement with global care and love to deal with global atrocities and
poverty—through which new forms of neoliberal governance are being encouraged. In such forms, as state support for eradication of social ills and
inequalities is diminished, the privileged white woman is made to function
as the face of the new neoliberal logic(s) of the nation—masking (as well as
justifying) the state's rollback function. In doing so, privileged white women
end up offering models of citizenship, responsibility, and civic engagement
that individualizes the notion of citizenly and global belonging as it delinks
these concepts from any notion of collectivity and state support. As a result,
such models of civic belonging also produce new, or rearticulate old, formations of racism and classism. Women of color, women in the Global South,
and working-class women are most affected by such models of belonging
that the media—as I have illustrated in this book—only serves to celebrate
through glamorous images of white female celebrities and their beautiful
bodies. White femininity, then, in such a context, plays a role in the production of what Imogen Tyler (2013) has termed "social abjection"—a process
by which the state constitutes its borders of belonging by making certain
populations "abject" and then blaming them for that abject condition.

If there is one thing that I would want the readers to take out of this book,
it is the complex and multifaceted role that white femininity (as a racial
formation) plays in the management of contemporary liberal logics of multiculturalism and cosmopolitanism. Although this is not necessarily a novel
claim, what becomes rather evident when we look across a range of media
images of celebrity and privileged white women in North Atlantic Western
nations, driven by neoliberal governance mechanisms, is the similarity of the
logics that often underlie those images, even when the specific context might
be different. Thus, logics of international adoption, active motherhood, global
motherhood, global humanitarianism, ethnic fashion, non-Western modes
of self-care, and more seem to define (privileged) white female subjectivity in the late 20th and early 21st centuries. In fact, one of the issues I have
highlighted in relation to this is how such logics are simultaneously informed
by class. It is the economically and culturally privileged white woman (and
sometimes the wealthy nonwhite woman) who embodies these logics. By
implication, working-class or poor whites are seen as being outside of these

cosmopolitan and multicultural reworkings of the nation. Their bodies often end up signifying the overt white prejudices that affluent, upper-class whites, with their hip global makeovers, wish to dissociate from (at least in their image) that they then (by implication) displace onto the working-class white body. The chapter on fashion especially demonstrated this.

But where is white femininity now—in these recession years—especially in the United Kingdom? This is important to probe given that in many Western nations, the 21st century recession seems to be reifying and hardening particular borders of belonging that further exclude, or make vulnerable, already disenfranchised groups—the working class, immigrants, people of color (especially disempowered ones), and so on. The recession has also been encouraging—certainly in the context of the United Kingdom—new kinds of cultural withdrawals that end up resurrecting many traditional logics of culture. "Austerity" is now trendy. And the language of austerity now begins to define new expressions of citizenship and responsibility. One of the current noteworthy trends in the United Kingdom is an emerging rhetoric of how privileged people (usually white upper class) are "working so hard" and how they have scaled back their lives to reflect on, and be sensitive to, these recession times. Indeed, the logic of austerity is being glamorized through the image of "hard work" and the principle of "do-it-yourself" often promoted by upper-class white people. Celebrity royalty have been particularly significant here. Kate Middleton's recycling of her clothes at different functions, Kate and William's initial rejection of a full-time nanny (although we now hear that they have employed a nanny) and their assertion that they want to raise Prince George as much as they can on their own, their life in the small cottage in Wales, Anglesey (where we even saw images of Kate doing her grocery shopping—pushing a grocery cart down an aisle), all seemed to work deliberately to evoke a very ordinary lifestyle of a couple who, though royalty, is as ordinary as any of us (we are meant to infer). In fact, in the last few years, the phrase "working royals" has acquired popularity to remind the public that the upper class and aristocracy also work like ordinary people—often more—and without complaints. Kate Middleton, after the birth of her baby, emerged from what the media dubbed her "maternity leave." The notion of maternity leave, we know, was historically instituted to *protect the female worker* from discrimination if she had to take time off to deliver, and then attend to, a baby (in lieu of being able to afford nanny care). Yet, now royalty is seen as needing maternity leave (as though royal members can "lose" their jobs and lifestyle or face workplace repercussion if they are "out" for a long time). And the implication is that the job of a middle- or working-class female worker is somehow equivalent to the likes of Kate Middleton. We are meant to recognize that "we are all in this together"—as the rhetoric of the Cameron government has repeatedly reminded Britons. Kate is also congratulated for "returning to work" so soon. Indeed, the rhetoric of Kate's return to work seems especially noteworthy in the light of Cameron government's recent attack on mothers who end up being "stay at home moms." The state and media rhetoric have represented such mothers as engaging in a lifestyle choice (by staying home) that the taxpayer should not have to bear. However, the fact of the matter is that many mothers (including single mothers) do not have the resources for proper childcare and are forced to stay at home to tend to their children. Differences of social inequalities are erased as a new logic and rhetoric of meritocracy and do-it-yourself individualism takes hold to justify the egregious rolling back of state support for disempowered publics in the United Kingdom—and especially those hit hard by the recession. As Biressi and Nunn (2013) write of contemporary class relations in the United Kingdom, "rich elites, especially those with inherited wealth, titles and power, also take care to advertise their labour and their social, cultural, and even financial contribution to the national good" (p. 198).

We have seen this in other examples as well that speak to the reification of traditional gender practices. The *Daily Mail* in October 2009 reported an increase in knitting groups in England.[1] Such knitting circles have apparently emerged to help people adopt a "make your own" attitude during the recession, as stated by the chief executive of *Hobby Crafts* in the report. TV presenter Kirstie Allsopp featured knitting in a new Channel 4 craft show, and new magazines such as *Mollie Makes*, *The Simple Things*, and *Making* have also emerged. Knitting has become glamorous—shedding, as the *Daily Mail* report notes, its "granny" image. Clearly, here we have another instance of how a national discourse of austerity is being glamorized and normalized through images and practices of affluent white women who are now made to look ordinary as they encourage other women to make their own clothes, instead of buying. Such images reconstruct affluent and upper-class white women through logics of thrift that we would normally associate with the lower-middle or even working class. In so doing, class and raced effects of austerity are minimized and the issue of "choice"—that is the *choice* to scale back one's material life versus not having anything in the first place that can be scaled back—is rendered obscure. As austerity is glamorized, it emerges as a new national logic signifying responsible citizenship. And those who are unable to exercise austerity—and depend on the state—are seen as somehow being undisciplined, work-shy, and morally irresponsible.

The thing is, however, that in the United Kingdom, as well as in the United States, the contemporary "recession" has been a white person's recession.

Lower- and working-class people (that includes several people of color) have hardly seen any improvement in their economic conditions since the 1980s and 1990s, when rolling back the state first emerged as a major mantra—not just during the Thatcher/Reagan years, but also during the Blair/Clinton years. Thus, it is not that there is a *sudden* "austerity" facing the poor. Their conditions have always been austere. It is only now when the middle and even upper middle class begin to feel the heat of the recession that austerity as a logic takes hold. And the inability to exercise austerity becomes projected onto the working class, people of color, and poor immigrants who become symptoms of a morally bankrupt society—as Cameron so strongly declared after the 2011 "riots" when he refused to say that the intersection of race and poverty had anything to do with the "looting" that took place.

Additionally such rhetorics of austerity are also resurrecting many traditional gendered logics of domesticity—such as knitting, as mentioned earlier, or making your own jams (or other similar food products). (Kate Middleton in particular has made this fashionable; we learned that in Anglesey she made jams, which she has given the royal family as Christmas gifts.) While such practices in and of themselves are not a problem, the issue is that it is women who are expected to take these up (we do not find images of men in knitting circles, for example). And often the women who are able to engage in these practices are ones who have the luxury of time to do so (and do not necessarily have the pressure to maintain or find jobs to supplement their families). Thus, white (upper-) class privilege already underlies these practices. Yet, these practices are unreflexively offered as solutions for our austere times for everyone.[2]

If white women (especially privileged white women who *exercise a choice* instead of being forced to be financially prudent) become symbolic sites for nationalizing the recession in ways that keep alive, indeed even harden, classed and raced boundaries, where issues of immigrants, as well as Muslims—the other "problem" of the British landscape in our times—are concerned we see white womanhood functioning as a site through which multiculturalism's apparent failure is being affirmed in the United Kingdom today. This is particularly seen in the context of Asian and Muslim men. The last few years in the United Kingdom have produced moral panics about Asian men, particularly of Pakistani origin, grooming and exploiting young white vulnerable girls for sex. Jack Straw, Labor party member, member of Parliament, and former Blair administration cabinet member, spoke out in outrage in 2011, targeting men of Pakistani heritage. He stated that they (men of Pakistani origin) see white girls as "easy meat." Noting that now that these "young men" are "in a western society . . . [they] act like any other young men, they're fizzing and popping with testosterone, they want some outlet for that, but Pakistani heritage girls are off-limits" and so, according to him, white young girls become easy targets for their sex exploitation.[3] Although Straw does acknowledge that sexual exploitation and violence are also engaged in by other offenders including white men, his main explanation is a cultural one. Men of Pakistani "heritage" (and note the link between "heritage" and the discourse of national "origins")—and we are to understand such men to be primarily Muslim men—because of their cultural upbringing end up targeting young white women because they cannot find an outlet for their testosterone in their "conservative" (we are to understand "sexually repressed") Muslim/Pakistani cultures. Newspapers such as the *Telegraph* have reiterated such rhetorics. In an issue in 2013, the *Telegraph* declared in its headline "We will regret ignoring Asian thugs who target white girls."[4] This was followed by a subheadline that stated, "What a god awful mess this country has got itself into with multiculturalism, and once again our fear of racism will lead to the betrayal of hundreds of young girls." These lines are immediately followed by a powerful photo of a young white girl, her face covered with her hands (suggesting both despair and shame). One notes the language of "we" and "our" betrayal of white girls. This young white girl in the photo is meant to stand in for "hundreds of young girls." And this photo visually tells us what the article could not explicitly in its written text: that the kinds of girls who have been "betrayed" by multiculturalism are white girls (the future of white national domesticity and the procreative future of the nation). Although it has been revealed since that underage Muslim girls (who in media reports are already assumed to be nonwhite and non-Western) and Asian girls have also been victimized by such gangs, the national outrage has taken on a cultural-identity dimension. Fury has been primarily expressed at the violation of young white girls (and less so for other girls). Thus, once again, Asian and Muslim men, in particular, are culturally criminalized in relation to white women. Instead of pursuing a complex probe into why and how such gangs are able to operate and what larger nationalist circumstances might be producing such situations, a rhetoric of violation of young vulnerable white girls ends up reproducing hard stereotypes about Asian men, solidifying current arguments against multiculturalism. This specter of pure and fragile white womanhood being defiled by nonwhite non-Western men—that has surfaced so many times in various national/colonial scripts in Britain and its empire—had been particularly powerful in Enoch Powell's famous (1968) Rivers of Blood speech. The speech evoked an image of an old widowed English woman who lived alone and was harassed by immigrants—"wide grinning piccaninnies" (as Powell offensively labeled them). That famous image seems to reemerge here in a different guise, to tell us how multiculturalism is not working. And it seems to matter little in this rhetoric that white men are also involved in shameful sexual violations. Yet, we do not offer a "cultural" explanation for their crimes, nor do we say that the whiteness is a threat to the nation's safety, or that white men's testosterones spill out of control—into sexual violence and trafficking—when they do not find "outlets" for their sexual urges.

While space does not permit a more detailed discussion of such issues, suffice it to note then we see two salient operations of white womanhood in these current times in the United Kingdom: (1) White womanhood becomes a site through which economic austerity is glamorized and justified, and through that class and raced inequalities are obscured; and (2) defiled white womanhood functions as a trope through which multiculturalism is being rendered a problem, justifying already preexisting rhetorics about the failure of multiculturalism. While I do not suggest that all aspects of the economic and cultural crises in the United Kingdom can be read off images of white womanhood, I do suggest that it is important to keep noting how signs and signifiers of white femininity are being mobilized to signify national crises around recession and multiculturalism. In contrast to the desired rhetoric of white womanhood during the Blair years that this book has traced, these Cameron years in the United Kingdom espouse a rhetoric of retreatism—signified solidly by the current image of Kate Middleton and her love for the countryside (she preferred to live in a remote village in Wales with William) or the images of her knee-length and usually arm-covered dresses. While novelist and twice Booker Prize winner Hilary Mantel's comments, in February 2013, about Kate being a plastic princess may have produced a national furor, her comments were illuminating to say the least.[5] Read closely, they certainly seem to suggest how Kate's "machine made" precision, don't rock the boat persona (as a contrast to Diana's) seems to fit well the retreatism of the Cameron times. Indeed, if the contours of white femininity shaped by the Diana phenomenon made Diana the ideal ambassador of New Labor's cosmopolitan and global values, then the safe outline of another version of white femininity presented by Kate Middleton's image seems to be making her the ideal (white national) face of the Cameron-led government. But one still has to wait to see how Kate's image unfolds over the years.

And Diana—is her image still powerful? Is she still being articulated and rearticulated to new times at this moment? I had stated earlier that Diana does not seem to die. She keeps emerging and reemerging for new articulations. This is how multifaceted her script is. The Diana biopic starring Naomi Campbell is about to be released in the United States just as this book is going into production. While I will not be able to see the film in its entirety, the trailer and the description suggest that it is based on the story of Hasnat Khan and Diana. To that extent, I think it would be rather interesting to analyze this representation of a Muslim man and a white woman—whose real lives crossed in the late 20th century but are now being revisualized in the second decade of the 21st century, when Islamaphobia is raging on both sides of the Atlantic and multiculturalism has been declared a failure by the British government. Further, an investigation into Diana's death has been recently reopened by Scotland Yard, in light of (apparently) new information, to determine whether her death was a conspiracy. It would be important to pay attention to how this story unfolds and what it might reveal about how a particular script of white femininity, which Diana signified in the late 20th and early 21st centuries, might now be expressing, as well as serving, anxieties of contemporary British nationalism.

I see this book as part of a larger conversation about white femininity in the context of nationalism and contemporary postcolonial relations in North Atlantic–situated Western nations. Indeed, there is so much to be probed and understood about the relations between white femininity and the nation in contemporary (Western) postcolonial contexts. I want to end by offering some thoughts on future directions for further work on white femininity and the nation. In the process of writing this book, I have been forced to recognize that there are some really important areas about white femininity about which we need to know more. These include, among others, issues such as the relations among white femininity, nation, and queer resistances; the contemporary militarization of white femininity;[6] white femininity and representations of Muslim men (which I have partly addressed in this book but more work needs to be done); white femininity and the contemporary environmental movement (worldwide); and white femininity, national identity, and transgendered subject positions. I have highlighted these areas, knowing there are many others, because these are important political issues of our times. And these issues are imbricated in the numerous desires and despairs of contemporary postcolonial relations as they inform the Global North and impact the Global South. Ultimately, we need more conversations on how race is increasingly becoming a slippery object (that is difficult to see in black and white ways or through predictable logics in the 21st century) where many of the earlier signs of whiteness are (seemingly) less visible or operable today, while new signs are continually being enacted under the guise of "progressive" global relations (of the 21st century) that are subtly articulating old nationalist racist logics in many Western nations as well as in middle European ones.

Notes

Chapter 1. White Femininity in the Nation, the Nation in White Femininity

Note to epigraph: Mayer, C. (2007, August 16). How Diana transformed Britain. *Time*. Retrieved from http://content.time.com/time/specials/2007/article/0,28804,1650830_1650834_1653460,00.html. Accessed August 9, 2009.

1. See here also the special issue on Diana and Democracy (1999) in *New Formations*, volume 36.

2. Tapia (2011) is an exception—especially in relation to Diana—that will be addressed later.

3. In a video produced by the *Daily Mail, Diana: A life in fashion* (1997), Collector's Edition.

4. Female force to be reckoned with: Princess Diana is immortalized in a "glowing" comic book. (2009, October 29). Retrieved from http://www.dailymail.co.uk/news/article-1223639/Female-force-reckoned-Princess-Diana-immortalised-glowing-comic-book.html. Accessed June 11, 2011.

5. I am thinking here of works by scholars such as Antoinette Burton, or Helen Callaway, both of whom have examined European women in the colonies during the time of high imperialism. The focus in such important works, however, is less on the issue of nation and national identity and more on the racialization of white women in the empire.

6. See also Arat-Koc (2010), Thobani (2010), and Moreton-Robinson, Casey, & Nicoll (2008). Although the last focuses on transnational whiteness, most of the essays in the volume except for the essay by Serisier (2008) focus on earlier colonial times.

7. Instead of citing specific works, I want to note specific scholars. I am referring here to many influential scholars' work on the nation such as Homi Bhabha, Gayatri

Spivak, Nira Yuval-Davis, Zillah Eisenstein, Sarah Radcliffe, Lisa Lowe, Lauren Berlant, Partha Chatterjee, Stuart Hall, Benedict Anderson, Eric Hobsbawm, and Ernest Gellner among others.

8. This particular point has been inspired by what I recall to be an observation made by Stuart Hall in the Draper lecture given at Queen Mary University of London on November 15, 2006. I was personally present in the audience. The title of the lecture was "Once More Around Cultural Identity." I tried to contact Queen Mary University during the writing of this book to secure a copy of the lecture to enable a fuller citation; however, they (the Events Department) informed me that do not have any recording of the lecture. Thus, I do not have any more precise citational information than my recollection of Hall's observation in that inspiring lecture. In 2007, in an interview by the *Guardian* (by Tim Adams), Hall makes a similar point when he notes that debates around the veil represent really "a lag between one modernity and another . . . If you come from a culture where relations between women and men are much more traditional you begin to see *what not wanting to be exposed to the gaze of a man really means*" (emphasis mine). Retrieved from http://www .theguardian.com/society/2007/sep/23/communities.politicsphilosophyandsociety. Accessed October 5, 2013.

9. Hardy, F. (2009, July 25). I won Miss England to prove being black is never an excuse for failure says Linford Christie's niece. *Daily Mail Online*. Retrieved from http://www.dailymail.co.uk/femail/article-1202029/I-won-Miss-England-prove-black -NEVER-excuse-failure-says-Linford-Christies-niece.html. Accessed May 31, 2010.

10. Cool Britannia lure launched. (1997, January 7). *The Guardian*, p. 5.

11. Cool Britannia is no media fad. (1998, August 27). *Marketing Week*, pp. 36–37.

12. See also Povinelli (2002) and Gunew (2004) in a different context.

13. Retrieved from wsiwyg://897/http://www.guardian.co.uk/quiz/questions/ 0,5961,211620,00.html. Accessed June 3, 2008.

14. The article ran on November 19, 1999.

15. The article ran on September 4, 1997.

16. NBC Nightly News. (1997, October 1). Retrieved from http://www.nbcuniversal archives.com/nbcuni/clip/5112930084_s03.do. Accessed January 6, 2003.

17. Ibid.

18. Ibid.

19. Ibid. These figures are from 6:30 P.M. broadcast.

20. These figures are from *New York Times*, September 10, 1997, Sec. C, 18, col. 5.

21. Last respects: Let her legacy be compassion. (1997, September 8). *The Mirror*. Retrieved from http://www.highbeam.com/doc/1G1-61059692.html. Accessed on December 20, 2004.

22. I do not mean to suggest here that Muslim men are always necessarily nonwhite or from the Middle East. Indeed, there are white Muslim men—although limited numbers of them. It is the case, however, that the mainstream discourse in the West generally focuses on nonwhite Muslim men from the Middle Eastern part of the world. And it is this discourse that I investigate here.

Chapter 2. Racialized Maternalisms

1. Blair calls for age of giving. (1997, October 1). *The Guardian*. Retrieved from http://www.theguardian.com/politics/1997/oct/01/speeches1. Accessed September 10, 2008.

2. Did bad parenting really turn these boys into killers? (2000, October, 31). *The Guardian*. Retrieved from http://www.guardian.co.uk/uk/2000/nov/01/bulger.family andrelationships. Accessed October 5, 2011.

3. Did bad parenting really turn these boys into killers?

4. Loneard, T., & Reilly, J. (2012, December 16). "She would get very upset that he wouldn't let her hug him": Dysfunctional relationship of Sandy Hook gunman and his mother. *The Daily Mail*. Retrieved from http://www.dailymail.co.uk/news/article -2249185/Nancy-Lanza-Did-paranoid-gun-crazed-mother-trigger-Sandy-Hook -Connecticut-killing-spree.html. Accessed October 5, 2011.

5. The making of John Walker Lindh. (2002, October 7). *Time*. Retrieved from http://www.time.com/time/magazine/article/0,9171,1003414,00.html. Accessed October 5, 2011.

6. Borger, J. (2002, October 4). Bright boy from the California suburbs who turned Taliban warrior. *The Guardian*. Retrieved from http://www.guardian.co.uk/world/2002/oct/05/usa.afghanistan. Accessed October 5, 2011.

7. This controversial image of Demi Moore has also been discussed by some others concerned with contemporary representations of the pregnant body—such as as Tyler (2001), Stabile (1994), Oliver (2012), Matthews & Wexler (2000), among others.

8. The new sexy moms. (1997, May 26). *People Weekly*, cover.

9. Mama Madonna. (1996, October 28). *People Weekly*, cover.

10. Cover. (2000, March 13). *People Weekly*.

11. Although Anita Harris's (2004) work has utilized the can-do versus at-risk tropes to discuss girlhood in particular, in this chapter, I deploy these notions to examine images of (white) postfeminist motherhood. I address the reasons for this utilization later in the chapter.

12. Douglas and Michaels (2004) have also offered a discussion of what they saw as Diana's "performance," "a carefully coordinated public relations campaign" where her photos with her children were to prove that she was the better parent (p. 127).

13. The phrases within quotation marks in Hill Collins's quote refers to words of an anonymous African American mother in 1904. Hill Collins draws on her words in the excerpt cited here.

14. Stephen had massive wounds. There is no way those boys didn't know what they are doing. I am so full of anger frustration and pain that I physically hurt all of the time; Doreen Lawrence tells for the first first time how her life has been destroyed by the racist killing of her eldest son. (1997, March 7). *Daily Mail*. Retrieved from http://www.highbeam.com/doc/1G1–110800198.html. Accessed October 6, 2011.

15. This is from the preface to the Kindle edition of the book, from Amazon, so I do not have the page numbers.

16. Retrieved from http://www.dailymail.co.uk/femail/article-2130941/Stephen -Lawrence-murder-Mother-Doreen-state-isolation-19-years-later.html. Accessed April 1, 2013.

17. See also Tapia (2011) for a very different discussion of death and the maternal.

18. I am using this phrase echoing Jhally and Lewis's (1992) concept of "enlightened racism" captured in the title of their book. Like enlightened racism, enlightened nationalism performs a mystifying function that obscures the distribution of cultural power and identities within a national polity.

19. The works of scholars such as Elizabeth Povinelli, Ann Marie-Fortier, Sneja Gunew, and Wendy Brown among others on national governance in late liberalism must also be acknowledged. My thinking on many such matters has been influenced by this rich body of scholarship.

20. See here also Marriott's (2007) important work on blackness and death where he argues that "racism also robs the black of his or her ability to live and so die as a free subject" (p. 234). Patterson's (1982) important and foundational work must also be acknowledged here.

21. Bedell, G. (1993, November 28). James Bulger: The death of innocence. *The Independent*. Retrieved from http://www.independent.co.uk/news/uk/crime/james -bulger-the-death-of-innocence-739586.html. Accessed October 2, 2010.

22. Kauffman, J. (1989, October 4). Princess Diana. *People*. Retrieved from http:// www.people.com/people/article/0,20063181,00.html. Accessed October 2, 2010.

23. Spice Girls honour Di at awards. (1997, September 5). *Daily Record* (Glasgow, Scotland). Retrieved from http://www.highbeam.com/doc/1G1–61004891.html. Accessed October 2, 2010.

24. This quote in the *Los Angeles Times* comes from Natasha Walter, author of *The New Feminism* (1999), from which the article drew.

25. These statistics were taken from the European Union's statistical unit, Eurostat, which was cited in: Doughty, S. (2011, April 1). Single mother Britain: U.K. has most lone parents of any major European nation. *The Daily Mail*. Retrieved from http:// www.dailymail.co.uk/news/article-1372533/Britain-lone-parents-major-Euro-nation. html#ixzz2bM4uEq1M. Accessed February 3, 2013.

26. Pearson, A. (2011, January 13). Why we all need a Tiger Mother. *The Telegraph*. Retrieved from http://www.telegraph.co.uk/education/8255804/Why-we-all-need-a -Tiger-Mother.html. Accessed September 4, 2013.

27. The real Elizabeth II. (2002, January 10). *The Telegraph*. Retrieved from http:// www.telegraph.co.uk/news/1399980/The-real-Elizabeth-II.html. Accessed September 4, 2013.

28. The latest reincarnation of white motherhood, reflecting Western national desires, is the "security mom" that has been analyzed so well by Grewal (2006).

29. The term is from Young's (1990) title of his book *White mythologies: Writing history and the West*.

Chapter 3. Fashioning the Nation

1. Howell (1998, p. 22).

2. Diva of style. (1996, March 1). *People* magazine. Retrieved from http://www .people.com/people/archive/article/0,20063566,00.html. Accessed October 6, 2011.

3. Andrew Morton in the *Daily Mail's* (1997) video, *Life in Fashion, Collector's Edition.*

4. Victor Edelstein, quoted in Howell (1998, p. 44).

5. Howell (1998, p. 44).

6. Retrieved from www.pbs.org/newshour/bb/remember/1997/diana.html. Accessed October 6, 2011.

7. Green, M. (1997, June 29). Love on the rocks. *People* magazine. Retrieved from http://www.people.com/people/archive/article/0,20113005,00.html. Accessed October 6, 2011.

8. Timmons, H. (2005, April 3). The once and future Camilla. *The New York Times.* Retrieved from http://www.nytimes.com/2005/04/03/fashion/03camilla.html?_r=0. Accessed October 6, 2011.

9. Cunningham, S. (1997, October 27). Britain is at the forefront of designer-led revolution. *The Times.*

10. Kamp, D. (1997, March). London swings! Again! *Vanity Fair.* Retrieved from http://www.vanityfair.com/magazine/archive/1997/03/london199703. Accessed February 20, 2013.

11. BOP Consulting. (2010). *Creative and Cultural Economy Series, Vol. 2. Mapping the creative industries: A toolkit.* London: British Council Creative Economy Unit.

12. Creative Industries Mapping Document, 1998. Department for Culture, Media and Sport. Retrieved from http://www.creativitycultureeducation.org/creative-industries-mapping-document-1998. Accessed August 12, 2013. (Also see discussion in *Mapping the creative industries: A toolkit.* British Council. Retrieved from http://www.britishcouncil.org/mapping_the_creative_industries_a_toolkit_2–2.pdf. Accessed August 11, 2013

13. Cherie Booth labors at gym. (1997, February 13). *The Times.*

14. (1997, June 19). *The Evening Standard.*

15. *Heat and Dust* is the famous Ivory Merchant Production that came out in 1983 based on the novel by Ruth Jhabvala, which won the Booker Prize in 1975. The main theme of the movie focuses on a white British woman who is in India during colonial times. She abhors stiff British social constraints and finds herself charmed by India and a Princely Nawab. I term this section *Heat and Dust* to signify a continuing logic of such fascination with India that is often expressed by the white female body.

16. Robson, J. (2002, May 21). *The Telegraph.* All set for an Indian summer. Retrieved from fashion.telegraph.co.hk/news-features/TMG32299784/All-set-for-an-Indian-summer.html. Accessed September 1, 2013.

17. The photo in the *Daily Mail* is in the article: Rawi, M. (2011; May 20). You look starry in that sari Mrs. Clegg: Miriam is pretty in pink at Asian women of achievement awards show. Retrieved from http://www.dailymail.co.uk/femail/article-1389147/Miriam-Clegg-pretty-pink-Asian-Women-Achievement-Awards-show.html. Accessed January 2, 2013. Interestingly, in this *Daily Mail* report, Teresa's salwar kameez was wrongly called a sari, illustrating an alarming dehistoricization and a "they are all the same" attitude.

18. Harvey, M. (1998, March 26). Sari chic: Cherie dazzles in a display of traditional eastern style. *The Daily Mail*, p. 13.

19. Suri, S. (1999, November 22). Behind the Tony bash. *Outlook*. Retrieved from outlookindia.com. Accessed November 12, 2012.

20. Foggo, D. (2002, January 6). Cherie's Indian outfits made by workers "on poverty pay." *The Telegraph*. Retrieved from http://www.telegraph.co.uk/news/worldnews/asia/india/1380567/Cheries-Indian-outfits-made-by-workers-on-poverty-pay.html. Accessed February 1, 2013.

21. Bevins, A. (1998, March 26). Blair vows to fight crime and racism. *The Independent*.

22. I kept fighting to win freedom. Satpal defended himself from a racist attacker. He ended up in 74 prisons. *Socialist Worker*, Issue 1807; July 6, 2002. Retrieved from http://socialistworker.co.uk/art/5167/I+kept+fighting+to+win+freedom. Accessed March 22, 2014.

23. Murderer freed after European court ruling. *Daily Mail*. Retrieved from http://www.dailymail.co.uk/news/article-123928/Murderer-freed-European-Court-ruling.html. Accessed September 12, 2003.

24. Quoted in Chaudhary, V. (1998, March 26). Blair hails Britain's super-rich Asians. *The Guardian*, p. 6.

25. Bhachu's (2004) important discussion of the history of salwar kameez in Britain, as it was made by different generations of diasporic Indians/Pakistanis is also worth noting. My focus, however, is its history in India.

26. A rather extreme example of this is that Chanel has now created super expensive limited edition saris to sell in India. The ones who will buy these will most likely be upper-class Indians chasing the Chanel name but buying their own national garments! Once again, we see a dehistoricization, as well as an intersection between a Western-driven global multiculturalism and upper-class relations in India.

27. Columnist Rituparna Chatterjee (2012) wrote a powerful blog post—a letter to Oprah—on the CNN-IBN (one of the largest television channels in India) website that circulated heavily. Chatterjee, R. (2012, July 23). *An open letter to Oprah Winfrey from an Indian who eats with her hand [web log post]*. Retrieved from http://ibnlive.in.com/blogs/rituparnachatterjee/2802/63722/an-open-letter-to-oprah-winfrey-from-an-indian-who-eats-with-her-hand.html. Accessed June 21, 2013. It is worth quoting at length from this blog:

> But which India have you [Oprah] come looking for? The one that shops at state-of-the-art supermarkets and vacations abroad or the one whining about their misery in tiny holes of homes with LCD televisions on the walls? The India that scrapes by with $200 a month but sends its children to subsidised government schools to pick up fluent English? The India of your press information—fascinating, with its many-headed goddesses and grimy, naked children playing by roadside hovels—or the India of the future—an economic superpower that looms large outside the range of an average American's myopic vision?

Chatterjee's comments call attention to the contradictions that make up the India that Oprah clearly seems to miss. She continues,

> Oprah, your comment about eating with the hand is really not that big a deal to us; we are used to gross Western ignorance regarding our ancient country. But as a responsible public figure about to air a show that will be beamed across the world, you should have done your homework. Using our hands to eat is a well established tradition and a fact none of us are ashamed of. Our economic distinction has nothing to do with it.
>
> A millionaire here eats the same way a pauper does. You have been to Asian nations. You should know that.
>
> In fact, we scoff at people who try to tackle their pizzas and rotis with cutlery. In one sweeping, general statement you linked the usage of cutlery to our progress. . . . Do you say you did not mean it as an offence? It is then an abominable insensitivity to Indian hospitality.

28. I have also discussed elsewhere the nation-centric engagements with multiculturalism in Western discourses such as in the United States. See Shome (2010) and Shome (2012).

Chapter 4. "Global Motherhood"

1. In saying this, I am not suggesting that "insides" and "outsides" of the nation are separate and independent. Indeed, the global and the national are interlinked relations. However, in the staging of national imaginations, this binary is often upheld—as in domestic versus foreign policies.

2. See also Chouliaraki (2006).

3. Tempest, M. (2002, September 2). Blair calls for the healing of Africa. Retrieved from http://www.guardian.co.uk/environment/2002/sep/02/greenpolitics.world summit2002. Accessed October 6, 2011.

4. Retrieved from http://www.oxfam.org.uk/what_we_do/issues/debt_aid/kwatkins _blair.htm. Accessed October 6, 2011.

5. *Q & A: Arms to Africa scandal.* (1998, May 10). BBC News. Retrieved http:// news.bbc.co.uk/2/hi/uk_news/90526.stm. Accessed October 6, 2011.

6. Hubbard, K. (1998, February 2). Touched by Diana. *People, 49(4).* Retrieved from http://www.people.com/people/archive/article/0,20124388,00.html. Accessed July 11, 2010.
This statement reproduced in *People* magazine was made by Debbie Tate, cofounder of a group of Washington homes for abused children.

7. Ibid. (This statement reproduced in *People* magazine was made by Roger Singleton, chief executive of a British charity.)

8. Christina Lamb, in *The Sunday Times* cited in B. MacArthur (1997) (Ed.). Requiem: Diana: Princess of Wales 1961–1997. *New York: Arcade.*

9. Retrieved from http://www.unicef.org/specialsession/photoessays/audrey/photo1 .htm. Accessed July 11, 2010.

10. Meg Ryan's "metaphysical" adoption. (2008, September 12). *Boston Globe*. Retrieved from http://www.boston.com/ae/celebrity/articles/2008/09/12/meg_ryans _metaphysical_adoption/. Accessed July 11, 2010.

11. Retrieved from http://www.dailymail.co.uk/tvshowbiz/article-1212510/Katherine -Heigl-Im-adopting-baby-girl-Korea.html. Accessed June 14, 2013.

12. Retrieved from www.usatoday.com/life/people/2006–10-23-madonna-oprah-x .htm. Accessed June 3, 2012.

13. Bono praises Madonna for African Adoption. (2006, November 13). Retrieved from www.exposay.com/bono-praises-madonna-for-adoption/v/6011. Accessed November 1, 2010.

14. The notion of ethics of care here is influenced by Michel Foucault's work.

15. This information is taken from the web site of International Adoption. Retrieved from http://www.internationaladoptionhelp.com/international_adoption/ international_adoption_guatemala_available_children. Accessed November 1, 2010.

16. See Dorow (2006) for a different discussion of maternal abandonment.

17. I am deliberately echoing here legendary Bengali feminist Marxist writer, Mahasweta Devi's (1997) short story "Breast Giver" in her book *Breast Stories* (1997) (translated and discussed by Gayatri Spivak).

18. Parrenas and Boris (2010) is another source that offers excellent discussions of how intimate care is being commodified under globalization.

19. The term is from Adrienne Rich (1980).

20. Retrieved from http:// politicalticker. Blogs.cnn.com/2008/01/11/mccains-start -speaking-about-their-children. Accessed September 7, 2010.

21. Cited in "John McCain-2008 Presidential Candidate." Retrieved from http:// lesbianlife.about.com/od/lesbianactivism/p/John McCain/htm. Accessed September 7, 2010.

22. Retrieved from www.dailymail.co.uk/tvshowbiz/article-412751/Agenlina-set -adopt-baby.html Accessed September 3, 2010.

23. Angelia Jolie: I'm on the pill. (2006, December 14). Retrieved from www .foxnews.com/story/0,2933,236522,00.html. Accesssed September 3, 2010.

24. Vineyard, J. (2006, November 1). Madonna calls uproar over adoption "racist" in new interview. *MTV*. Retrieved from http://www.mtv.com/news/articles/1544540/ madonna-calls-adoption-uproar-racist.jhtml. Accessed November 1, 2010.

25. Confessions on a TV show: Oprah hears Madonna's side of the story. (2006, October 25). *The Guardian*. Retrieved from www.guardian.co.uk/world/2006/oct/26/ arts.usa. Accessed November 1, 2010.

26. Lilie Chouliaraki (2013) has argued that there has been an "epistemic shift" in the communication of humanitarianism. Whereas in the past there was an "other-oriented morality, where doing good to others is about our common humanity and asks nothing back," now we have the "emergence of a self-oriented morality, where doing good to others is about 'how I feel' and must, therefore, be rewarded by minor gratifications to the self . . . the confessions of our favorite celebrity, the thrill of the rock concert and Twitter journalism . . ." (pp. 3–4).

27. Lynch, J. (2005, December 19). Happy Father's Day. *People*. Retrieved from www.people.com/people/archive/article/0,20145123,000.html. Accessed November 3, 2010.

28. Angelina Jolie: Her mission and motherhood. (2006, June 23). *Anderson Cooper 360 Degrees*. Retrieved from http://transcripts.cnn.com/TRANSCRIPTS/0606/23/acd.02.html. Accessed November 3, 2010.

29. Domestic vs international adoption: Are celebrities overlooking American children. (2009, April 3). Retrieved from http://www.foxnews.com/entertainment/2009/04/03/domestic-vs-international-adoption-celebrities-overlooking-american-children/. Accessed November 3, 2010.

30. I thank one of the reviewers for pushing me to think about this point.

31. Negra (2010) has an interesting discussion on the Jolie-Pitt family that is worth looking at.

Chapter 5. White Femininity and Transnational Masculinit(ies)

1. At this time, few were aware that Diana's "real love," as alleged by many reports, was Pakistani doctor, Hasnat Khan. Most understood that she and Dodi were romancing when they died.

2. An excellent book that does this is Massad (2008). In an inverted gesture, Massad focuses on how Arabs represent sexuality (including Western sexuality) and how understanding those frameworks enable us to provincialize Western frames of sexuality, which then come across as primitive and deviant.

I want to also mention a visual project that in recent years has been actively working to challenge dominant representations of Arab and Muslim men on our global screens. Canadian-Iraqi photojournalist Tamara Abdu Hadi's (2009) project "Picture an Arab Man" has collected numerous photos of Arab men that were taken while traveling the world. These images are oppositional to the violent, aggressive, and macho images of Muslim men shown in mainstream media. Such visual projects constitute important geopolitical steps toward creating alter images of Muslim men that can be accessible and visible in the West so that we can see the Muslim man through frames of complexity, dignity, justice, and humanity.

3. Cited in: Egyptian media questions the death of Di and Dodi. (1997, September 1). *Deutsche Presse-Agentur*. Retrieved from LexisNexis. Accessed 3 September 2012.

4. Ibid.

5. Iranian magazine claims Diana assassinated for loving a Moslem. (1997, September 19). *Deutsche Presse-Agentur*. Retrieved from LexisNexis. Accessed September 3, 2012.

6. Cited in: Egyptians hail one of their own for snapping up royal prize. (1997, August 14). *Agence France Presse* (International News). Retrieved from LexisNexis. Accessed September 3, 2012. Please note that although this article appeared two weeks before Diana's death, its framing of the Dodi-Diana relationship as a race with a prize is significant for this perception only seems to have increased in many Middle Eastern circles after the tragedy.

7. Gadhafi says British agents killed Diana, Dodi Fayed (1997, September 28). Associated Press. Gadhafi is also reported to have described the Diana–Dodi car crash as an "odious racist, religious and ethnic crime contrary to all laws, human rights and civilization." See: Kadhafi sees British and French hand in Diana's death. (1997, September 2) *Africa News*. Numerous other newspapers and Middle Eastern columnists, not all of whom are cited here, have similarly reflected such views. So this is not just a view of Gadhafi, who the West usually liked to see as "crazy."

8. Cited in: Qadhafi says Diana, Dodi deaths "arranged" by Secret Services. (1997, September 3). *BBC Summary of World Broadcasts*. (Original source: Libyan TV, Tripoli, in Arabic [1997, September 1]).

9. Will's tragic plea/Prince wanted Di to ditch Dodi. (1997, September 1). *Hobart Mercury*.

10. Jemima Khan in a November 2008 issue of *Vogue* ran an article on several British white women (like her) who had converted to Islam. See: Leap of Faith. (2008, November). *Vogue*, pp. 123–126.

11. Islamic Human Rights Commission.(2002). Untitled report. Available from the Islamic Human Rights Commission, PO Box 598 Wembley, HA9 7XH.

12. Cited in: Islamic Human Rights Commission. (1998, August 1). Islamophobia: Fact not fiction. Retrieved from http://ihrc.org.uk/show.php?id=706. Accessed June 10, 2012.

13. Runnymede Trust is a think tank set up in 1968 in the United Kingdom to advise the government on race-related issues.

14. Jack Shaheen's recent *Reel Bad Arabs* (2001) provides an excellent archive of close to 900 films focused on the figure of the Arab.

15. The *Daily Mail* in a report by Jack Doyle posted on January 5, 2011 and based on a study by the multifaith group Faith Matters, noted that 5,200 men and women have adopted Islam over the previous year. Almost two-thirds of them were women and more than 70% were white. The average age was 27 years. Retrieved from http://www .dailymail.co.uk/news/article-1343954/100–000-Islam-converts-living-UK-White -women-keen-embrace-Muslim-faith.html. Accessed June 10, 2010. The report by Faith Matters can be directly accessed online. Also, numerous other leading newspapers have confirmed the same. Cambridge University, as of 2011, has been engaged in a study on this subject of conversion to Islam in Britain.

16. See English and Harris (2008).

17. I am fully aware here that there are Muslim cultures and states even in parts of Asia—beyond the Middle East. But I am referring to the Middle East here because the Middle East, in Western imaginations, is primarily seen as constituting Muslim nations. And hence stereotypes of Middle Easterners become the same as those of Muslims (when, in fact, there are Arabs in the Middle East who may not be Muslims).

18. This is a theme that never changes; it is almost always there in representations of Arab/Muslim men. See also Canton (2000), which offers a different read as it focuses more on white men playing Arab sheikhs; Shaheen (2001); Shohat (2011); and Taylor (2007), among others.

19. Retrieved from http://www.vanityfair.com/society/features/1997/12/dodi-fayed -199712. Accessed June 20, 2010.

20. Obituaries section. (2003, 8 January). *The Telegraph*. Retrieved from http://www.telegraph.co.uk/news/obituaries/1418179/Mohammed-al-Fassi.html. Accessed June 23, 2012.

21. Allen, N. (2009, 11 November). Fort Hood shooter Nidal Malik Hasan visited lap dancing club. Retrieved from http://www.telegraph.co.uk/news/worldnews/northamerica/usa/6546905/Fort-Hood-killer-Nidal-Malik-Hasan-visited-lapdancing -club. Accessed February 4, 2013.

22. Another recent film is *Cairo Time* (2010). The film is replete with Orientalist narratives. Particularly relevant here is the same old theme of a white woman being followed by Egyptian men (and the implication that they are again lusting for the white woman).

23. Jones, J. (2003, April 14). Look at the size of those missiles. *The Guardian*. Retrieved from http://www.guardian.co.uk/culture/2003/apr/15/artsfeatures.iraq. Accessed November 10, 2012.

24. Retrieved from http://abcnews.go.com/Politics/OTUS/osama-bin-laden-death -anniversary-10-things-learned/story?id=16253928#.UMwUB-R9J8E. Accessed September 2, 2013.

25. Goldman, R. (2011 October 20). The seven weirdest things about Moammar Gadhafi. ABC News web site. Retrieved from http://abcnews.go.com/International/weirdest-things-moammar-gadhafi/story?id=14779142#.UMleneR9J8E. Accessed August 20, 2012.

26. See: Documentary shows Saddam's weird behavior. (2002, November 22) *Good Morning America*. ABC News web site. Retrieved from http://abcnews.go.com/GMA/story?id=125576&page=1#.UMlg5-R9J8E. Accessed March 4, 2011.

27. An unauthorized look at Saddam Hussein. (2002, November 26). *Good Morning America*. ABC News web site. Retrieved from http://abcnews.go.com/GMA/story?id=125578&page=1#.UMlkb-R9J8H. Accessed July 5, 2013.

28. Retrieved from http://www.dailymail.co.uk/news/article-1281480/CIA-plot-air -fake-Saddam-Hussein-gay-sex-tape-prior-2003-Iraq-invasion.html. Accessed June 10, 2010. See also: Harris, P. (2010, May 26). CIA's secret Iraq weapon revealed: a Saddam gay sex tape. *The Guardian*.

29. Stein, J. (2010, May 25). CIA unit's wacky ideal: Depict Saddam as gay. *The Washington Post*. Retrieved from http://voices.washingtonpost.com/spy-talk/2010/05/cia_group_had_wacky_ideas_to_d.html. See also: Saddam Hussein in "gay video." (2010, May 27). *The Mirror*. Retrieved from http://www.mirror.co.uk/news/uk-news/saddam-hussein-in-gay-video-224262. Accessed January 4, 2012. Tourni, H. (2010, May 27). CIA plotted faking Saddam Hussein sex video. *Gulf News. Retrieved from* http://gulfnews.com/news/region/iraq/cia-plotted-faking-saddam-hussain-sex-video -1.633160. Accessed January 4, 2012.

30. Retrieved from http://www.dailymail.co.uk/news/article-1281480/CIA-plot -air-fake-Saddam-Hussein-gay-sex-tape-prior-2003-Iraq-invasion.html. Accessed January 4, 2012. See also Harris (2010, May 26). CIA's secret Iraq weapon revealed.

31. Haritaworn, Tauqir, and Erdem's (2008) cogent discussion of "gay imperialism" is also worth mentioning.

32. See also Allen (2010). In a different context, see the discussion of good and bad diversity by Lentin and Titley (2011).

Chapter 6. Cosmopolitan Healing

1. Browne, A. (2001, January 20). Antidote to the stiff upper lip. *The Observer*. Retrieved from http://www.theguardian.com/uk/2001/jan/21/theobserver.uknews. Accessed June 3, 2012.

2. Retrieved from www.nationalaccountsofwellbeing.org. Accessed June 3, 2012.

3. O'Sullivan, J. (1997, September 8). Diana's devotees join the new religion. *The Independent*. Retrieved from http://www.independent.co.uk/voices/dianas-devotees-join-the-new-religion-1238118.html. Accessed June 3, 2012.

4. One thinks here of scholars such as Angela McRobbie, Rosalind Gill, Lisa Blackman, Diane Negra, Beverly Skeggs, and others who have drawn our attention to the rhetoric of "freedom" through which new postfeminist subjectivities are envisioned in contemporary cultures.

5. See also Sean Redmond's (2007) discussion of Kate Winslett's idealized whiteness.

6. Julia Roberts may adopt Indian child. (2010, October 1). *The Economic Times*. Retrieved from http://articles.economictimes.indiatimes.com/2010-10-01/news/27578501_1_julia-roberts-indian-child-eat-pray-love. Accessed July 18, 2012.

7. Angelina Jolie and Brad Pitt to have a Hindu wedding next year? (2010, December 14). *Zee News India*. Retrieved from http://zeenews.india.com/entertainment/celebrity/angelina-jolie-and-brad-pitt-to-have-a-hindu-wedding-next-year_77565.htm. Accessed June 3, 2012.

8. Corliss, R. (2001, April 15). The power of yoga. *Time* magazine. Retrieved from http://www.time.com/time/health/article/0,8599,106356-1,00.htm. Accessed July 18, 2012.

9. Some work, for instance, has been done on the appropriation of Native American cultural rites and spiritual practices. See Crowley (2011) or Donaldson (1999).

10. Retrieved from www.facingthechallenge.org. Accessed July 18, 2012.

11. God and guidance for glossy bible. (2004, April 7). *The Telegraph* (Calcutta). Retrieved from http://www.telegraphindia.com/1040407/asp/foreign/story_3096181.asp. Accessed July 20, 2010.

12. Ibid.

13. Cited in: Bedell, G. (1995, November 26). Emotions without tears. *The Independent*. Retrieved from http://www.independent.co.uk/opinion/emotion-without-tears-1583747.html. Accessed July 19, 2012.

14. Di cures all her ills with weird water therapy. (1993, June 1). *The Globe*.

15. Cooke, R. (2007, October 6). Wheatgrass juice sun salutations and a colonic—or two: Just what the celebrity doctor ordered. *The Guardian*. Retrieved from http://

www.guardian.co.uk/lifeandstyle/2007/oct/07/healthandwellbeing.features. Accessed July 18, 2012.

16. Ibid.

17. Cohen, N. (2002, December 8). Ev'rybody must get stones. Retrieved from http://www.theguardian.com/politics/2002/dec/08/cherieblair.labour1. Accessed July 18, 2012.

18. PM, wife in rebirth ritual. (2001, December 16). *The Sunday Telegraph* (Sydney). Retrieved from LexisNexis. Accessed August 6, 2012.

19. Duchess of Cornwall resorts to Shirodhara. (2010, September 30). *The Deccan Herald*. Retrieved from http://www.deccanherald.com/content/100907/ipl-2012.html. Accessed August 6, 2012.

20. Cherie's cranks. (2002, December 6). *The Mirror*. Retrieved from http://www.highbeam.com/doc/1G1–94967299.html. Accessed August 6, 2012.

21. Seaman, A., & Thomas, D. (2007, July 4). Is Cherie Blair misunderstood or bonkers? *The Daily Mail*. Retrieved http://www.dailymail.co.uk/femail/article-465798/Is-Cherie-Blair-misunderstood-bonkers.html. Accessed August 6, 2012.

22. Pasternak, A. (2009). Thailand spaces, where they excavate the "sediments of sadness" from your soul. *The Daily Mail*. Retrieved from http://www.dailymail.co.uk/travel/article-1203826/Thailand-spas-excavate-sediments-sadness-soul.html. Accessed July 20, 2012.

23. Arun Saldhana (2007), in his study of whites visiting Goa (India), has used "psychedelic whiteness" to refer to practices of whites whereby—through embracing drugs, spiritual sites, counterculture exotic resorts such as Goa, alternative music, and so on—they attempt to escape whiteness but in so doing also recreate whiteness in such locales. Psychedelic whiteness conceptually invokes the culture of LSD and mental trips.

24. See also Dei, Hall, & Rosenberg (2000).

For a significantly different, but nonetheless interesting and novel, discussion of the marketing of the "primitive" and "ethnicity" by natives of the Global South that cater to the terms of recognition set by the Global North, see Comaroff and Comaroff (2009).

25. Elizabeth Povinelli's (2006) *The Empire of Love* has brilliantly shown how practices of intimate love (and spirituality is a kind of intimate love) function as modes of governance in late liberalism through which unequal forms of distributions of power occur. See also Ahmed (2010), Berlant (1997, 2004), Fortier (2008), and Sedgwick (2003).

26. David Arnold's (1993) work is important for this point here, as is Parama Roy's (2010). For another interesting discussion, see Langford (2002).

Afterword

1. Levy, A. (2009, October 7). The wonder of wool . . . of how knitting is once again helping us through the hard times. *The Daily Mail*. Retrieved from http://www.daily

mail.co.uk/femail/article-1218575/Wool-sales-soar-celebrity-fans-recession-help
-knitting-cast-unfashionable-image.html. Accessed October 3, 2013.

2. Negra and Tasker (2014) promises to offer an excellent discussion of the politics of gender in these recession years. My book is going into production as this book appears. Hence I have not been able to review it as I would like, but can only note from the description of the book and the authors involved that it promises to offer exciting discussions.

3. White girls seen as 'easy meat' by Pakistani rapists, says Jack Straw. (2011, January 8). *The Guardian*. Retrieved from http://www.theguardian.com/world/2011/jan/08/jack-straw-white-girls-easy-meat. Accessed October 3, 2013.

4. Oxford grooming gang: We will regret ignoring Asian thugs. (2013, May 15). *The Telegraph*. Retrieved from http://www.telegraph.co.uk/news/uknews/crime/10060570/Oxford-grooming-gang-We-will-regret-ignoring-Asian-thugs-who-target-white-girls.html. Accessed October 3, 2013.

5. Mantel, H. (2013). Royal Bodies. *London Review of Books, 35*(4). Retrieved from http://www.lrb.co.uk/v35/n04/hilary-mantel/royal-bodies. Accessed November 4, 2013.

6. Some of Vron Ware's recent work seems to have begun exploring this.

References

Adams, T. (2007, September 22). Cultural hallmark: Interview with Stuart Hall. *The Guardian*. Retrieved from http://www.theguardian.com/society/2007/sep/23/communities.politicsphilosophyandsociety. Accessed October 5, 2013.

Ahmed, S. (2004). Affective economies. *Social Text, 22,* 117–139.

Ahmed, S. (2007). A phenomenology of whiteness. *Feminist Theory, 8*(2), 149–168.

Ahmed, S. (2010). *The promise of happiness.* Durham, NC: Duke University Press.

Ahuja, A. (1998, May 15). Can papers be accused of racism? *The Times,* p. 47.

Alexander, J. (1997). Erotic autonomy as a politics of decolonization. In M. J. Alexander& C. Mohanty (Eds.), *Feminist genealogies, colonial legacies and democratic futures* (pp. 63–100). New York: Routledge.

Alexander, J. (2006). *Pedagogies of the sacred.* Durham, NC: Duke University Press.

Ali, M. (2012). *The untold story.* New York: Scribner.

Allen, C. (2010). *Islamophobia.* Farnham, UK: Ashgate Publishing.

Allen, K., & Osgood, J. (2009). Young women negotiating maternal subjectivities: The significance of social class. *Studies in the Maternal, 1*(2). Retrieved from http://www.mamsie.bbk.ac.uk/documents/allen-osgood.pdf. Accessed January 15, 2012.

Alsultany, E. (2012). *Arabs and Muslims in the media.* New York: New York University Press.

Anagnost, A. (2000). Scenes of misrecognition: Maternal citizenship in the age of transnational adoption. *Positions, 8*(2), 299–421.

Anderson, B. (1983). *Imagined communities.* New York: Verso.

Ang, I., Barcan, R., Grace, H., Lally, E., Lloyd, J., & Sofoulis, Z. (1997). (Eds.). *Planet Diana: Cultural studies and global mourning.* Kingswood, NSW, Australia: Research Centre in Intercommunal Studies, University of Western Sydney, Nepean.

Anthias, F., & Yuval-Davis, N. (1989). (Eds.) *Woman-nation-state.* Basingstoke, UK: Palgrave.

Apter, E. (2001). On translation in a global market. *Public Culture, 13*(1), 1–12.

Apter, E. (2006). *The translation zone: A new comparative literature.* Princeton, NJ: Princeton University Press.

Arat-Koc, S. (2010). New whiteness(es), beyond the colour line? In S. Razack, M. Smith, & S. Thobani (Eds.), *States of race* (pp. 147–168). Toronto: Between the Lines Press.

Arnold, D. (1993). *Colonizing the body.* Durham, NC: Duke University Press.

Back, L. (2010). Whiteness in the dramaturgy of racism. In P. Hill Collins & J. Solomos (Eds.), *The Sage handbook of race and ethnic studies* (pp. 444–468). London: Sage.

Backer, K. (2012). *From MTV to Mecca.* Charleston, SC: Arcadia Books.

Banerjea, K. (2000). Sounds of whose underground? The fine tuning of diaspora in an age of mechanical reproduction. *Theory, Culture & Society, 17*(3), 64–79.

Banet-Weiser, S. (1999*). The most beautiful girl in the world: Beauty pageants and national identity.* Berkeley: University of California Press.

Banet-Weiser, S. (2007). What's your flava? Race and postfeminism in media culture. In Y. Tasker & D. Negra (Eds.), *Interrogating postfeminism* (pp. 201–226). Durham, NC: Duke University Press.

Barnard, M. (2002). *Fashion as communication.* New York: Routledge.

Bashford, A. (2006). Global biopolitics and the history of world health. *History of the Human Sciences, 19*(1), 67–88.

Bedell, G. (1993, November 28). James Bulger: The death of innocence. *The Independent.* Retrieved from http://www.independent.co.uk/voices/james-bulger-the -death-of-innocence-there-are-no-meanings-to-be-found-in-james-bulgers-murder -says-geraldine-bedell-except-that-it-shows-us-hell-1507265.html. Accessed October 2, 2010.

Bennett, T. (1995). *The birth of the museum.* London: Routledge.

Berger, J. (1972). *Ways of seeing.* London: Penguin.

Berlant, L. (1997). *The queen of America goes to Washington city.* Durham, NC: Duke University Press.

Berlant, L. (2000). Intimacy: A special issue. In L. Berlant (Ed.), *Intimacy* (pp. 1–8). Chicago: University of Chicago Press.

Berlant, L. (2004). (Ed.). *Compassion: The culture and politics of an emotion.* New York: Routledge.

Bhabha, H. (1990). *Nation and narration.* New York: Routledge.

Bhabha, H. ([1994] 2004). *Location of culture.* Milton Park, UK: Routledge Classics.

Bhachu, P. (2004). *Dangerous designs.* London: Routledge.

Billig, M. (1995). *Banal Nationalism.* London: Sage.

Biressi, A., & Nunn, H. (2013). *Class and contemporary British culture.* London: Palgrave Macmillan.

Blackman, L. (2004). Self help, media cultures and the production of female psychopathology. *European Journal of Cultural Studies, 7*(2), 219–236.

Blair, T. (1996). *New Britain: My vision of a young country.* London: Fourth Estate.

Blee, K. (2002). *Inside organized racism: Women in the hate movement.* Berkeley: University of California Press.

Blunt, A. (1999). The flight from Lucknow: British women travelling and writing home, In J. Duncan & D. Gregory (Eds.), *Writes of passage* (pp. 92–113). New York: Routledge.

Boltanski, L. (1999). *Distant suffering: Politics, morality and the media.* Cambridge: Cambridge University Press.

Borger, J. (2002, October 4). Bright boy from the California suburbs who turned Taliban warrior. *The Guardian.* Retrieved http://www.guardian.co.uk/world/2002/oct/05/usa.afghanistan.

Bower, T. (2001). *Fayed: The unauthorized biography.* London: Pan Books.

Braidotti, R. (1997). In the sign of the feminine: Reading Diana. *Theory and Event, 1,* 4. Retrieved from http://muse.jhu.edu/journals/theory_and_event/v001/1.4braidotti.html. Accessed October 10, 2010.

Briggs, L. (2003). Mother, child, race, nation: The visual iconography of rescue and politics of transnational and transracial adoption. *Gender and History, 15*(2), 179–200.

Briggs, L. (2006). Making "American" families: Transnational adoption and U.S. Latin America foreign policy. In A. Stoler (Eds.), *Haunted by empire: Geographies of intimacy in North American history* (pp. 344–364). Durham, NC: Duke University Press.

Briggs, L. (2010). Foreign and domestic: Adoption, immigration and privatization. In R. Parrenas & E. Boris (Eds.), *Intimate labors: Culture, technologies, and the politics of care* (pp. 49–62). Stanford, CA: Stanford University Press.

Brown, Y. (2001). *Imagining the New Britain.* New York: Routledge.

Butler, J. (2009). *Frames of war.* New York: Verso.

Butler, J. (2012). *Parting Ways.* New York: Columbia University Press.

Campbell, B. (1999). *Diana, Princess of Wales: How sexual politics shook the nation.* London: Women's Press.

Canton, S. (2000). "The Sheik: Instabilities of race and gender in transatlantic popular culture of the early 1920's." In H. Edward (Ed.), *Noble dreams wicked pleasures: Orientalism in America, 1870–1930* (pp. 99–119). Princeton, NJ: Princeton University Press.

Carrette, J., & King, R. (2005). *Selling spirituality: The silent takeover of religion.* New York: Routledge.

Carrillo-Rowe, A. (2000). Locating feminism's subject: The paradox of white femininity. *Communication Theory, 10*(1), 64–80.

Carroll, H. (2011). *Affirmative reaction: New formations of white masculinity.* Durham, NC: Duke University Press.

Cartwright, L. (2003). Photographs of "waiting children": The transnational adoption market. *Social Text, 74,* 83–109.

Castaneda, C. (2002). *Figurations: Child, bodies, worlds.* Durham, NC: Duke University Press.

Chatterjee, P. (1991). Whose imagined community? *Millennium: Journal of International Studies, 20*(3), 521–526.

Chen, T., & Zamperini, P. (2003). Introduction. Fabrications [Special issue]. *Positions, 11*(2), 261–269.

Cherniavsky, E. (1995). *That pale mother rising.* Bloomington: Indiana University Press.

Cherniavksy, E. (2006). *Incorporations: Race, nation, and the body politics of capital.* Minneapolis: University of Minnesota Press.

Chouliaraki, L. (2006). *The spectatorship of suffering.* London: Sage Publications.

Chouliaraki, L. (2013). *The ironic spectator: Solidarity in the age of post-humanitarianism.* Cambridge, UK: Polity Press.

Chow, R. (1990). Violence in the other country. In C. Mohanty, A. Russo, & L. Torres (Eds.), *Third world women and the politics of feminism* (pp. 81–100). Bloomington: Indiana University Press.

Chua, A. (2011). *Battle hymn of the tiger mother.* New York: Penguin.

Colebrook, C. (2006). Introduction. Beauty [Special issue]. *Feminist Theory, 7*(2), 131–142.

Comaroff, J., & Comaroff, J. (2009). *Ethnicity Inc.* Chicago: University of Chicago Press.

Cooks, J., & Simpson, J. (Eds.). (2007). *Whiteness, pedagogy and performance: Dis/placing race.* Lanham, MD: Lexington Books.

Cool Britannia is no media fad. (1998, August 27). *Marketing Week*, pp. 36–37.

Cool Britannia lure launched. (1997, January 7). *The Guardian*, p. 5.

Coombe, R. (1998). Intellectual property, human rights and sovereignty. *Indian Journal of Global Legal Studies, 6*(1), 59–115.

Coombe, R., & Herman, A. (2004). Rhetorical virtues: Property, speech and the commons on the World Wide Web. *Anthropological Quarterly, 77*(3), 559–574.

Corner, J., & Harvey, S. (1991). *Crosscurrents of national culture.* New York: Routledge.

Coward, R. (1999a, November 19). The little visitor. *The Guardian.* Retrieved from http://www.guardian.co.uk/politics/1999/nov/20/tonyblair.uk1. Accessed April 3, 2013.

Coward, R. (1999b). *Sacred cows: Is feminism irrelevant to the new millennium?* London: Harper Collins.

Coward, R. (2007). *Diana: The portrait (anniversary edition).* Kansas City, MO: Andrews McMeel Publishing.

Craik, J. (1994). *The face of fashion.* New York: Routledge.

Craik, J. (2009). *Fashion: The key concepts.* Oxford, UK: Berg.

Crang, P. (2010). Contemporary British Asian fashion designers. In C. Breward, P. Crang, & R. Crill (Eds.), *British Asian style* (pp. 78–87). London: V & A Publishing.

Crenshaw, C. (1997). Resisting whiteness's rhetorical silence. *Western Journal of Communication, 61,* 253–278.

Crewe, L., & Goodrum, A. (2000). Fashioning new forms of consumption: The case of Paul Smith. In S. Bruzzi & P. Church (Eds.), *Fashion cultures* (pp. 25–48). Milton Park, UK: Routledge.

Crowley, K. (2011). *Feminism's new age.* Albany: State University of New York Press.

Davin, A. (1997). Imperialism and motherhood. In F. Cooper & A. Stoler (Eds.), *Tensions of empire: Colonial cultures in a bourgeois world* (pp. 87–151). Berkeley: University of California Press.

Davy, K. (1997). Outing whiteness: A feminist lesbian project. In M. Hill (Ed.), *Whiteness: A critical reader.* New York: New York University Press.

Dei, G. J., Hall, B., & Rosenberg, D. (2000). *Indigenous knowledges in global contexts*. Toronto: University of Toronto Press.

Deliovsky, K. (2010). *White femininity: Race, gender, and power*. Black Point, Nova Scotia: Fernwood Publishing Company.

Devi, M. (1997). Breast giver. In *Breast stories* (G. C. Spivak, Trans.). Kolkata, India: Seagull Books.

Diana: A life in fashion. (1997). Video. [collector's edition]. London, UK: Daily Mail.

The Diana Years. (1997). *People* [commemorative edition]. New York: Time Inc. Home Entertainment.

Diana: An extraordinary life. (1998). Orbis Publishing Ltd. (Phoenix Illustrated Edition).

DiPiero, T. (2002). *White men aren't*. Durham, NC: Duke University Press.

Donaldson, L. (1999). On medicine women and white shame-ans: New age Native Americanism and commodity fetishism as pop culture feminism. *Signs: Journal of Women in Culture and Society, 24*(3), 677–696.

Dorow, S. (2006). *Transnational adoption*. New York: New York University Press.

Douglas, S. (2010). *Enlightened sexism*. New York: Macmillan.

Douglas, S., & Michaels, M. (2004). *The Mommy myth*. New York: Free Press.

Driver, S., & Martell, L. (1998). *New Labour: Politics after Thatcherism*. Malden, MA: Polity Press.

Dubrofsky, R. (2006). The Bachelor: Whiteness in the harem. *Critical Studies in Media Communication, 23*(1), 39–56.

Durham, M. (2001). Displaced persons: Symbols of South Asian femininity and the returned gaze in U.S. media culture. *Communication Theory, 11(2)*, 201–217.

During, S. (1994). Rousseau's patrimony: Primitivism, romance and becoming other. In. F. Barker, P. Hulme, & M. Iverson (Eds.), *Colonial discourse/postcolonial theory* (pp. 47–71). Manchester, UK: Manchester University Press.

Dwyer, C. (2010). From suitcase to showroom: British Asian retail spaces. In. C. Breward, P. Crang, & R. Crill (Eds.), *British Asian style* (pp. 148–159). London: V & A Publishing.

Dwyer, C., & Crang, P. (2002). Fashioning ethnicities. *Ethnicities, 2*, 410–430.

Dyer, R. (1979). *Stars*. London: British Film Institute.

Dyer, R. ([1986] 2004). *Heavenly bodies: Film stars and society*. London: Macmillan.

Dyer, R. (1988). White. *Screen, 29*(4), 44–64.

Dyer, R. (1997). *White*. New York: Routledge.

Ecclestone, K. (2007). Resisting images of the "diminished self": The implications of emotional wellbeing and emotional engagement in education policy. *Journal of Education Policy, 22*(4), 455–470.

Ecclestone, K., & Hayes, D. (2008). *The dangerous rise of therapeutic education*. London: Routledge.

Ehrenreich, B., & Hochschild, A. (2002). *Global women*. New York: Henry Holt & Company.

Eisenstein, Z. (1996). *Hatreds*. New York: Routledge.

Eisenstein, Z. (1998). *Global obscenities*. New York: New York University Press.

Eng, D. L. (2003). Transnational adoption and queer diasporas. *Social Text, 21* (no. 3 76), 1–37.

English, R., & Harris, P. (2008, January 15). Diana's mother called her a whore for sleeping with Muslim men. *The Daily Mail.* Retrieved from www.dailymail.co.uk/news/article-508191. Accessed June 10, 2012.

Enloe, C. (1990). *Bananas, beaches and bases: Making feminist sense of international politics.* Berkeley: University of California Press.

Enloe, C. (2000). *Maneuvers.* Berkeley: University of California Press.

Entwistle, J. (2000). *The fashioned body: Dress and modern social theory.* Cambridge, UK: Polity.

Espiritu, Y. (2008). *Asian American women and men.* Lanham, MD: Rowman & Littlefield.

Etzioni, A. (1993). *The parenting deficit.* London: Demos.

Ewing, K. P. (2008). *Stolen honor.* Stanford, CA: Stanford University Press.

Fairclough, N. (2000). *New Labour, new language?* London: Routledge.

Feldstein, R. (2000). *Motherhood in black and white: Race and sex in American liberalism, 1930–1965.* Ithaca, NY: Cornell University Press.

Feng, P. (2002). *Identities in motion: Asian American film and video.* Durham, NC: Duke University Press.

Ferguson, S. (2012). *Finding Sarah: A duchess' journey to find herself.* New York: Atria Paperback.

Fitzpatrick, M. (2001). *The tyranny of health.* New York: Routledge.

Ford, R. (1998, April 13). Blacks and Asians "imprisoned" by fear of violence. *The Times,* p. 5.

Forna, A. (2000). Mothers of Africa and the diaspora: Shared maternal values among black women. In K. Owusu (Ed.), *Black British culture and society: A text and reader* (pp. 391–406). London: Routledge.

Fortier, A. (2008). *Multicultural horizons: Diversity and the limits of the civil nation.* New York: Routledge.

Frankenberg, R. (1993). *White women, race matters.* Minneapolis: University of Minnesota Press.

Franklin, S. (2000). What's wrong with New Labor politics? *Feminist Review, 66,* 138–142.

Franklin, S., Lury, C., & Stacey, J. (2000). *Global nature, global culture.* London: Sage Publications.

Furedi, F. (2004). *Therapy culture: Cultivating vulnerability in an uncertain age.* New York: Routledge.

Furedi, F. (2005). The age of unreason: Celebrities, healers and new age gurus transmit the message that normal human beings cannot do it on their own. (2005, November 18). *The Spectator.* Retrieved from http://www.frankfuredi.com/articles/unreason-20051118.shtml. Accessed June 3, 2012.

Furedi, F. (2006, May 22). Why the "politics of happiness" makes me mad. *Spiked.* Retrieved from http://www.spiked-online.com/newsite/article/311#.Uzc3IahdV8E. Accessed March 3, 2012.

Gee, D. (Director). (1988). *Slaying the dragon* [Documentary]. United States: Asian Women United of California.

Giddens, A. (1991). *Modernity and self identity.* Stanford, CA: Stanford University Press.

Gill, R. (2007). Postfeminist media culture: Elements of a sensibility. *European Journal of Cultural Studies, 10*(2), 147–166.

Gillies, V. (2006). *Marginalised mothers: Exploring working class experiences of parenting.* Milton Park, UK: Routledge.

Gilroy, P. (1997). Elton's crooning, England's dreaming. *Theory and Event, 1,* 4. Retrieved from http://muse.jhu.edu/journals/theory_and_event/v001/1.4gilroy.html. Accessed June 10, 2012.

Gilroy, P. (2005). *Postcolonial melancholia.* New York: Columbia University Press.

Gitlin, T. (1979). Prime time ideology: The hegemonic process in television entertainment. *Social Problems, 26*(3), 251–266.

Glenn, E., Chang, G., & Forcey, L. (Eds.). (1994). *Mothering: Ideology, experience, and agency* (pp. 56–74). New York: Routledge.

Goldman, M. (1998). *Privatizing nature: Political struggles for the global commons.* New Brunswick, NJ: Rutgers University Press.

Gole, N. (2011). *Islam in Europe: The lure of fundamentalism and the allure of cosmopolitanism.* Princeton, NJ: Markus Weiner.

Goodrum, A. (2005). *The national fabric: Fashion, Britishness, globalization.* Oxford, UK: Berg.

Gopinath, G. (2005). *Impossible desires.* Durham, NC: Duke University Press.

Gordon, A. (1997). *Ghostly matters.* Minneapolis: University of Minnesota Press.

Graham, T., & Blanchard, T. (1998). *Dressing Diana.* London: Weidenfeld & Nicholson.

Grewal, I. (1996). *Home and harem.* Durham, NC: Duke University Press.

Grewal, I. (2005). *Transnational America: Feminisms, diasporas, neoliberalisms.* Durham, NC: Duke University Press.

Grewal, I. (2006). "Security Moms" in the early twentieth century United States. *Women Studies Quarterly, 34*(1&2), 25–39.

Griffin, R. (2002). Afterthought: Redressing the balance in historiography. In W. Parkings (Ed.), *Fashioning the body politic* (pp. 217–226). Oxford, UK: Berg.

Gunew, S. (2004). *Haunted nations. The colonial dimensions of multiculturalism.* London: Routledge.

Gupta, A., & Ferguson, J. (1997). Beyond "culture": Space, identity and the politics of difference. In A. Gupta & J. Ferguson (Eds.), *Culture, power, place* (pp. 33–51). Durham, NC: Duke University Press.

Hall, C. (2000). Introduction: Thinking the postcolonial, thinking the empire. In C. Hall (Eds.), *Cultures of empire: A reader* (pp. 1–36). New York: Routledge.

Hall, S. (1997). Old identities and new identities, old ethnicities and new ethnicities. In A. D. King (Ed.), *Culture, globalization, and the world system* (pp. 41–68). Minneapolis: University of Minnesota Press.

Hall, S. (2000, October 14). A question of identity (II). Special report: What is Britain? *The Observer.* Retrieved from http://www.guardian.co.uk/uk/2000/oct/15/britishidentity.comment1. Accessed June 10, 2010.

Hall, S. (2006, November). Once more around cultural identity. Lecture delivered at Queen Mary University, London.

Hall, S. (2007). *Plenary lecture*. Presented at Cultural Studies Now Conference, University of East London. Retrieved from http://culturalstudiesresearch.org/?page_id=12. Accessed October 20, 2011.

Hancock, P., Hughes, B., Jagger, E., Patterson, K., Russell, R., Tulle-Winton, E., & Tyler, M. (2000). *The body, culture, and society*. Buckingham, UK: Open University Press.

Handy, C. (1997 October 24). Welcome to the new renaissance. *The Evening Standard*, p. 21.

Hage, G. (2000). *White nation: Fantasies of white supremacy in a multicultural society*. Annandale, NSW, Australia: Pluto Press.

Hage, G. (2003). *Against paranoid nationalism: Searching for hope in a shrinking society*. Sydney: Pluto Press.

Haritaworn, J., Tauqir, T., & Erdem, E. (2008). Gay imperialism. In A. Kuntsman & E. Miyake (Eds.), *Out of place*. York, UK: Raw Nerve Books.

Harris, A. (2004). *Future girl: Young women in the twenty-first century*. New York: Routledge.

Hay, D. (2002). The spirituality of adults in Britain—Recent research. *Scottish Journal of Healthcare Chaplaincy, 5*(1), 4–9.

Hays, S. (1996). *The cultural contradictions of motherhood*. New Haven, CT: Yale University Press.

Hebdige, D. (1987). *Cut 'n' mix culture*. London: Methuen Press.

Heelas, P. (1996). *The new age movement*. Cambridge, MA: Blackwell Publishers.

Heelas, P., & Woodhead, L. (2005). *The spiritual revolution*. Malden, MA: Blackwell.

Higson, A. ([1993] 2006). Re-presenting the national past: Nostalgia and pastiche in heritage films. In L. Friedman (Ed.), *Fires were started* (pp. 91–109). West Sussex, UK: Wallflower Press.

Hill, M. (2004). *After whiteness*. Durham, NC: Duke University Press.

Hill Collins, P. (1994). Shifting the center: Race, class and feminist theorizing about motherhood. In E. Glenn, G. Chang, & L. Forcey (Eds.), *Mothering: Ideology, experience, and agency* (pp. 56–74). New York: Routledge.

Hill Collins, P. (1999). Producing mothers of the nation: Race, class, and contemporary U.S. population policies. In N. Yuval-Davis (Ed.), *Women, citizenship, and difference* (pp. 118–129). London: Zed Books.

Holden, A. (1997). *Diana, her life and legacy*. New York: Random House.

Holland, S. (2000). *Raising the dead*. Durham, NC: Duke University Press.

Holmes, S., & Negra, D. (2011). Introduction. In S. Holmes & D. Negra (Eds.), *In the limelight and under the microscope: Forms and functions of female celebrity* (pp. 1–16). London: Continuum Publishing.

Holmes, S., & Redmond, S. (2010). Editorial. *Celebrity Studies, 1*(1), 1–10.

hooks, b. (2011). *All about love: New visions*. New York: Harper Collins.

Howell, G. (1998). *Diana: Her life in fashion*. London: Pavilion Books Ltd.

Hurtado, A. (1996). *The color of privilege*. Ann Arbor: University of Michigan Press.

Hutnyk, J. (1998). Adorno at Womad: South Asian crossovers and the limits of hybridity talk. *Postcolonial Studies, 1*(3), 401–426.

Hutnyk, J. (2000). *Critique of exotica*. London: Pluto Press.

Hutton, W. (1997, September 14). New Britain: We've changed . . . but what will we become? *The Observer*, p. 24.

Hyder, R. (2004). *Brimful of Asia*. Aldershot, UK: Ashgate.

Ingraham, C. (1999). *White weddings: Romancing heterosexuality in popular culture*. New York: Routledge.

Jacques, M., & Hall, S. (1997, April 13). Blair: Is he the greatest Tory since Thatcher? *The Observer*, p. 31.

Jan Mohammed, A. (2005). *The death-bound subject: Richard Wright's archaeology of death*. Durham, NC: Duke University Press.

Jeffords, S. (1988). *The remasculinization of America: Gender and the Vietnam War*. Bloomington: Indiana University Press.

Jeffords, S. (1994). *Hard bodies: Hollywood masculinity in the Reagan era*. New Brunswick, NJ: Rutgers University Press.

Jenkins, A. (2009, February 6). Death of the yummy mummy: They made us feel so inadequate but at last they're being credit crunched to extinction. *The Daily Mail*. Retrieved from http://www.dailymail.co.uk/femail/article-1136923/Death-Yummy-Mummy-They-feel-inadequate-theyre-credit-crunched-extinction.html. Accessed October 6, 2011.

Jhally, S. & Lewis, J. (1992). *Enlightened racism: The Cosby show, audiences, and the myth of the American dream*. Boulder, CO: Westview Press.

Johnson, B. (1997, September 3). Where is this—Argentina? *The Daily Telegraph*, p. 22.

Jolly, M. (1998). Introduction. In M. Jolly & K. Ram (Eds.), *Maternities and modernities* (pp. 1–25). Berkeley: University of California Press.

Kandiyoti, D. (1991). Identity and its discontents. *Millenium, 20*(3), 429–443.

Kang, M. (2010). *The managed hand: Race, gender and body in beauty service work*. Berkeley: University of California Press.

Kaplan, A. (1992). *Motherhood and representation*. London: Routledge.

Kaplan, C. (1995). A world without boundaries: Body shop's trans/national geographic. *Social Text, 43,* 45–66.

Kaplan, C. (2001). Hillary Rodham Clinton's Orient: Cosmopolitan travel and global feminist subjects. *Meridians, 2*(1), 219–240.

Kaplan, C., Alarcon, N., & Moallem, M. (Eds.) (1999). *Between woman and nation*. Durham, NC: Duke University Press.

Karla, V., & Hutnyk, J. (1998). Brimful of agitation, authenticity, and appropriation: Madonna's "Asian Kool." *Postcolonial Studies, 1*(3), 339–355.

Kauffman, J. (1989, October 4). Princess Diana. *People*. Retrieved from http://www.people.com/people/article/0,20063181,00.html. Accessed October 2, 2010.

Kay, R., & Levy, G. (1998). *Diana: The untold story*. London: Boxtree.

Kear, A., & Steinberg, D. (Eds.). (1999). *Mourning Diana*. New York: Routledge.

Kennedy-Pipe, C. & Vickers, R. (2003). Britain in the international arena. In P. Dunleavy, A. Gamble, R. Heffernan, & G. Peele (Eds.), *Developments in British politics* (pp. 321–337). Basingstoke, UK: Palgrave Macmillan.

Kiernan, K., Land, H., & Lewis, J. (1998). *Lone motherhood in twentieth century Britain: From footnote to front page*. Oxford, UK: Clarendon Press, Oxford University Press.

Kim, E. (2011). *Slaying the Dragon: Reloaded*. San Francisco: Asian Women United.

Kim-Puri, J. H. (2005). Conceptualizing gender-sexuality-state-nation: An introduction: *Gender and Society, 19*(2), 137–159.

Kincheloe, J., & Steinberg, S. (1998). Addressing the crisis of whiteness: Reconfiguring white identity in a pedagogy of whiteness. In J. Kincheloe, S. Steinberg, N. Rodriguez, & R. Chennault (Eds.), *White reign: Deploying whiteness in America* (pp. 3–30). New York: St. Martin's Griffin.

Kipnis, L. (1997). White trash girl: Interview [with J. Reeder]. In M. Wray & A. Newitz (Eds.), *White trash: Race and class in America* (pp. 124–129). New York: Routledge.

Kondo, D. (1997) *About face: Performing race in fashion and theater*. New York: Routledge.

Ladd-Taylor, M., & Umansky, L. (Eds.). (1998). *Bad mothers: The politics of blame in twentieth century America*. New York: New York University Press.

Ladies Home Journal. (1990, February). Vol. 107(2).

Langford, J. (2002). *Fluent bodies*. Durham, NC: Duke University Press.

Larsen, N. (2001). *Determinations*. New York: Verso.

Lau, K. J. (2000). *East of Eden*. Philadelphia: University of Pennsylvania Press.

Lawrence, D. ([2006] 2011 Kindle version). *And still I rise*. London: Faber & Faber.

Lentin, A., & Titley, G. (2011). *The crises of multiculturalism: Racism in a neoliberal age*. London: Zed Press.

Leonard, M. (1997). *Britain: Renewing our identity*. London: Demos.

Lipovetsky, G. (1994). *Empire of fashion: Dressing modern democracy*. Princeton, NJ: Princeton University Press.

Lister, R. (1996). Introduction: In search of the "underclass." In C. Murray, *Charles Murray and the Underclass* (pp. 1–18). London: the IEA Health and Welfare Unit.

Littler, J. (2008). "I feel your pain": Cosmopolitan charity and the public fashioning of the celebrity soul. *Social Semiotics, 18*(2), 237–251.

Liu, L. (1999). Introduction. In L. Liu (Ed.), *Tokens of exchange: The problem of translation in global circulation*. Durham, NC: Duke University Press.

Lomax, E. (1999). Diana Al Fayed: Ethnic marketing and the ends of racism. In J. Richards, S. Wilson, & L. Woodhead (Eds.), *Diana: The making of a media saint* (pp. 74–97). London: I. B. Taurus and Co. Ltd.

Loneard, T., & Reilly, J. (2012, December 16). "She would get very upset that he wouldn't let her hug him": Dysfunctional relationship of Sandy Hook gunman and his mother. *The Daily Mail*. Retrieved from http://www.dailymail.co.uk/news/

article-2249185/Nancy-Lanza-Did-paranoid-gun-crazed-mother-trigger-Sandy
-Hook-Connecticut-killing-spree.html. Accessed October 5, 2011.

Ma, S. (2000). *The deathly embrace: Orientalism and Asian American identity*. Minneapolis: University of Minnesota Press.

Madison, S. (2013). Dressing out-of-place: From Ghana to Obama commemorative cloth on the US American Red Carpet. In. K Hansen & S. Madison (Eds.), *African dress: Fashion, agency, performance*. New York: Bloomsbury.

Maira, S. (2002). Temporary tattoos: Indo-chic fantasies and late capitalist orientalism. *Meridians, 3*(1), 134–160.

Malkki, L. (1994). "Citizens of humanity": Internationalism and the imagined community of nations. *Diaspora, 3*(1), 41–68.

Mamdani, M. (2002). Good Muslim, bad Muslim: A political perspective on culture and terrorism. *American Anthropologist, 104*(3), 766–775.

Mamdani, M. (2005). *Good Muslim, bad Muslim*. New York: Three Leaves Press, Doubleday.

Mannur, A., & Sahni, P. (2011). What can brown do for you? Indo chic and fashionability of South Asian inspired styles. *South Asian Popular Culture, 9*(2), 117–190.

Marie-Fortier, A. (2008). *Multicultural horizons*. Milton Park, UK: Routledge.

Marre, D. & Briggs, L. (2009). (Ed.). *International adoption: Global inequalities and the circulation of children*. New York: New York University Press.

Marriott, D. (2007). *Haunted life: Visual culture and black modernity*. New Brunswick, NJ: Rutgers University Press.

Massad, J. (2002). Re-orienting desire: The gay international and the Arab world. *Public Culture, 14*(2), 361–386.

Massad, J. (2008*). Desiring Arabs*. Chicago: University of Chicago Press.

Matthews, S., & Wexler, L. (2000). *Pregnant pictures*. New York: Routledge.

Mayer, C. (2007, August 16). How Diana transformed Britain. *Time*. Retrieved http://content.time.com/time/specials/2007/article/0,28804,1650830_1650834_1653460,00.html. Accessed March 3, 2012.

Mayer, T. (2000). Gender ironies of nationalism: Setting the stage. In T. Mayer (Ed.), *Gender ironies of nationalism* (pp. 1–24). New York: Routledge.

Mbembe, A. (2003). Necropolitics. *Public Culture, 15*(1), 11–40.

McClintock, A. (1993). Family feuds: Gender, nationalism and the family. *Feminist Review, 44*, 62–80.

McClintock, A. (1995). *Imperial leather*. New York: Routledge.

McClintock, A., Mufti, A., & Shohat, E. (Eds.) (1997). *Dangerous liaisons*. Minneapolis: University of Minnesota Press.

McGee, M. (2005). *Self Help Inc: Makeover culture in American life*. New York: Oxford University Press.

McGhee, D. (2005). *Intolerant Britain: Hate, citizenship and difference*. Berkshire, UK: Open University Press.

McGuigan, J. (2001). British identity and "the people's princess." *The Sociological Review, 48*(1), 1–18.

McIntosh, P. (1988). *White privilege, male privilege.* Working paper of the Wellesley Center.

McIntyre, B. (1999, December 15). Posh foils baby snatcher. *The Guardian.* Retrieved from http://www.guardian.co.uk/uk/1999/dec/16/7. Accessed October 6, 2011.

McRobbie, A. (1998). *British fashion design: Rag trade or image industry.* Boca Raton, FL: Taylor & Francis.

McRobbie, A. (2000). Feminism and the third way. *Feminist Review, 64,* 97–112.

McRobbie, A. (2009). *The aftermath of feminism.* London: Sage.

McRobbie, A. (2011, April 8). *Top girls? Young women and the sexual contract.* Lecture for the Harriet Taylor Mill-Institute for Economic and Gender Research at Berlin School of Economics and Law. Retrieved from http://www.harriet-taylor-mill.de/pdfs/sonst/HTMI_Lecture_McRobbie.pdf. Accessed June 10, 2012.

Melamed, J. (2006). The spirit of neoliberalism: From racial liberalism to neoliberal multiculturalism. *Social Text, 24*(4), 1–24.

Merck, M. (Ed.). (1998). *After Diana: Irreverent elegies.* New York: Verso.

Miles, R. (1999). Racism as a concept. In M. Blumer & J. Solomos (Eds.), *Racisms* (pp. 344–355). Oxford, UK: Oxford University Press.

Miller, M. (1999, November 27). Wife's pregnancy delivers political boost for British premier. *Los Angeles Times.* Retrieved from http://articles.latimes.com/1999/nov/27/news/mn-37967. Accessed April 3, 2013.

Miller, T. (2008). *Makeover nation.* Columbus: Ohio University Press.

Minha, T. (1992). Film as translation. Interview with Scott McDonald. In T. Min-ha Framer, *Framed* (pp. 111–136). New York: Routledge.

Moallem, M. (1999). Transnationalism, feminism, and fundamentalism. In C. Kaplan, N. Alarcon, & M. Moallem (Eds.), *Between woman and nation* (pp. 320–348). Durham, NC: Duke University Press.

Modood, T. (1994). Political blackness and British Asians. *Sociology, 28*(4), 859–876.

Modood, T. (1998). Anti-essentialism, multiculturalism and the "recognition" of religious groups. *The Journal of Political Philosophy, 4*(6), 378–399.

Modood, T. (2005). *Multicultural politics: Racism, ethnicity and Muslims in Britain.* Minneapolis: University of Minnesota Press.

Mohanram, R. (2007). *Imperial white: Race, diaspora, and the British empire.* Minneapolis: University of Minnesota Press.

Moon, D. (1999). White enculturation and bourgeois ideology: The discursive production of "good (white) girls": In T. Nakayama & J. Martin (Eds.), *Whiteness: The communication of social identity* (pp. 177–197). Thousand Oaks, CA: Sage.

Moon & Flores (2000). Antiracism and the abolition of whiteness. *Communication Studies, 51,* 97–115.

Moorti, S. (2007). Out of India. In A. Valdivia (Ed.), *A companion to media studies* (pp. 293–309). Malden, MA: Blackwell.

Moreton-Robinson, A., Casey, M., & Nicoll, F. (Eds). (2008). *Transnational whiteness matters.* Plymouth, UK: Lexington Books.

Morley, D., & Robbins, K. (Eds.). (2001). *British cultural studies: Geography, nationality, and identity*. Oxford, UK: Oxford University Press.

Morrison, B. (2003, February 5). Life after James. *The Guardian*. Retrieved from http://www.guardian.co.uk/uk/2003/feb/06/bulger.ukcrime. Accessed June 15, 2011.

Morton, A. ([1992] 1998). *Diana: Her true story*. New York: Pocket Books, Simon and Schuster.

Mouffe, C. (2005). *On the political*. New York: Routledge.

Mulvaney, J. (2002). *Diana & Jackie: Maidens, mothers, myths*. New York: St. Martin's Press.

Mulvey, L. (1975). Visual pleasure and narrative cinema. *Screen, 16*(3), 6–18.

Najmi, A., & Srikanth, R. (2002). *White women in racialized spaces*. Albany: State University of New York Press.

Nakayama, T., & Krizek, R. (1995). Whiteness: A strategic rhetoric. *Quarterly Journal of Speech, 81,* 291–309.

Nakayama, T., & Martin, J. (Eds.). (1999). *Whiteness: The communication of social identity*. Thousand Oaks, CA: Sage.

Nash, M. (2012). *Making "postmodern" mothers*. Basingstoke, UK: Palgrave.

Nasrawi, S. (1997, December 26). Arab conspiracy theories abound about Princess Diana's death. Associated Press. Retrieved from http://www.apnewsarchive.com/1997/Arab-conspiracy-theories-abound-about-Princess-Diana-s-death/id-d868bb1afa3d54eb4f1db610bb9ba0d5. Accessed October 20, 2012.

Nava, M. (1999). Diana and race: Romance and the reconfiguration of race. In A. Kear & D. Steinberg (Eds*.), Mourning Diana: Nation, culture, and the performance of grief* (pp. 108–119). New York: Routledge.

Nava, M. (2007). *Visceral cosmopolitanism*. Oxford, UK: Berg Press.

Nayar, P. (2009). *Seeing stars: Spectacle, society and celebrity culture*. New Delhi: Sage Publications.

Negra, D. (2001). *Off-white Hollywood: American culture and ethnic stardom*. New York: Routledge.

Negra, D. (2009). *What a girl wants: Fantasizing the reclamation of self in postfeminism*. New York: Routledge.

Negra, D. (2010). Picturing family values. *The Velvet Light Trap*, 65, 60–61.

Negra, D., & Tasker, Y. (Eds.) (2014). *Gendering the recession*. Durham, NC: Duke University Press.

Nelson, D. (1998). *National manhood*. Durham, NC: Duke University Press.

Niessen, S. (2011). Re-orienting fashion theory. In L. Welters & A. Lillethun (Eds.), *The Fashion Reader* (pp. 150–155). Oxford, UK: Berg.

Nye, J. (2005). *Soft power*. Cambridge, MA: Perseus Books.

O'Bryne, R. (2009). *Style city: How London became a fashion capital*. London: Francis Lincoln Limited.

Oliver, K. (2012). *Knock me up, knock me down: Images of pregnancy in Hollywood films*. New York: Columbia University Press.

Ono, K., & Pham, V. (2009). *Asian Americans and the media*. Malden, MA: Polity.

Orleck, A. (1997). Overview: Good motherhood as patriotism: Mothers on the right. In A. Jetter, A. Orleck, & D. Taylor (Eds.), *The politics of motherhood*. (pp. 225–228). Hanover, NH: University Press of New England.

Orth, M. (1995, September). Holy war at Harrods. *Vanity Fair*, pp. 70–98.

Ortiz, A., & Briggs, L. (2003). The culture of poverty, crack babies, and welfare cheats: The making of the "healthy white baby crisis." *Social Text*, *21* (no. 3 76), 39–57.

Owen, N. (1997). *Diana: The People's Princess*. [*Reader's Digest* commemorative tribute]. London: Carlton Books Ltd.

Parameswara, R., & Cardoza, K. (2009). Melanin on the margins: Advertising and the cultural politics of fair/light/white beauty in India. *Journalism and Communication Monographs*, *11*, 213–274.

Parkins, W. (2002). *Fashioning the body politic*. Oxford, UK: Berg.

Parrenas, R., & Boris, E. (2010). (Eds.). *Intimate Labors: Culture, technologies and the politics of care*. Stanford, CA: Stanford University Press.

Patterson, O. (1982). *Slavery and social death*. Cambridge, MA: Harvard University Press.

Patton, C. (1992). From nation to family: Containing African AIDS. In H. Abelove, D. Halperan, & M. Barale (Eds.), *Lesbian and gay studies reader* (pp. 127–138). New York: Routledge.

Pearson, A. (2011, January 13). Why we all need a tiger mother. *The Telegraph*. Retrieved from http://www.telegraph.co.uk/education/8255804/Why-we-all-need -a-Tiger-Mother.html. Accessed September 4, 2013.

Pfeil, F. (1994). *White guys*. New York: Routledge.

Phelan, P. (1993). *Unmarked*. New York: Routledge.

Phoenix, A. (1996). Social constructions of lone motherhood: A case of competing discourses. In E. Silva (Ed.), *Good enough mothering? Feminist perspectives on lone mothering* (pp. 175–190). London: Routledge.

Pollock, S., Bhabha, H., Breckenridge, C., & Chakrabarty, D. (2000). Cosmopolitanisms. *Public Culture*, *12*(3): 577–589.

Povinelli, E. (2002). *The cunning of recognition*. Durham, NC: Duke University Press.

Povinelli, E. (2006). *The empire of love*. Durham, NC: Duke University Press.

Pratt, M. L. (1992). *Imperial eyes*. New York: Routledge.

Prideaux, S. (2004). From organization theory to third way: Continuities and contradictions underpinning Amitai Etzioni's communitarian. In S. Hale, W. Leggett, & L. Martell (Eds.), *The third way and beyond* (pp. 128–146). Manchester, UK: Manchester University Press.

Projansky, S. (2001). *Watching rape*. New York: New York University Press.

Projansky, S. (2007). Mass magazine cover girls: Some reflections on postfeminist girls and postfeminism's daughters. In Y. Tasker & D. Negra (Eds.), *Interrogating postfeminism* (pp. 40–72). Durham, NC: Duke University Press.

Projansky, S., & Ono, K. (1999). Strategic whiteness as cinematic racial politics In T. Nakayama & J. Martin (Eds.), *Whiteness: The communication of social identity* (pp. 149–174). Newbury Park, CA: Sage.

Puar, J. (2007). *Terrorist assemblages.* Durham, NC: Duke University Press.

Pupavac, V. (2001). "Therapeutic governance": Psychosocial intervention and trauma risk management. *Disasters, 25*(4), 358–372.

Puri, J. (2004). *Encountering nationalism.* Malden, MA: Blackwell.

Puwar, N. (2002). Multicultural fashion . . . stirrings of another sense of aesthetics and memory. *Feminist Review, 71*(1), 63–87.

Puwar, N. (2003). Exhibiting spectacle and memory. *Fashion Theory, 7(3/4),* 257–274.

Radcliffe, S., & Westwood, S. (1996). *Re-making the nation.* New York: Routledge.

Rafael, V. (2000). *White love.* Durham, NC: Duke University Press.

Rajagopal, A. (1999). Celebrity and the politics of charity: Memories of a missionary departed. In A. Kear & D. Steinberg (Eds.), *Mourning Diana* (pp. 126–141). Routledge: New York.

Ram, K., & Jolly, M. (1998). *Maternities and modernities.* Berkeley: University of California Press.

Ranchod-Nilsson, S., & Tetreault, M. (2000). Introduction. In. S. Ranchod-Nilsson & M. Tetreault (Eds.), *Women, states, and nationalism* (pp. 1–17). New York: Routledge.

Razack, S. (2002). *Race, space and the law: Unmapping a white settler society.* Toronto, ON: Between the Lines Press.

Redmond, S. (2007). The whiteness of stars: Looking at Kate Winslet's unruly white body. In S. Redmond & Su Holmes (Eds.), *Stardom and celebrity: A reader* (pp. 263–274). London: Sage Publications.

Redmond, S., & Holmes, S. (2007). Introduction. In S. Redmond & S. Holmes (Eds.), *Stardom and celebrity: A reader* (pp. 1–12). London: Sage Publications.

Reynolds, T. (2005). *Caribbean mothers: Identity and experience in the UK.* London: Tufnell Press.

Rich, A. (1980). Compulsory heterosexuality and lesbian existence. *Signs, 5,* 631–660.

Richards, J., Wilson, S., & Woodhead, L. (Eds.). (1999). *Diana: The making of a media saint.* London: I. B. Taurus and Co Ltd.

Richardson, J. (2004). *(Mis)representing Islam.* Amsterdam: John Benjamin's Publishing.

Roberts, D. (1997). Unshackling black motherhood. *Michigan Law Review, 95*(4), 938–964.

Roberts, D. (1999). *Killing the black body: Race, reproduction and the meaning of liberty.* New York: Vintage.

Robinson, S. (2000). *Marked men.* Durham, NC: Duke University Press.

Rojek, C. (2001). *Celebrity.* London: Reakton Books.

Rose, N. (1989). *Governing the soul: The shaping of the private self.* New York: Routledge.

Roy, P. (2010). *Alimentary tracts: Appetites, aversions, and the postcolonial.* Durham, NC: Duke University Press.

Runnymede Commission. (2000). *Report on the future of multi-ethnic Britain.* London: Runnymede Trust. Retrieved from www.runnymedetrust.org. Accessed June 10, 2010.

Said, E. (1978). *Orientalism.* New York: Vintage Books.

Saldhana, A. (2007). *Psychedelic white: Goa trance and the viscosity of race*. Minneapolis: University of Minnesota Press.

Savran, D. (1998). *Taking it like a man: White masculinity, masochism, and contemporary culture*. Princeton, NJ: Princeton University Press.

Sedgwick, E. (2003). *Touching feeling*. Durham, NC: Duke University Press.

Serisier, T. (2008). Laura Bush and Dan Brown: Whiteness, feminism, and the politics of vulnerability. In A. Moreton-Robinson, M. Casey, & F. Nicoll (Eds.), *Transnational whiteness matters* (pp. 147–164). Plymouth, UK: Lexington Books.

Shah, S. (Eds.). (1997). *Dragon ladies: Asian American feminists breathe fire*. Cambridge, MA: South End Press.

Shaheen, J. (2001). *Reel bad Arabs: How Hollywood vilifies a people*. New York: Olive Branch Press.

Sharma, S. (1996). Noisy Asians or "Asian noise"? In S. Sharma, J. Hutnyk, & A. Sharma (Eds.) *Dis-orienting rhythms: The politics of new Asian dance music* (pp. 32–57). London: Zed Books.

Sharma, S. Hutnyk, J., & Sharma, A. (1996). (Eds.) *Dis-orienting rhythms: The politics of new Asian dance music*. London: Zed Books.

Sharpe, J. (1993). *Allegories of empire*. Minneapolis: University of Minnesota Press.

Shiva, V. (1999). *Biopiracy: The plunder of nature and knowledge*. Cambridge, MA: South End Press.

Shohat, E. (2011). *On the image of the Sheikh* [video lecture]. In *Reclaiming identity: Dismantling Arab stereotypes* (video). Arab American National Museum Online Exhibit. Retrieved from http://www.arabstereotypes.org/. Accessed January 12, 2013.

Shohat, E., & Stam, R. (1994). *Unthinking Eurocentrism*. New York: Routledge.

Shome, R. (1996). Race and popular cinema: The rhetorical strategies of whiteness in city of joy. *Communication Quarterly, 44*(4), 502–518.

Shome, R. (2000). Outing whiteness. *Critical Studies in Media Communication, 17*(3), 366–371.

Shome, R. (2001). White femininity and the discourse of the nation: Remembering Princess Diana. *Feminist Media Studies, 1*, 323–342.

Shome, R. (2006). Transnational feminism and communication studies. *Communication Review, 9*(4), 255–266.

Shome, R. (2010). Internationalizing critical race communication studies: Transnationality, space and affect. In R. Halualani & T. Nakayama (Eds.), *Critical intercultural communication* (pp. 149–170). Malden, MA: Blackwell

Shome, R. (2012). Mapping the limits of multiculturalism in the context of globalization. *International Journal of Communication, 6*. Retrieved from www.ijoc.org. Accessed 3 April, 2013.

Shukla, S. (2003). *India abroad*. Princeton, NJ: Princeton University Press.

Skeggs, B. (2005). The making of class and gender through visualizing moral subject formation. *Sociology, 39*(5), 965–982.

Smith, A. (2005). *Conquest: Sexual violence and the American genocide.* Cambridge, MA: South End Press.

Smith, S. B. (1997, December). Dodi's life in the fast lane. *Vanity Fair.* Retrieved from http://www.vanityfair.com/society/features/1997/12/dodi-fayed-199712. Accessed August 12, 2012.

Snell, K. (2000). *Diana: Her last love.* London: Granada.

Spivak, G. (1988). Can the subaltern speak? In L. Grossberg & C. Nelson (Eds.), *Marxism and the interpretation of culture* (pp. 271–313). Urbana: University of Illinois Press.

Spivak, G. (1993). *Outside in the teaching machine.* New York: Routledge.

Spivak, G. (1999). *A critique of postcolonial reason.* Cambridge, MA: Harvard University Press.

Spivak, G. (2001). Questioned on translation: Adrift. *Public Culture, 13*(1), 13–22.

Spivak, G. (2003). *Death of a discipline.* New York: Columbia University Press.

Stabile, C. (1994). *Feminism and the technological fix.* Manchester, UK: Manchester University Press.

Stokes, M. (2001). *The color of sex.* Durham, NC: Duke University Press.

Stoler, A. (1995). *Race and the education of desire.* Durham, NC: Duke University Press.

Stoler, A. (2002). *Carnal knowledge and imperial power.* Berkeley: University of California Press.

Stoler, A. (2006). *Haunted by empire.* Durham, NC: Duke University Press.

Stone, R. (2013). *Hidden stories of the Stephen Lawrence inquiry, personal reflections.* Bristol, UK: Policy Press, University of Bristol.

Suri, S. (1997, December 1). Cherie's sari diplomacy. *Outlook.* Retrieved from http://www.outlookindia.com/article.aspx?204647. Accessed February 20, 2013.

Suri, S. (October 12, 1998). We're there. *Outlook.* Retrieved from http://www.outlookindia.com/article.aspx?206311. Accessed February 20, 2013.

Sweeney, G. (1997). The king of white trash culture: Elvis Presley and the aesthetics of excess. In A. Newitz & M. Wray (Eds.), *White trash: Race and class in America* (pp. 113–130). New York: Routledge.

Talley, A. (1997, March). London fashion streets ahead. *Vanity Fair,* pp. 126–138.

Tapia, R. (2011). *American pietas: Visions of race, death and the maternal.* Minneapolis: University of Minnesota Press.

Tasker, Y., & Negra, D. (2007). Introduction: Feminist politics and postfeminist culture. In Y. Tasker & D. Negra (Eds.), *Interrogating postfeminism* (pp. 1–26). Durham, NC: Duke University Press.

Taylor, D. (2003). *The Archive and the Repertoire: Performing Cultural Memory in the Americas.* Durham, NC: Duke University Press.

Taylor, [Jessica]. (2007). And you can be my sheikh. *Journal of Popular Culture, 40*(6), 1032–1051.

Taylor, [John A.]. (2000). *Diana, self-interest, and British national identity.* West Port, CT: Praeger.

Thobani, S. (2007). *Exalted subjects*. Toronto: University of Toronto Press.

Thobani, S. (2010). White innocence, Western supremacy: The role of Western feminism in the "war on terror." In S. Razack, M. Smith, & S. Thobani (Eds.), *States of race* (pp. 127–146). Toronto, ON: Between the Lines Press.

Toynbee, P. (1997, October 23). In defence of Islamophobia: Religion and the state. *The Independent*, p. 23.

Treichler, P. (1999). *How to have theory in an epidemic: Cultural chronicle of AIDS*. Durham, NC: Duke University Press.

Trimble, S. (2008). (Un)usual suspects: Mothers, masculinities, monstrosities. In A. O'Reilly (Ed.), *Feminist mothering* (pp. 177–190). Albany: State University of New York Press.

Trinh, T. Min-ha. (1992). *Framer framed*. New York: Routledge.

Turner, G. (2004). *Understanding celebrity*. London: Sage Publications.

Turner, L. (2000, September 30). Meet the e-mother. *The Guardian*. Retrieved from http://www.guardian.co.uk/theobserver/2000/oct/01/life1.lifemagazine1.

Twine, F. W., & Gallagher, C. (2008). The future of whiteness: A map of the "third wave." *Ethnic and Racial Studies, 29*(2), 260–280.

Tyler, I. (2001). Skin-tight: Celebrity, pregnancy and subjectivity. In S. Ahmed & J. Stacey (Eds.), *Thinking through the skin* (pp. 69–83). London: Routledge.

Tyler, I. (2008). "Chav mum, chav scum": Class disgust in contemporary Britain. *Feminist Media Studies, 8*(2), 17–34.

Tyler, I. (2011). Pregnant beauty: Maternal femininities under neoliberalism. In R. Gill & C. Scharff (Eds.), *New femininities: Postfeminism, neoliberalism, and subjectivity* (pp. 21–36). Basingstoke, UK: Palgrave.

Tyler, I. (2013). *Revolting subjects: Social abjection and resistance in neoliberal Britain*. London: Zed Books.

Urry, J. (2000). *Sociology beyond societies*. New York: Routledge.

Visveswaran, K. (2010). *Un/common cultures: Racism and rearticulation of cultural difference*. Durham, NC: Duke University Press.

Volkman, T. (2003). Transnational adoption. *Social Text, 21* (no. 1 74), 1–5.

Walby, S. (2006). Gender approaches to nations and nationalisms. In G. Delanty & K. Kumar (Eds.), *The Sage handbook of nations and nationalisms* (pp. 118–128). London: Sage Publications.

Walter, N. (1999). *The new feminism*. London: Virago Press.

Walter, T. (Ed.). (1999). *The mourning for Diana*. Oxford, UK: Berg.

Ward, D. (2001, June 18). Alternative spirituality "rising fast." *The Guardian*. Retrieved from http://www.theguardian.com/uk/2001/jun/18/religion.world. Accessed February 3, 2013.

Ware, V. (1992). *Beyond the pale*. New York: Verso

Ware, V. (2001). Perfidious Albion: Whiteness and the international imagination. In B. Rasmussen, E. Klineberg, I. Nexica, & M. Wray (Eds.) *The making and unmaking of whiteness* (pp. 184–212). Durham, NC: Duke University Press.

Ware, V., & Back, L. (2001). *Out of whiteness*. Chicago: University of Chicago Press.

Warning of riots unless police improve attitude to Asians (discussion of report by British Home Office). (1997, December 10). *The Times*, p. 6.

Warren, J. (2003). *Performing purity: Whiteness, pedagogy and the reconstitution of power*. New York: Peter Lang.

Werbner, P., & Yuval-Davis, N. (Eds.). (1999). *Women, citizenship, and difference*. London: Zed Books.

West, L. (2009). Nation. In P. Essed & D. Goldberg (Eds.), *A companion to gender studies* (pp. 145–159). Malden, MA: Blackwell.

What is Britain? (n.d.) *The Guardian*. Retrieved from http://www.guardian.co.uk/quiz/questions/0,5961,211620,00.html. Accessed June 20, 2012.

Wiegman, R. (1995). *American anatomies*. New York: Routledge.

Wiegman, R. (2012). *Object lessons*. Durham, NC: Duke University Press.

Wilding, R. (1997). Afterimages of being. In Re-Public (Ed.), *Planet Diana: Cultural studies and global mourning* (pp. 145–148). Sydney: Research Centre in Intercommunal Studies: University of Western Sydney.

Wilson, E. (1985). *Adorned in dreams*. London: Virago.

Wong, Sau-ling C. (1994). Diverted mothering: Representations of caregivers of color in the age of "multiculturalism." In E. Glenn, G. Chang, & L. Forcey (Eds.), *Mothering: Ideology, experience, and agency* (pp. 67–91). New York: Routledge.

Wood, R. (1998). *Diana: The people's princess*. Austin, TX: Steck-Vaughn Company.

Wood, G., & Newman, J. (2005). From Welfare to wellbeing regimes: Engaging new agendas. Paper presented New Frontiers of Social Policy, Arusha, Tanzania.

Young, R. (1990). *White Mythologies: Writing history and the West*. New York: Routledge.

Yuval-Davis, N., & Anthias, F. (Eds.) (1989). *Woman-nation-state*. Basingstoke, UK: Macmillan.

Yuval-Davis, N. (1997a). *Gender and nation*. London: Sage Publications.

Yuval-Davis, N. (1997b). Women, citizenship, and difference. *Feminist Review, 57,* 4–27.

Zacharias, U. (2003). The smile of Mona Lisa: Postcolonial desire, nationalist families, and the birth of consumer television in India. *Critical Studies in Media Communication, 20*(4), 388–406.

Zuberi, N. (2001). *Sounds English: Transnational popular music*. Urbana: University of Illinois Press.

Index

RAKA SHOME is a media, communication and cultural studies scholar. She has held faculty appointments at the London School of Economics, Arizona State University, the University of Washington, and served as the 2011–12 Inaugural Harron Family (Visiting) Endowed Chair of Communication at Villanova University.

The University of Illinois Press
is a founding member of the
Association of American University Presses.

Composed in 10.5/13 Adobe Minion Pro
by Lisa Connery
at the University of Illinois Press
Manufactured by Sheridan Books, Inc.

University of Illinois Press
1325 South Oak Street
Champaign, IL 61820-6903
www.press.uillinois.edu